THE
BATTLE
FOR
GOD

Responding to the Challenge
of Neotheism

NORMAN L. GEISLER • H. WAYNE HOUSE
with Max Herrera

kregel
PUBLICATIONS

Grand Rapids, MI 49501

The Battle for God: Responding to the Challenge of Neotheim

© 2001 by Norman L. Geisler and H. Wayne House

Published in 2001 by Kregel Publications, a division of Kregel, Inc., P.O. Box 2607, Grand Rapids, MI 49501. For more information about Kregel Publications, visit our Web site: www.kregel.com.

ISBN 0-8254-2735-5

Printed in the United States of America

2 3 / 05 04 03 02

Contents

Acknowledgments

SOURCE CITATIONS IN TEXT follow the Author-Date citation style. Complete references can be found in the sources, pages 323–29. Cross-references and substantive notes follow the standard footnote citation style.

Scripture quotations marked NJB are from the New Jerusalem Bible, © 1985, Doubleday.

Scripture quotations marked NLT are from the *Holy Bible,* New Living Translation, © 1996. Used by permission of Tyndale House Publishers, Inc., Wheaton, Illinois 60189. All rights reserved.

Scripture quotations marked NRSV are from the New Revised Standard Version of the Bible, © 1989 by the Division of Christian Education of the National Council of the Churches of Christ in the USA. Used by permission.

Scripture quotations marked RSV are from the *Revised Standard Version.* © 1946, 1952, 1971, 1973 by the Division of Christian Education of the National Council of the Churches of Christ in the United States of America.

Scripture quotations marked TANAKH are from the traditional Hebrew Torah.

Scripture quotations marked TEV are from *Today's English Verion, Good News Bible*—New Testament. © American Bible Society 1966, 1971, 1976.

Scripture quotations marked TCNT are from *The Twentieth Century New Testament.* © Fleming H. Revell, 1904.

CHAPTER ONE

Neotheism and the Doctrine of God

EVANGELICALISM HAS FACED several crucial battles in the past two generations: the battle for the Bible . . . the battle for Creation . . . the battle for the Resurrection. . . . None is more important, however, than the battle that now must be faced— the battle for God.

Just what is the battle for God? It is the theological debate now being waged in the halls of academia and in the pulpits of America over the nature of God. Nothing is more fundamental to the survival of evangelical Christianity than the outcome of this struggle. For every other major doctrine of the faith is based on the doctrine of God. For example, the claims that the Bible is the Word of God and that Christ is the Son of God are entirely dependent on what is meant by *God*. What sort of God has communicated in Scripture and visited humanity in the Son? If by *God* we mean the impersonal Force of the *Star Wars* version of Zen Buddhism, then saying that Christ is God's Son is to make Him no higher than a guru.

If by God we mean the finite bumbler as portrayed by Rabbi Harold Kushner (1989), then He is not powerful enough to overcome death, and He is in need of our forgiveness. To say the Bible is the Word of such a being is not to offer any ultimate consolation in our struggle against sickness, sin, and death.

SEVEN MAJOR VIEWS OF GOD

To set the stage for our understanding of neotheism, the new challenge to the traditional Christian view of God, it is helpful to discuss the seven views of God in the marketplace of ideas.[1] Each view has a name and its own distinguishing set of characteristics.

Among major religions, only the faith of orthodox Judaism, Christianity, and Islam can, strictly speaking, be called theist. *Theism* denotes a supernatural, infinite, personal Being who created the material universe and who transcends it. The theist God can and does intervene in the world in a supernatural way from time to time.

Deism is like theism, minus miracles. It affirms that there is an infinite, personal Creator of the universe. Deists, however, deny that He sustains the world or that He intervenes supernaturally in it. Famous deists have included François-Marie Voltaire (1694–1778) and Thomas Paine (1737–1809).

Pantheism denotes a God who is identical to the universe. It literally means "God is All, and All is God." This view is embraced by traditional Hinduism, some forms of Buddhism, Christian Science, and many forms of contemporary New Age belief. The media has helped popularize this view.

Panentheism literally means "All in God or God in All." Panentheism is a hybrid of theism and pantheism. Panentheists hold that God is in the world as a soul is in a body or a mind in a brain. Since God has two poles, one spiritual and one physical, this view is also called *bipolar* or *dipolar theism*. Furthermore, since this view believes that God is in a continual process of change, it is labeled *process theology* or *organicism*. Another label for this position is *neoclassical theism* (as opposed to *classical theism*). The founder of this view was Alfred North Whitehead (1861–1947), and some of his significant disciples

---

1. For a more detailed description of these seven views of God see Norman L. Geisler and William Watkins, *Worlds Apart: A Handbook on World Views* (Grand Rapids: Baker, 1989).

have been Charles Hartshorne, Shubert Ogden, John Cobb, and Lewis Ford.

Finite godism claims that God is limited in power and perfection. He created the world but does not control it. This position is as ancient as Plato (428 B.C.–348 B.C.) and as young as Rabbi Kushner. John Stuart Mill (1806–1873) and William James (1842–1910) were finite godists, as were Edgar S. Brightman (1884–1953) and Peter Bertocci (b. 1910).

Polytheism, the belief in many gods, characterized religious life back in ancient Babylon, Egypt, Greece, and Rome. Modern manifestations are found in Mormonism, occultism, and witchcraft. One form of polytheism, called *henotheism*, believes that one finite god is supreme over others.

Atheism is a denial that any gods exist. This view is most militantly embraced by Marxism. Atheism extends to some forms of Buddhism, and most forms of secular humanism. Major atheists include Ludwig Feuerbach (1804–1872), Karl Marx (1818–1883), Friedrich Nietzsche (1844–1900), and Sigmund Freud (1856–1939).

NEOTHEISM: THE NEW "KID" ON THE BLOCK

Recently a group of Christian thinkers carved out a new concept of God by combining aspects of panentheism, or process theology, with traditional theism. This view is sometimes called the *openness view* of God or *free-will theism*, since it stresses that a libertarian view of human freedom leaves the future open to us and to God. Neotheism has adopted important dimensions of process theology, and for this reason poses a serious threat to the classical theism that evangelical Christianity embraces. It presents one of the most serious threats to Christian orthodoxy.

Since they represent the "new kid on the block," neotheists work hard to make their ideas clear, distinct, and appealing. Since neotheists want to be accepted as members in good standing within the orthodox theist camp, they have put their best foot forward in describing their view. Neotheists list five characteristics of their position.

1. God not only created this world *ex nihilo* but can (and at times does) intervene unilaterally in earthly affairs.

2. God chose to create us with incompatibilistic (libertarian) freedom—freedom over which he cannot exercise total control.

3. God so values freedom—the moral integrity of free creatures and a world in which such integrity is possible—that he does not normally override such freedom, even if he sees that it is producing undesirable results.

4. God always desires our highest good, both individually and corporately, and thus is affected by what happens in our lives.

5. God does not possess exhaustive knowledge of exactly how we will utilize our freedom, although he may well at times be able to predict with great accuracy the choices we will freely make (Pinnock et al. 1994, 156).

To get these five points in focus, compare theism, panentheism, and neotheism.[2]

Theism and Neotheism

The similarities between neotheism and traditional (or classical) theism are such that neotheism may be viewed as a mutant form of theism. In both views, God is a personal, infinite, all-powerful Creator, who created the world from nothing. He is also able to perform miracles and defeat evil. He knows all that is possible to know and is an independent, self-existing, and Necessary Being.

Neotheism and Process Theology

But despite the similarities between theism and neotheism, there are marked differences, all of which are borrowed from process theology. Like the process view, and unlike traditional theism, neotheists affirm that God is temporal, changing, and

---

2. For a more detailed comparison, see Norman L. Geisler, *Creating God in the Image of Man?* (Minneapolis: Bethany, 1997), ch 4.

complex (as opposed to simple in Being). He has potential to become and does not have infallible knowledge of future free choices. He does not have absolute control of the world and is capable of learning.

Neotheists and panentheists are close enough in belief that some prefer to call neotheism a form of process theology. Neotheism does differ, however, from the panentheism of Whitehead and Hartshorne. Neotheism, like classical theism, ostensibly affirms God's infinity, necessity, ontological independence, transcendence, omnipotence, omnipresence, and omniscience.[3] Likewise, it shares with traditional theism the belief in *ex nihilo* creation and direct divine, supernatural intervention in the world. Process theology denies all of these doctrines.

The Nature of Neotheism

A brief introduction to the characteristics of neotheism will set the stage for more in-depth analysis. Several promoters of this new theism, Clark Pinnock, Richard Rice, John Sanders, William Hasker, and David Basinger, collaborated on a volume entitled *The Openness of God*. All of these scholars had written works of their own on the topic.[4] Other Christian thinkers share

---

3. However, as we shall see, some of these are qualified either explicitly or implicitly.

4. Contributors of books to this area include Richard Rice, *God's Foreknowledge and Man's Free Will* (Minneapolis: Bethany House, 1980); Ronald H. Nash, ed., *Process Theology* (Grand Rapids: Baker, 1987); Gregory A. Boyd, *Trinity and Process* (New York: Peter Lang, 1992); and (cowritten with Edward K. Boyd) *Letters from a Skeptic* (Wheaton, Ill.: Victor, 1994); J. R. Lucas, *The Freedom of the Will* (Oxford: Clarendon, 1970); and *The Future: An Essay on God, Temporality and Truth* (Oxford: Blackwell, 1989); P. T. Geach, *Providence and Evil* (Cambridge: Cambridge University Press, 1977); Richard Swinburne, *The Coherence of Theism* (Oxford: Clarendon, 1977); Thomas V. Morris, *Our Idea of God: An Introduction to Philosophical Theology* (Downers Grove, Ill.: InterVarsity, 1977); David Basinger, *The Case for Freewill Theism: A Philosophical Assessment* (Downers Grove, Ill.: InterVarsity, 1996); Randall Basinger, *Exhaustive Divine Sovereignty*; William Hasker, *God, Time and Knowledge* (Ithaca, N.Y.: Cornell University Press, 1989); and John Sanders, *The God Who Risks: A Theology of Providence* (Downers Grove, Ill. InterVarsity, 1998).

similar views or have expressed sympathy for this position.[5] A popular attempt to provide a biblical basis for this view is found in Gregory Boyd's *God of the Possible* (2000).

While there are similarities between the new theism and classical theism, it does not fit comfortably in this category. For example, neotheism denies God's immutability, eternality, simplicity, and pure actuality. It denies God's infallible foreknowledge of future free acts and, as a consequence, God's complete sovereignty over human events. Another important difference between theism and neotheism concerns human free choice. Neotheists accept a libertarian view of free will. They believe that free will is meaningless with a God who completely foreknows, fore-determines, and controls all events of human history.

By a *libertarian* or *incompatibilist* view of free will, neotheists mean "an agent is free with respect to a given action at a given time if at that time it is within the agent's power to perform the action and also in the agent's power to refrain from the action" (Pinnock et al. 1994, 136–37). To be free under the libertarian view, one must have both the "inner freedom" (with no overwhelming desire to the contrary) and "outer freedom" (with no external restraints) to perform the act. On the compatibilists' view, one need only have the "outer freedom" from external restraints. The libertarian view is that one must be free in both desire and decision, the compatibilists' view that one need only be free to decide. Desire and inclination are never fully free.

Most of these are serious enough deviations from the view of God shared by orthodox Christians over nearly two millennia to warrant giving the innovation another name to distinguish it from classical theism.

---

5. These include Stephen T. David, *Logic and the Nature of God* (Grand Rapids: Eerdmans, 1983); Linda Zagzebski, *The Dilemma of Freedom and Foreknowledge* (New York: Oxford, 1991); Alvin Plantinga, *Does God Have a Nature* (Milwaukee: Marquette University Press, 1980); and Nicholas Wolterstorff, "God Everlasting." in *God and the Good:* Essays in honor of Henry Stob, ed. Clifton Orlebeke and Lewis Smedes (Grand Rapids: Eerdmans, 1975).

THE NAMES OF NEOTHEISM

Perhaps one should simply accept the neotheists' own name for their theology, the "openness of God" view or "free will theism." However, this is not desirable for several reasons. For one thing, neither title is really descriptive or simple. Classical theism also claims to hold to human and divine free will. The title "openness of God" is cumbersome and cryptic. Open to what? Open in what way? It seems better to call the view what it is and claims to be, a significant modification of traditional theism in the direction of process theology. It is a new theism. Indeed, it offers itself as a third alternative to theism and panentheism. Pinnock correctly positions it "between classical and process theism." Whatever one calls this view, it challenges central assumptions of classical theism and attacks the view of God that holds together important doctrines of the Christian worldview.

THE CHALLENGE OF NEOTHEISM

Evangelical "Rubicon"

In his 1978 presidential address before the Evangelical Theological Society, Stanley Gundry expressed concern about the direction of evangelicalism. Evangelicals had been tainted, he believed, because they were accommodating critical scholarship ("Evangelical Theology: Where Should We Be Going?" 3–4). Since that time, in many evangelical circles, this accommodation has relaxed into acceptance. Now evangelicalism has moved another step in accommodating liberal theology. If Gundry was right that accommodating an errant view of Scripture posed significant problems for the future of evangelicalism, what will the future hold if evangelicals accept a form of finite godism. If enough evangelicals embrace neotheism, historic orthodoxy will be dead. Evangelicals must once again establish a line of demarcation, a boundary outside of which a Christian cannot be called evangelical . . . or even orthodox.

What Is at Stake

In the debate over biblical inerrancy, there could be dialogue with other orthodox Christians regarding how narrowly to understand the term inerrant.[6] Collegial connection is more problematic in a debate about the nature of God's infinitude, in which those who reject fundamental attributes of God unwittingly identify themselves with the unorthodox, rather than with the historic church (Beckwith and Parrish 1991, 129). The challenge to biblical orthodoxy is real.

Though we do not question the sincerity of those evangelicals who advocate neotheism, we do question their understanding of God's nature and the benefits of neotheism to the Christian life.[7]

If God is not infinite in His attributes, then many cherished beliefs and expectations of Christians are suspect. The Christian's confidence in God, His Word, our salvation, and our daily dependence on God come into grave doubt. Neotheism is a major challenge to the church's historic view and profession of God. However, neotheists often underestimate the extent of their deviation from historic Christianity. Note the words of Boyd, "Next to the central doctrines of the Christian faith, the issue of whether the future is exhaustively settled or partially open is relatively unimportant. It certainly is not a doctrine Christians should ever divide over. Still, I have to confess that the perspective I came to embrace has had a rather profound impact on my life" (Boyd 2000, 8). Boyd seems to believe that whether God

---

6. For example, James Orr, Edward J. Carnell, and Berkeley Mickelsen.
7. We speak here of statements by some neotheists who believe that a more limited view of God's nature provides comfort or assurance to believers in distress. See, for example, Gregory Boyd, *The God of the Possible* and *Letters from a Skeptic*. Similar to Boyd's pastoral concerns, John Sanders, in *The God Who Risks*, seems to come to neotheism out of personal tragedy, rather than dispassionate investigation. See the critique of Sanders's book by A. B. Caneday, "Putting God at Risk: A Critique of John Sanders's View of Providence," *Trinity Journal* 20 NS (1999):131–63, at http://msnhomepages.talkcity.com/IvyHall/kainosman/a_critique_of_john_sanders.htm#_edn2.

exhaustively knows the future is a minor matter. On the contrary, the implications of his denial are staggering. If God does not know the future for the reasons that neotheists argue, this deficiency permeates His nature. This issue is more important than are contemporary controversies involving almost any other area of theology.

AREAS OF CONCERN

Who is God? If this seems an over-obvious question to ask of a Christian, it is because the answer is of the utmost importance. The true God is the One who has clearly revealed Himself in Scripture.[8] A denial at this point has a serious effect on doctrine and practice.

The Effect on Our Worship

One might believe that a Christian naturally worships the true God, or that we all mean the same thing when we speak of God. This is not the case. The Israelites were the people of God who were delivered by the true God and received His written revelation. However, they distorted this revelation to the point that God resembled the pagan gods their Canaanite neighbors worshiped. Christians today may do the same thing. Many worship a god of their own creation, rather than the One who has revealed Himself. To speak of God in ignoble or distorted terms is idolatry.

The Effect on Our View of Scripture

The Scripture cannot rise above its Creator. This is especially true regarding prophecy. A "limited" omniscience necessarily means shortsighted prophets with little more prescience than their pagan counterparts (Beckwith 1993, 357–62). Though God may be an excellent "guesser," innumerable possibilities exist

---

8. We are not discounting the fact that God has also revealed Himself in nature (Psalm 19; Romans 1) but the special revelation of God presents a more complete picture.

within neotheism. Prophecy that is not qualified with certain preconditions might not come true. Even if one argues that God determines some things, while leaving most matters undetermined, this moves the argument nowhere.

Every determined act of God connects with, and must be influenced by, undetermined, free acts of humans. God's knowledge remains fallible.

The Effect on Our Assurance of Salvation

Even our salvation is called into question by neotheist theology. There may be some uncertainty affecting us that God has not considered. He cannot be certain that He has correctly envisioned even the nature of eternity, if He Himself lives within the temporal dimension. There may be unseen hurdles. Lacking infinite wisdom, He may not be as wise in this issue as He or we have imagined.

The Effect on Hermeneutics

The nature of hermeneutics is affected by this debate. The neotheist is unwilling to recognize the metaphorical expressions in reference to God changing His mind or repenting or regretting. This leaves biblical interpretation in a hermeneutic quagmire. If such clearly analogical statements must be taken literally, are we able to consider anything as metaphorical? What about statements that God walked in the garden of Eden, that He forgets our sins, or indications that He lacks present and past knowledge of events and persons. If the difference between analogical and literal language is abandoned, Bible interpretation regarding God in all of His attributes will move in dangerous directions.

The Effect on Our Practical Life

Daily living issues have given impetus to neotheism, but the practical concerns of daily life are troubled by implications of this view for ethics and sanctification. As A. W. Tozer has said,

Figure 1. The God of Theism and of Neotheism

Theism	Neotheism
Wisdom and foreknowledge	
God knows all things, past, present, and future.	God knows past and present, but learns future, free events.
Emotions	
God is impassible: Nothing can hurt or act upon Him. He acts out of His grace and mercy.	God is passible: He can be hurt and acted upon. We can make God feel pain.
Transcendence over time	
God is eternal (nontemporal).	God is temporal.
Simplicity of Being	
God is simple, not composed of parts. He is absolutely and indivisibly one in essence.	God is composite, made of parts.
Changeableness	
God is immutable: He does not change. He is perfect, and any change would be for the worse.	God is mutable: Change does not necessarily mean imperfection.
Authority and rule	
God sovereignly reigns over all things. Not one atom in the universe is outside His control, efficiently or permissively. God allows us to participate in His plan of salvation, but He does not need us.	God is sovereign, but He needs our help to be able to carry out His plan of salvation. God does not control free events. He cannot guarantee in advance how everything will turn out.
Power	
God is omnipotent: He can do anything that does not contradict His nature. He gives but does not give away power. His power is infinite.	God is omnipotent: He can do all things that are not contradictory. He gives away power. Thus, He is not infinite in power.
Fallibility	
God is infallible: He cannot err in any respect.	God is fallible: He can err, and Scripture states that He has erred.

A right conception of God is basic not only to systematic theology but to practical Christian living as well. It is to worship what the foundation is to the temple; where it is inadequate or out of plumb the whole structure must sooner or later collapse. I believe there is scarcely an error in doctrine or a failure in applying Christian ethics that cannot be traced finally to imperfect and ignoble thoughts about God (Tozer 1961, 10).

Geerhardus Vos also speaks to this concern:

The divine omniscience is most important for the religious life. The very essence of religion as communion with God depends on His all-comprehensive cognizance of the life of man at every moment. Hence, it is characteristic of the irreligious to deny the omniscience of God (Psalm 10:11, 13; 94:7–9; Isaiah 29:15; Jeremiah 23:23; Ezekiel 8:12; 9:9). Especially along three lines this fundamental religious importance reveals itself:
a. it lends support and comfort when the pious suffer from the misunderstanding and misrepresentation of men;
b. it acts as a deterrent to those tempted by sin, especially secret sin, and becomes a judging principle to all hypocrisy and false security;
c. it furnishes the source from which man's desire for self-knowledge can obtain satisfaction (Psalm 19:12; 51:6; 139:23, 24; Orr 1929: "Omniscience").

CONCLUSION

As shown in figure 1, the contrast between historical Christian orthodoxy and neotheism is stark in their views of God. The challenge of neotheism is both theological and practical. Ideas have consequences, and basic theological ideas have eternal consequences. The concept of God is foundational in any worldview. Hence, neotheism challenges Christian belief at its root. The entire superstructure of theology will fall if the foundation is destroyed. Evangelicals have a divinely given responsibility to maintain the faith once for all delivered to the saints (Jude 3). This is particularly true in reference to the Being of God.

CHAPTER TWO

Omniscience

AT THE CORE OF neotheism is the belief that God does not have infallible foreknowledge of future acts. This stands in stark contrast to the virtually unanimous view of the historical Christian church from the earliest times. Further, the biblical and theological ground undergirding classical theism, and orthodox Christianity built upon it, is solid.

Christians and Jews, from their earliest recorded histories, have united in their affirmation that God knows all things exhaustively (past, present, and future, actual and contingent). Their confession is not based on wishful thinking, but on a multitude of biblical texts that affirm the all-knowing nature of God.[1] As Geerhardus Vos correctly comments, "Scripture everywhere teaches the absolute universality of the Divine knowledge" (*ISBE:* "Omniscience").

BIBLICAL PERSPECTIVE ON OMNISCIENCE

The exhaustive totality of God's knowledge is asserted or assumed throughout Scripture. That omniscience can be broken down into affirmations:

---

1. Lewis Sperry Chafer and Geerhardus Vos give practical reasons that come from the omniscience of God. See Lewis Sperry Chafer, *Systematic Theology*, 8 vols. (Dallas: Dallas Seminary Press, 1947). 1.197–98; and Geerhardus Vos, "Omniscience," in *ISBE*.

God's Exhaustive Knowledge

God's knowledge of Himself and His creation is infinite. It is exhaustive of everything external to Him (Isa. 40:28) and internal to Himself within the members of the Trinity (Matt. 11:27; 1 Cor. 2:11). He has perfect knowledge of Himself (*scientia necessaria*, "necessary knowledge"), and He has exhaustive knowledge of all else. He knows everything immediately, not by acquired understanding (Ps. 139:1-6). Psalm 147:5 says, "Great is our Lord and mighty in power; his understanding has no limit." The term *infinite* testifies that there is no limit upon God's knowledge. Literally, it is without number.[2] The Scripture says that nothing is hidden from Him (Heb. 4:13). He has a knowledge of everything that is external to Himself in His creation (*scientia libera*, "free knowledge," Acts 15:18).[3] In anthropomorphic expression, Scripture says that God's eyes run everywhere (Job 24:23-24; Pss. 33:13-15; 139:13-16; Prov. 15:3; Jer. 16:17).

God Knows His Creation Minutely and Intimately.

His exhaustive knowledge includes the smallest elements of creation to the most important matters. He knows the exact number of hairs on our heads (Matt. 10:30) and the number of days each of us will live (Ps. 139:16). His knowledge extends to all human activities (Ps. 33:13-15) and the other created

---

2. Heb.: *ʾeyin mispar*; LXX: *ouk arithmo*, and Vul.: *non est numerus*.
3. Richard Longenecker says, "The interpretation of v. 18 is notoriously difficult. Aleph, B, and C, together with the Coptic and Armenian versions, read 'that have been known for ages' (*gnosta ap aionos*). To accept this reading is to understand the clause as part of a conflated biblical citation that extends from v.16 through v.18 (as RSV, NEB, JB, TEV, NIV), probably alluding to Isaiah 45:21. But A and D, together with Bodmer P74 and the major Latin and Syriac versions, read 'known to the Lord from eternity is his work' (*gnoston ap aionos estin to kyrio to ergon autou*); and E and P, together with the Byzantine text, read 'known from eternity to God are all his works' (*gnosta ap aionos esti to theo panta ta erga au tou*)." *Expositor's Bible Commentary* (Grand Rapids: Zondervan, 1980; CD-ROM ed. Oak Harbor, Wash.: Logos Research Systems), Acts 15:18.

order (Matt. 10:29), seeing (Heb. *rāʾāh*) human actions but looking inside the heart to determine the very internal thoughts and motives (Heb. *mahăšābā*) of the heart (1 Sam. 16:7; 1 Kings 8:39; 1 Chron. 28:9; Ps. 139:1–4; Prov. 15:3; Ezek. 11:5).[4] Indeed, God has the ability to look inside the heart. This allows Him to perceive whether actions mirror actual heart intent (Heb. 4:13). He gives work for good (Isa. 44:28; Eph. 2:10) and sees those that do evil (Gen. 6:5; Luke 22:22; Rev. 2:23).

God's Certain Foreknowledge

Since God dwells in eternity, He has comprehensive insight (*praescientia*, "knowledge before") into all past, present, and future reality.[5] To God, the past is as real as though it was happening in the present. The future is as certain as though it was the past. For Paul affirms in Romans 4:17 that God "calls those things which do not exist as though they did" (see Isa. 46:10). God brings to pass all things that He has planned in

---

4. Regarding *rāʾāh*, see F. Brown, S. Driver, and C. Briggs, *Enhanced Brown-Driver-Briggs Hebrew and English Lexicon*, (Oak Harbor, Wash.: Logos Research Systems, 2000). Scripture indicates that God does not only see human actions, but His knowledge extends to the inward thoughts and motives. According to Genesis 6:5, before God destroyed the earth, He had not only observed the actions of mankind but also looked into the hearts. The noun derivative *mahăšābā* has three basic meanings: "thought," "plan," and "invention." All three correspond to basic variations noted for the verb. It is used to mean "thought" in Gen. 6:5b: "Every inclination of the thoughts of his heart was only evil all the time." See R. Laird Harris, *Theological Wordbook of the Old Testament*, (Chicago: Moody, 1980).

5. Stephen Charnock explains the relationship: "The knowledge of one thing is not in God before another, one act of knowledge doth not forget [forego] another. In regard of the objects, one thing is before another, one year before another, one generation of men before another; one is the cause, the other is the effect. In the creatures there is such a succession, and God knows there will be such a succession; but there is no such order in God's knowledge, for he knows all those successions by one glance, without any succession of knowledge in himself" (Stephen Charnock, *The Existence and Attributes of God* [ET Grand Rapids: Sovereign Grace, 1971], 223).

eternity, even as each of His creatures acts freely, doing as he or she wills. God knows perfectly all that He has purposed (Isa. 14:26, 27; 46:10, 11; Dan. 4:35; Eph. 1:11). All of the future is certain in the mind of God, and each future event will follow from the decree of God. As A. H. Strong says, "God knew free human actions as possible, before he decreed them; he knew them as future, because he decreed them" (Strong 1907-9, 357).[6]

In this regard, God has known eternally all historical developments, including all that would happen to His people Israel (Dan. 2:36-43; 7:4-8) and all that would pertain to Jesus the Messiah (cf. Acts 2:29-36). He now knows all the future events that will transpire on the earth (Matt. 24:25; Revelation 6-19).

God's Contingent Knowledge

Not only does God know with complete certainty all of the future, He also knows what would have happened had He decreed otherwise. These possible scenarios and the free decisions they would have triggered are never actual (*scientia de futuro conditionata*, "conditional/provisional knowledge of the future"). As revealed in Scripture, God knew that the town of Keilah would betray David to Saul if David remained where he was (1 Sam. 23:11-13). He knew that Tyre and Sidon would have repented had they seen the miracles that were done by Jesus in Bethsaida and Chorazin (Matt. 11:21). He knew that

---

6. Though generally all would recognize that God's decree does not precede His foreknowledge chronologically, there is difference of opinion whether the decree may precede the foreknowledge in a logical manner. Strong believes that "Logically, though not chronologically, decree comes before foreknowledge" (*Systematic Theology*, 357). This is also accepted by Francis Turretin, *Institutes of Elenctic Theology*, ed J. T. Dennison Jr.; trans. G. M. Giger (Phillipsburg, N.J.: Presbyterian and Reformed, 1992), I.3.12.18, and William G. T. Shedd, *Dogmatic Theology*. 2d ed., 3 vols. (Nashville: Thomas Nelson, 1980), I.397, but rejected by Augustine, Anselm, and Aquinas (SCG, I.76), and Lewis Sperry Chafer. They insist that in the mind of God these are interrelated and simultaneous.

Sodom would not have been destroyed if they had seen the works done in Capernaum (Matt. 11:23).[7]

Those who hold to "middle knowledge" (*scientia media*) claim that God knows all possible worlds, and so His decisions are based on these foreseen free actions.[8] However, God is a simple and independent Being. Hence, His knowledge and being are identical. Thus, God's knowledge cannot be any more dependent than His Being (Geisler 1999: "Middle Knowledge").[9]

KNOWLEDGE AND GOD'S OTHER ATTRIBUTES

God's knowledge of all things is from the vantage point of eternity, so that the past, present, and future are all encompassed in one ever-present "now" to Him (see Acts 15:17–18). He is the Alpha and the Omega, the beginning and the end, the first and the last (Isa. 46:10; Rev. 1:8, 17). He encompasses time, though He is not in time. God's timelessness directly correlates with His exhaustive knowledge (*ISBE:* "Omniscience").[10]

Even as Scripture speaks of God's foreknowledge, this expression is an accommodation to human understanding (Rom. 8:29; 1 Peter 1:2). God knows all in eternity, but the events He knows occur in time and appear from the human standpoint to be known *beforehand* (Thiessen 1949, 81).[11] God's coordinate foreknowing and foredetermining (His decrees) together comprise His comprehensive plan for His creation. His decrees are the basis for all that occurs in time and space (Isa. 41:22–27; Amos 3:7).

---

7. Although this particular passage may be a hypothetical hyperbole indicating the severity of Capernaum's sin.

8. For a discussion of *scientia media*, see Charles Hodge, *Systematic Theology*, 1.398–400, and Caspar Wistar Hodge, "Foreknowledge," in *ISBE*.

9. We will look at God as a simple and independent Being in ch. 5.

10. We will return to this point in chapter 3. See Vos, "Omniscience."

11. Some desist from the view that God has all knowledge before Him, with His actions viewed as past, present, and future from human perspective. See discussion in H. Orton Wiley, *Christian Theology*, 3 vols. Kansas City: Beacon Hill, 1940–43): 1.357–58.

God's knowledge, then, closely relates to His sovereignty. He has created all things, He sustains them, and He upholds them moment by moment. All things conform to His perfect plan (Eph. 1:11). J. I. Packer says, "The idea that God could know, and foreknow, everything without controlling everything seems not only unscriptural but nonsensical" (Packer 1993, 32).

The Bible relates God's knowledge to His omnipresence. Knowing all things means the mind of God is ever present and at work in every moment (*ISBE:* "Omniscience"). Just as nothing happens outside God's presence, nothing bypasses His purview (Ps. 147:5; Prov. 15:3; Jer. 23:23–24; Heb. 4:13). This connection is borne out especially in Psalm 139, where God's knowledge of the psalmist is closely related to the presence of God wherever the psalmist might be (vv. 7–12).

The fact that God knows the future sets Him apart from the false gods of the nations (Isa. 44:7–9), proving that He is God. In fact, the lack of certain knowledge of the future characterized the pagan deities (Isa. 41:23).

Some would argue that God's foreknowledge is conditioned by the acts of His creatures (Pope n.d., 1.318ff; Wiley 1940–43, 1.357). However, God does not simply know because man chooses to act. Though His knowledge of man's free acts is not causative, it is decretive.[12] Strong corrects Pope, when he argues that "in eternity there could be no cause of the future existence of the universe, other than God Himself, since no other being existed. Consequently, God's determination to create involved also a determination of all the actual results of that creation; or, in other words, God decreed those results" (Strong 1907–9, 356).

The omni-knowledge of God is not contrary to human free choice. Lewis Sperry Chafer (1871–1952) explains, "If the question be asked whether the moral agent has freedom to act

---

12. God, of course, is the ultimate and primary cause of all things. But He is not the immediate cause of our free acts. Free agents are the immediate efficient cause of all their free acts.

otherwise than as God foresees he will act, it may be replied
that the human will because of its inherent freedom of choice
is capable of electing the opposite course to that divinely
foreknown; but he will not do so. If he did so, that would be
the thing which God foreknew. The divine foreknowledge does
not coerce; it merely knows what the human choice will be"
(Chafer 1947, 1.196). He then addresses the protest of the
Socinians (sounding remarkably like today's neotheists), who
assert that until the human choice is made, it cannot be a subject
of knowledge, so that even God is not able to know what the
choice would be. He responds that "What God foreknows is
certain, not because He foreknows it, but because He has
decreed it" (Chafer 1947, 1.196). The men who crucified Christ
did precisely what prophets a thousand years before had said
they would. God determined what they would do, even to the
point of someone jeering, "He trusts in the LORD; let the LORD
rescue him. Let him deliver him, since he delights in him" (Ps.
22:8; cf. Matt. 27:43). As predicted, they parted and cast lots
for His garments (Ps. 22:18; cf. John 19:24). Within their own
experience, these men said and did precisely what they freely
chose to; yet they said and did only what had been divinely
determined and hence divinely foreknown (Acts 2:23).

THEOLOGICAL SUPPORT FOR OMNISCIENCE

In addition to the biblical data, there are important
theological arguments for God's omniscience, with particular
reference to His infallible foreknowledge of future free acts.
Some of these are drawn from other attributes of God, which
are defended in later chapters.

The Argument from God's Infinity

Both theists and neotheists agree that God is infinite (without
limits). But God's knowledge is identical to His nature, since
He is a simple Being (see ch. 5). So God must know according
to His Being. Therefore, God must know infinitely. But to be
limited in knowledge of the future is not to know infinitely.

Hence, God's infinite knowledge must include all future events. If it did not, then He would be limited in His knowledge.

The Argument from God's Causality

All effects preexist in their efficient cause, since a Cause cannot produce what it does not posssess. It cannot give what it does not have. But God is the First Cause of all that exists or will exist. Hence, the future (with all of its free actions) preexists in God. By knowing Himself, God knows all future free actions. God knows Himself infallibly and eternally. Thus, He has infallible and eternal knowledge of all free actions that will ever occur.

The Argument from God's Necessity

Both theists and neotheists agree that God is a Necessary Being. But a Necessary Being has no possibility of not existing. And what has no possibility of not existing is Pure Existence. But Pure Existence or Pure Actuality has no potentiality. And since potentiality is a limitation in being, then a Being of Pure Actuality has no limitations in its Being. But God's knowledge is identical to His Being. Therefore, God's knowledge must be without any limitation. That is, it is infinite.

The Argument from the Nature of Reality

Reality includes both the actual and the possible. Only the impossible is not real. But God's knowledge extends to all that is real. If it did not, then He would not be all-knowing, since there would be something that He did not know. But if God knows the possible as well as the actual, then God must know the future, since the future is possible, not impossible. If it were impossible, then it would never happen. Hence, God must know all that will be actualized in the future, including all future free acts.

The Argument from God's Eternality

God is an eternal Being. His knowledge of the world is from eternity. But an eternal Being knows eternally. And eternal knowing is not limited by time. Thus, God's knowledge is not limited by time. He knows the future with the same eternal glance with which He knows the past or present. Thus, there is no problem of foreseeing future events. God simply sees them in His eternal present.

The Argument from God's Perfection

God is an absolutely perfect Being. Hence, His knowledge, as identical to His Being, must be absolutely perfect too. And as an absolutely perfect Being God must know Himself perfectly.

But to know Himself perfectly means to know not only His own nature but to know all possible ways others can participate in the perfections of that nature. This means that God's perfect knowledge includes all the ways creatures can and will participate in God's perfections. Nothing, then, in the future free acts of man can be unknown to God from eternity. If it were, then God's knowledge of Himself would not be perfect.

HISTORICAL SUPPORT FOR OMNISCIENCE

Not only is the classical view of God's omniscience firmly grounded in Scripture, but it is also virtually unanimously supported in the fathers of the church. This is true from the very beginning.

The Early Fathers and Omniscience

The early fathers, apologists, and theologians of the church are in unison affirming the exhaustive knowledge of God. Though the term omniscience is not used by them, foreknowledge being the favored word, the ideas stated in Scripture concerning this doctrine are clearly believed by them and taught in their writings.[13]

---

13. A fifth-century father, Fulgentius (467-532), bishop of Ruspe, says, "The eternal firmness and firm eternity of God's predestinating will consist not only in the ordaining of works. God also knows in advance the number of the elect. No one of that full number may lose his eternal

Justin Martyr (c. 100–165?) affirmed that God knows from all eternity those that He has chosen unto salvation. For example, Justin says that Christ would remain in heaven until "the number of those who are foreknown by Him as good and virtuous is complete, on whose account He has still delayed the consummation" (*First Apology* 45 in *ANF* 1:178). God knows beforehand persons to be saved by repentance, some not yet born (*First Apology* 28 in *ANF* 1:172). Justin also argues that when Christians speak of future events being prophesied, one should not understand this to refer to fatalism but to "God foreknowing all that shall be done by all men, and it being His decree that the future actions of men shall all be recompensed according to their several value (*First Apology* 44 in *ANF* 1:177).

Tatian (c. 110–172), a disciple of Justin's, attributes this foreknowledge of God, through prophecy, as one of the reasons for his conversion to Christianity: "and I was led to put faith in these by . . . the foreknowledge displayed of future events" (*Address to the Greeks* 29 in *ANF* 2.77).

Cyprian (200–258) says that this foreknowledge of God by the Holy Spirit through the apostles serves the church in teaching it how to live for Christ (*Epistles of Cyprian to the People of Thibaris* 55.6 in *ANF* 5.349).

Irenaeus (c. 120–202) says that God (here the Holy Spirit) foreknew the doctrines of the evil teachers (*Against Heresies* 3.21.9 in *ANF* 1.453). As well, God is fully knowledgeable of those persons who will not believe: "If, therefore, in the present time also, God, knowing the number of those who will not believe, since He foreknows all things, has given them over to unbelief, and turned away His face from men of this stamp,

---

grace, nor may any outside that total attain the gift of eternal salvation. For God, who knows all things before they come to pass, is not confused about the number of the predestined, any more than he doubts the effectiveness of the works he has ordained." Fulgentius, *On the Truth of Predestination* 3.6. *Ancient Christian Commentary*, 8.112–13; *Corpus Christianorum Series Latina* (Turnhout, Belgium: Brepols, 1953–), 91A:525.

leaving them in the darkness which they have themselves chosen for themselves" (*Against Heresies* 4.29.2 in *ANF* 1.502). Irenaeus also connects the establishment of the Christian faith with God's foreknowledge through prophecy, "in order that our faith might be firmly established; and contained a prophecy of things to come, in order that man might learn that God has foreknowledge of all things" (*Against Heresies* 4.32.2 in *ANF* 1.506).

Clement of Alexandria (c. 150–220?) says, "For He shows both things: both His divinity and His foreknowledge of what would take place" (*Instructor* 1.9 in *ANF* 2.228). Other fathers are in concert that God dwells in eternity and knows all future things from that eternal fulcrum.

Tertullian (160–220) responds to Marcion's (2d century) denial of God's foreknowledge by holding in tension foreknowledge and foreordination as two sides of the same answer. He feels confident to do this because inspiration of the prophets so clearly establishes foreknowledge:

> But what shall I say of His prescience, which has for its witnesses as many prophets as it inspired? After all, what title to prescience do we look for in the Author of the universe, since it was by this very attribute that He foreknew all things when He appointed them their places, and appointed them their places when He foreknew them? (*Against Marcion* 2.5 in *ANF* 3.301).

Tertullian adds, "There is sin itself. If He had not foreknown this, He would not have proclaimed a caution against it under the penalty of death" (*Against Marcion* 2.5 in *ANF* 3.301). At the same time, however, Tertullian says, this foreknowledge did not interfere with God's gift of freedom of choice, even to perish by the choice to sin (*Against Marcion* 2.7, 4.41 in *ANF* 3.303, 3.419).[14]

---

14. Also see *The Instructor* 1.9 (*ANF* 2.228).

Contrary to neotheists, Tertullian presents Judas's betrayal of Jesus to be according to the predictions of Scripture and also known by Christ (*Against Marcion* 4.41 in *ANF* 3.419). *The Constitutions of the Holy Apostles*, written sometime between the late 100s and 325, state what the author alleged to be the words of the apostles regarding Jesus' foreknowledge of the betrayer (*Constitutions of the Holy Apostles* 5.3.14 in *ANF* 7.444). The accuracy of the text may be doubtful, but it shows the attitude of the early church, in which the Lord's foreknowledge as God was indisputable.

Origen (c. 185–254), in his work against Celsus, contends that God observed in His foreknowledge those who would walk worthy of Him and would serve faithfully until death (Origen, *Against Celsus* 7.44 in *ANF* 4.629). God knows the future of all things, including human sins (Ambrosiaster *Commentary on Paul's Epistles* in *Oden* 2001, 235). These include evil acts against Christ and against Christians. Of the persecutions Christians faced, Justin says, "It was foreknown that these infamous things should be uttered against those who confessed Christ, and that those who slandered Him, and said that it was well to preserve the ancient customs, should be miserable. Hear what was briefly said by Isaiah; it is this: 'Woe unto them that call sweet bitter, and bitter sweet'" (*First Apology* 49 in *ANF* 1.179).

Further, Origen said that foreknowledge is not a term to use for God's knowledge of evil. Nonetheless, he believed that God's knowledge was universal:

> In Scripture, words like foreknew and predestined do not apply equally to both good and evil. For the careful student of the Bible will realize that these words are used only of the good. . . . When God speaks of evil people, he says that he never knew them. . . . They are not said to be foreknown, not because there is anything which can escape God's knowledge, which is present everywhere and nowhere absent, but because everything which is evil is considered to be unworthy of his knowledge or of his foreknowledge.

(*Commentary on the Epistle to the Romans* 4.86, 88, 90 in Oden 2000, 6:235)

Origen does not deny the exhaustive knowledge of God in his statements but demonstrates that God's actual knowledge includes all things, though He views the acts of good and the evil to be in a different relationship to Him.

Lactantius (250–325) wrote that Jupiter's lack of fore-knowledge was unbefitting a god and disproved his deity (*Divine Institutes* 1.11 in *ANF* 7.20). Other fathers argue also for foreknowledge being necessary to God. In writings of an uncertain date that are wrongly attributed to Clement of Rome (c. 97), the author uses an *a fortiori* argument that if God gave prophetic foreknowledge to Adam and to Moses, how could He not also have foreknowledge (*Clementine Homilies* 3.43–44 in *ANF* 8.246–47)?

Other early Fathers affirmed the same. Hippolytus (c. 160–236) says that God is "fully acquainted with whatever is about to take place, for foreknowledge also is present to Him" (*Refutation of All Heresies* 10.28).[15] Similarly, Gregory Thaumaturgus (c. 213–c. 270) indicates that, regarding God's foreknowledge, what is about to occur is as though it has already happened, because it has been made certain by God (*A Metaphrase of the Book of Ecclesiastes* 3 in *ANF* 6.11).

The Medieval View of Omniscience

The great theologians of the Middle Ages were unanimous in their view of God's omniscience. God knows all things, past, present, and future. He knows all things actual and potential. Further, His knowledge is infallible. He cannot be wrong about anything He knows. The only limits on God's knowledge are that God cannot know what is impossible to know. He knows what will be and what could be, but He cannot know what

---

15. Dates vary as to early fathers. We have chosen to use those dates found in *ANF* 10.277–399.

cannot be. God cannot know what is contradictory. God is a rational Being, and as such, He cannot know what is irrational or contradictory. The three great theologians of the medieval period were Augustine of Hippo (354–430), Anselm of Canterbury (c.1033–1109), and Thomas Aquinas (1224–1274). Their view forms the basis of what is known as *classical theism*.

Augustine

Augustine dominated the early medieval church. His prolific writings set forth with force and clarity the concept of God proclaimed by the great early fathers of the church. He proclaimed the infallible foreknowledge of God about all future events, including those resulting from free actions. He wrote of God: "His vision is utterly unchangeable. Thus, He comprehends all that takes place in time—the not-yet existing future, the existing present, and the no-longer-existing past—in an immutable and eternal present" (*City of God* 1983 ET 11.21). Further, Augustine declared, "Neither does His attention pass from thought to thought, for His knowledge embraces everything in a single spiritual contuition." Thus, "His knowledge of what happens in time, like His movement of what changes in time, is completely independent of time" (*City of God* 1983 ET 11.1).

As to the relation between God's absolute and unchangeable foreknowledge and human free will, Augustine held that God's "foreknowledge cannot be deceived" (*City of God* 5.10). God infallibly foreknows exactly how we are going to use our free choice. "The conclusion is that we are by no means under compulsion to abandon free choice in favor of divine foreknowledge, nor need we deny—God forbid!—that God knows the future, as a condition for holding free choice" (*City of God* 1983 ET 5.10). Hence, "a man does not sin because God foreknew that he would sin. Nay, it cannot be doubted but that it is the man himself who sins when he does sin, because He, whose foreknowledge is infallible, foreknew . . . that the man himself would sin, who if he wills not, sins not. But if he shall not will to sin, even this did God foreknow" (*City of God* 1983 ET 5.10).

In brief, for Augustine God infallibly foreknew from all eternity exactly how each creature would use his free choice. Hence, future free acts are determined from the vantage point of God's omniscience, but not from the standpoint of our free choice.

Anselm

Following the lead of his medieval mentor, Augustine, Anselm of Canterbury set forth in more reasoned form the classical view of God found in the earlier fathers. Anselm argued that God's omniscience included infallible foreknowledge of everything. "For He foreknows every future event. But what God foreknows will necessarily occur in the same manner as He foreknows it to occur" (*Trinity, Incarnation, and Redemption*, 153). This infallible foreknowledge includes free acts. "For God, who foresees what you are willingly going to do, foreknows that your will is not compelled or prevented by anything else; hence this activity of the will is free" (*Trinity, Incarnation, and Redemption*, 154). So, "to foreknow something implies that that thing is going to happen. . . . And so, if God foreknows something, then it is necessary that the thing occur" (*Trinity, Incarnation, and Redemption*, 157–58).

Anselm hastens to point out that God's necessary foreknowledge does not make the event necessary. "For, although He foreknows all future events, nevertheless He does not foreknow every future event as occurring by necessity. . . . He foreknows that some things are going to occur through the free will of rational creatures" (*Trinity, Incarnation, and Redemption*, 158). Anselm sees no difference in God's foreknowledge regarding whether an event happens through free will. God "sees only what is true—whether this results from necessity or from freedom" (*Trinity, Incarnation, and Redemption*, 161).

The Anselmian perspective is that "God who knows all truth and only truth, sees all things just as they are—whether they be free or necessary; and, conversely, as He sees them so they are" (*Trinity, Incarnation, and Redemption*, 159). The implication is that God's knowledge of everything, including future free acts, is necessary, unchangeable, eternal, and immutable (*Trinity, Incarnation, and Redemption*, 162–63).

Since God knows from eternity, Anselm reasons, "the foreknowledge of God is not properly called foreknowledge. For all things are always present to Him, and so He does not have foreknowledge of future things, but knowledge of present things" (*Truth, Freedom, and Evil* 185). Anselm reasons that the future is present to God in eternity. Thus, God does not have to foresee or wait to see or prognosticate the future. It is present to Him from all eternity. In fact, since He is the cause of all things, the future preexists in God in all eternity. Thus God sees it in Himself as its Cause from all eternity. All truth exists eternally in the "Supreme Truth [who] has no beginning and no end," for He Himself is truth (*Truth, Freedom, and Evil* 192).[16]

As for prediction of free events, Anselm held that they were made infallibly and with necessity. He wrote of the predictions about Christ:

> If, then, it be said that it was necessary for him to die of his single choice, because the antecedent faith and prophecy were true, this is no more than saying that it must be because it was to be. . . . But such a necessity as this does not compel a thing to be, but only implies a necessity of its existence. There is an antecedent necessity which is the cause of a thing, and there is also a subsequent necessity arising from the thing itself. . . . Wherever there is an antecedent necessity, there is also a subsequent one; but not vice versa. . . . By this subsequent and imperative necessity, was it necessary (since the belief and prophecy concerning Christ were true, that he would die of his own free will), that it should be so. (*Cur Deus Homo?* 18[a]).

16. See also *Cur Deus Homo?* 18[a].

Aquinas

Thomas Aquinas argued that all knowing involves a knower and a known. But in self-knowledge the knower and known are identical. Hence, God can only know Himself through Himself (*Summa Theologica* 1a.14.2). God knows Himself by Himself and in Himself. And since God is eternal, immutable, and simple, it follows that He knows Himself eternally, immutably, and simply (see ch. 2–4 for discussions of each of these areas).

Furthermore, for Aquinas, God also knows Himself perfectly. Something is known perfectly when its potential to be known is completely realized. And there is no unactualized potential in God, since He is complete, Pure Actuality. Therefore, God knows Himself perfectly. His self-knowledge is completely actual (*Summa Theologica* 1a.14.3).

What is more, for Aquinas, God's knowledge is identical with His essence. For if God's acts of knowledge were really distinct from His essence, then they would be related as actuality to potentiality. But there can be no potentiality in God. Therefore, God's knowledge and essence are really identical (*Summa Theologica* 1a.14.4). This does not mean that God cannot know things other than Himself. For God is the efficient Cause of all things. All effects preexist in their efficient cause. Whatever exists must preexist in God, who is its efficient cause, and God knows Himself perfectly. But to know Himself perfectly entails knowing all of the various kinds of perfection in Himself. He also must know perfectly those to whom He has given His likeness. Therefore, it follows that God knows whatever exists perfectly insofar as all preexists in Him (*Summa Theologica* 1a.14. 5).

Aquinas affirms that the fact that God is unchanging does not mean He cannot know changing things. For God knows everything in one eternal now including the past, present and future. And God knows the future before it happens in time. Therefore, when time changes, God's knowledge does not change, since He knew in advance it would change. In other words, God knows what we do but not in the way we do, that is, in successive time frames. God knows the whole of time from (within) eternity, but He knows what is before and what is after the temporal now of human history (*Summa Theologica* 1a.14.15). God's knowledge is not simply of the actual; He also knows the potential. He knows both what is and what could be, for God can know whatever is real in any way that it can be known. Now both the actual and the potential are real. Only the impossible has no reality (*Summa Theologica* 1a.14.9). Hence, God cannot know what is impossible to know, since contradictions do not fall under the omniscience of God. However, God can know future contingents, that is, things that are dependent on free choice. For the future is a potential that preexists in God. And God knows whatever exists in Himself as the cause of those things (*Summa Theologica* 1a.14.13).

Further, since God is a timeless Being, He knows all of time in one eternal present. But, the future is part of time. Therefore, God knows the future, including the free acts to be performed in it. Of course, whatever God knows is known infallibly, since God cannot err in His knowledge. And since God knows future contingents, it follows that they too are known infallibly. They are contingent with regard to their immediate cause (human free choice), but necessary with regard to God's knowledge. God can do this without eliminating free choice, for an omniscient Being can know whatever can be known. Certainly a timeless Being can know a necessary end that is caused by a contingent means.

Therefore, as an omniscient Being, God knows as necessarily true all future contingents. He knows necessarily what will be. That is, if something will occur and God infallibly knows it will occur, then it necessarily must occur. An omniscient Mind cannot be wrong about what it knows. Therefore, the statement "Everything known by God must necessarily be" is true, if it refers to the statement of the truth of God's knowledge. The statement is false if it refers to the necessity of the contingent events (*Summa Theologica* 1a.14.4).

In summation, from Augustine the "Medieval Monolith" to

Aquinas the "Angelic Doctor," there was one voice on the omniscience of God. God has infallible knowledge from all eternity of everything that would ever occur, including all free actions. This infallible knowledge does not diminish the freedom of the creature, since God knew for sure (determined) what they would do (by a free act).

Omniscience from the Reformation

The Reformers, generally, follow the thinking of Augustine in their formulation of God's omniscience: God knows all things past, present, and future.

Luther

Martin Luther (1483–1546) interprets the all-knowing of God as coming from the determination of His will, saying that God "foreknows nothing contingently, but that He foresees, purposes, and does all things according to His own immutable, eternal and infallible will" (*Bondage of the Will*, 80). When Luther uses the term *contingent*, he does not mean that God's knowledge is always *scientia necesaria* and not *scientia libera*. Luther uses *contingently* to speak of human actions that are independent of God's determinations, like the Greek concept of fate (*Bondage of the Will*, 80–81).[17] His meaning is clear from his discussion of the Latin: "Lest we be deceived over our terms, let me explain that being done contingently does not, in Latin, signify that the thing done is itself contingent, but that it is done by a contingent and mutable will—such as is not to be found in God!" (*Bondage of the Will*, 81). For Luther, something is contingent "when our will or hand fastens on something presented to us as if by chance, without our having previously thought or planned anything about it" (*Bondage of the Will*, 81). Thus, he believed that God knows all reality regarding Himself and all things outside of Himself. This knowledge is necessary because God wills everything, rather than because the created

---

17. See also Hodge, "Foreknow; Foreknowledge," in *ISBE*.

order possesses complete independence and God only observes. In fact, we know that He is actively involved.[18]

Moreover, in deciding the future that He knows, God does not do so by "necessity," in the sense of compulsion, that is, against His will, which is free (*Bondage of the Will*, 81). God has complete and infallible foreknowledge of all future events, including those flowing from free choice.

Calvin

John Calvin (1509-1564) speaks of the patriarch Joseph's comments to Pharaoh that his knowledge of the future was dependent on the revelation of what God Himself would do (Genesis 41). It was not that he had some special knowledge of the future. Calvin says,

> We hence infer, that God does not indolently contemplate the fortuitous issue of things, as most philosophers vainly talk; but that he determines, at his own will, what shall happen. . . . Wherefore, in predicting events, he does not give a response from the tables of fate, as the poets feign concerning their Apollo, whom they regard as a prophet of

---

18. Mark Chavalas distinguishes the exercise of divine will and kinds of causation: "Many think of divine will and natural causation in exclusive terms. They cannot exist together. But to seek a divine origin for an event because of the inability of our present understanding to provide a satisfactory natural explanation is a fallacy. This is a determination to be made from the other side of omniscience. To see a divine effect does not mean the termination of natural causes. Explanations of an event in natural and unnatural terms are not exclusive but compatible. In the ancient Near East, as well as in Israel, kings imputed victory to the gods without denying that human agents took part. Divine causation in Scripture was not usually those events that interrupted the sequence of natural causes but those that usually exhibited how God was at work in them. But one needs to find a balance in order to understand how to interpret an event historically." Mark W. Chavalas, "The Historian, the Believer, and a Study in the Supposed Conflict of Faith And Reason," *in* *JETS* 36.2 (June 1993): 157.

events which are not in his own power, but declares that whatever shall happen will be his own work.[19] (John Calvin, *Commentary on Genesis*, 658)

Moreover, Calvin states, "God foreknew what the end was to be before he made him, and foreknew so ordained by His decree. Should anyone inveigh against the prescience of God, he does it rashly and unadvisedly" (*Institutes of the Christian Religion* 3.23.7).[20]

For Calvin, foreknowledge does not mean conditioning by the creature. He states,

> When we attribute prescience to God, we mean all things always were, and ever continue, under his eye; that to his knowledge there is no past or future, but all things are present, and indeed so present, that is not merely the idea of them that is before him (as those objects are which we retain in our memory), but that he truly sees and contemplates them as actually under his immediate inspection. This prescience extends to the whole circuit of the world, and to all creatures. (*Institutes of the Christian Religion* 3.21.5)

Arminius

In most ways, the perspective of Jacobus Arminius (1560–1609) concerning God's future knowledge is consistent with that of Calvin, Luther, and the orthodox church through the centuries. Arminius, in contrast to the Socinians, believed that God understands all things. He has complete knowledge of Himself and His creatures' actions in the past, present, and future. His knowledge covers the necessary and the contingent,

---

19. See Isaiah 45:7.
20. Calvin seems to share the perspective of Strong, Shedd, and Turretin regarding the logical relation of God's decree and foreknowledge.

the good and the bad.[21] Arminius expresses God's omniscience in eloquent and precise terms:

> He knows things substantial and accidental of every kind; the actions and passions, the modes and circumstances of all things; external words and deeds, internal thought, deliberations, counsels, and determinations, and the entities of reason, whether complex or simple. All these things, being jointly attributed to the understanding of God, seem to conduce to the conclusion, that God may deservedly be said to know things infinite. (*Writings of James Arminius* 2.4.31)

This knowledge is not learned but infinitely intuitive, in eternity not time, immeasurable and immutable, by a single and undivided act (*Writings of James Arminius* 2.4.32).

Turretin

Francis Turretin (1623–1687) sets forth four aspects of God's knowledge: It is (1) perfect, (2) undivided, (3) distinct, and (4) immutable. His knowledge is perfect in that He knows all things by Himself, by His essence and His knowledge is in eternity, not in time. His knowledge is undivided since He knows all things intuitively and noetically, rather than by learning or reasoning (discursively and dianoetically). His knowledge is distinct in that He knows at one glance so that nothing, even the smallest thing, escapes His knowledge. Lastly, His knowledge is immutable because there is no change. He knows everything in all facets by immutable cognition (*Institutes of Elenctic Theology*, 207).

Jerome (c. 345–c. 419) made an unfortunate diminution of God's foreknowledge by claiming that it is "unworthy of the

---

21. "God knows himself *entirely* and *adequately*. For He is all Being, light and eye. He also knows other things *entirely;* but *excellently,* as they are in Himself and in his understanding; *adequately,* as they are in their proper natures" (*Writings of James Arminius* 2.4.1.32).

divine majesty to let it down to this, that it should know how
many gnats are born or die every moment, number of cinches
and fleas on earth" (*Commentariorum in Abucuc* 1.1 IPL 25.1286).
Turretin says that such a view is very injurious towards God
(*Institutes of Elenctic Theology*, 207). He counters by mentioning
that God knows the hairs on our heads and sparrows that fall
(Matt. 10:29–30), that all things are naked and open to Him
and manifest in His sight (Heb. 4:13) and that God knows the
number of stars and calls them by name (Ps. 147:4). He
concludes, "Yea, since all things (even the greatest) are the
smallest before him in comparison with his infinity (as Isa. 40:15
magnificently says) and, as it were, nothing, the knowledge of
all things should be denied of him if the smallest are removed
from his notice" (*Institutes of Elenctic Theology*, 208).

After a lengthy discussion of contingent knowledge, Turretin
concludes that "when God conceives future contingent things
as certainly future, he does not conceive of them otherwise than
they are; but he knows them relatively to the decree as
necessarily about to take place and determinate which, relative
to their cause, he knows as indeterminate and contingently
future" (*Institutes of Elenctic Theology*, 212). Turretin explains the
contingency by primary and secondary causes: "God foreknows
them both in himself and in his decree (as the first cause), and
so they are necessary on account of the immutability of the
decree and the infallibility of foreknowledge; and God
foreknows them in the second causes on which they proximately
and immediately depend, which are per se indefinite, and so
they are contingent things" (*Institutes of Elenctic Theology*, 212).

Edwards

Jonathan Edwards (1703–1758) shares the historic and
orthodox view of God's exhaustive knowledge, particularly that
of foreknowledge, seeing it as evidence of God's "peculiar glory,
greatly distinguishing him from all other beings" (*A Careful and
Strict Inquiry* 11.1.4.109). In reference to the nature of God's
foreknowledge, Edwards contends that for God not to know

beforehand is to deny God the ability to foretell the future. God, instead, is limited to uncertain guesses. For if God does not foreknow "the future volitions of moral agents, then neither can he certainly foreknow those events which are consequent and dependent on these volitions" (*A Careful and Strict Inquiry* 2.11.96–97).

In reacting to the suggestion by other theologians that God does not know the actions of His free creatures, Edwards says that God "must have little else to do but to mend broken links as well as he can, and be rectifying his disjointed frame and disordered movement in the best manner the case will allow." He then muses as to the tremendous and miserable disadvantages of God governing the world without being able to discover major things that may befall his world, for which, if He knew, He could plan accordingly (*A Careful and Strict Inquiry* 11.4.111). The tradition in favor of God's infallible foreknowledge of all events is virtually unbroken to modern times.

NEOTHEISTS' TEXTUAL OBJECTIONS

Neotheists have leveled serious biblical and theological objections against the traditional view of omniscience. Perhaps the most basic objection is that language about God's interaction with human beings should not be taken anthropomorphically.

God's Changing Mind

Neotheists argue that traditional theologians are inconsistent. On the one hand, they take literally those passages of Scripture where God is portrayed as knowing and/or controlling the future. On the other hand, they deny the literal meaning of passages that speak of God changing His mind or knowing the future only in terms of possibilities. Gregory Boyd says this differentiation is unneeded unless one assumes that the future is already settled. "If we don't assume that the future is entirely settled, there is an easy way to integrate the motif of future determinism with the motif of future openness" (Boyd 2000, 14–15).

Boyd then explains that the issue of "openness" does not relate to the nature of God but to the nature of the future:

> Though open theists are often accused of denying God's omniscience because they deny the classical view of foreknowledge, this criticism is unfounded. Open theists affirm God's omniscience as emphatically as anybody does. The issue is not whether God's knowledge is perfect. It is. The issue is about the nature that God perfectly knows. More specifically, what is the content of the reality of the future? Whatever it is, we all agree that God perfectly knows it. (Boyd 2000, 15–16)

Boyd adds that the future "consists partly of settled realities and party of unsettled realities" (Boyd 2000, 16).

An important issue of definition must be taken up with Boyd as he makes such statements. His argument hinges on the meaning of the words *reality* and *realities*. If the future truly is "open," it is ridiculous to speak of the content of its reality or that this reality can be in some sense "settled." Yet, can there be such a thing as an *unsettled* reality, if by reality we mean what is objectively to happen in the time-and-space future. *The American Heritage Dictionary* defines *reality* as:

> 1. The quality or state of being actual or true. 2. One, such as a person, an entity, or an event, that is actual . . . 3. The totality of all things possessing actuality, existence, or essence. 4. That which exists objectively and in fact. (4th ed., 2000)

According to this definition, something that is unsettled is only a possibility. Something that is a reality is certain or settled. Similar confusion of terms occurs elsewhere in the argument. Boyd illogically speaks of an infinite Being who has finite abilities. God is a partly omniscient deity. Boyd and his open-theist colleagues cannot have it both ways. There are no square circles. When the entire view of God is laid out before us, we are left with the inescapable conclusion that this is a finite god, a being different from the God who is.

Neotheists' unwillingness to accept anthropomorphic language regarding God's knowledge leads them to conclusions they may not have envisioned. If we refuse to treat as metaphorical any language about the mind of God, He does not know the present or the future exhaustively. In the interaction between Yahweh and Abraham in Genesis 18:20–33, the text portrays God as not having adequate information to know whether there were enough righteous in Sodom to spare the city. Indeed, Abraham negotiates God down from fifty to ten as the cut-off.

God also seems to have imperfect knowledge of the present in Isaiah 6:8: "And I heard the voice of the Lord, saying, 'Whom shall I send, and who will go for us?' Then I said, 'Here am I! Send me.'" Literalistic (non-figurative) interpretation of this question means God truly did not know whom to send. There are reasons why neotheists have fallen into this untenable position.

First, Boyd fails to understand that God may sound indefinite to us because He desires to speak in terms that solicit a response from us. He wants to involve the hearer in the implications of the answer. God uses language of sequential thought and indecision to communicate, not to satisfy a lack in His knowledge.

Second, if neotheists persist in taking these anthropomorphisms as literal descriptions, they reduce God to a finite being. He is no longer the infinite Creator who condescends to speak in human terms and thought patterns so that we can understand. If neotheists wish to speak of God as omniscient regarding only certain portions of the future, they are fudging on the meaning of *omniscient*. For example, a student declares, "My math teacher is omniscient." Upon further questioning, however, we learn that he means only that she has an unlimited knowledge of multiplication tables. Would we not think that this enthusiastic student had fudged on the meaning of omniscient?

Third, the hermeneutic employed by neotheists leads to other serious theological problems. If God is not omniscient, is He also not omnipresent? God interacts with human beings in the language of space. God calls out to Adam and Eve, asking, "Where are you?" (Gen. 3:9). Did God not know where Adam was when He inquired regarding his whereabouts? But if a nonspatial God found it necessary to enter into spatial dialogue in order to have a proper conversation with spatial creatures, why cannot the same nontemporal God use temporal concepts in dialogue with temporal creatures? Implicitly, the omnipresence of God is at stake if we do not understand this passage in a figurative sense regarding God's attributes. The text implies that God was located in one space and Adam in another.

Fourth, following neotheism's literalistic interpretation, we would have to conclude that God moves from place to place. In Exodus 3:7–8, Yahweh encounters Moses on Mount Horeb and reveals that He has been observing His people in Egypt and has empathized with their suffering. Then He reveals that He has now "come down" to deliver them. Surely we should not understand this literally, as God moving from one place to another. An omnipresent Being does not have to go anywhere. God is not spatial and does not move in time and space. But for communication, He uses expressions that are understandable to finite humans who move in time and space. Such nonliteral descriptions of divine activity enable personal interaction.

Knowing and Causing

According to Boyd, God knows all things that He has planned or determined to know. He chooses not to determine or plan anything involving the free choices of human beings. To defend this viewpoint, he turns to two passages on God's sovereignty and omniscience:

> Remember the former things of old, For I am God, and there is no other; I am God, and there is none like Me, declaring

the end from the beginning, and from ancient times things that are not yet done, saying, 'My counsel shall stand, And I will do all My pleasure,' calling a bird of prey from the east, The man who executes My counsel, from a far country. Indeed I have spoken it; I will also bring it to pass. I have purposed it; I will also do it. (Isa. 46:9–11)

Long ago, I foretold things that happened, From My mouth they issued, and I announced them; Suddenly I acted, and they came to pass. Because I know how stubborn you are (Your neck is like an iron sinew And your forehead bronze), Therefore I told you long beforehand, Announced things to you ere they happened — That you might not say, "My idol caused them, My carved and molten images ordained them. You have heard all this; look, must you not acknowledge it? As of now, I announce to you new things, Well-guarded secrets you did not know. Only now are they created, and not of old; Before today you had not heard them; You cannot say, 'I knew them already.'" (Isa. 48:3–7 TANAKH)

Strangely, Boyd declares that the passages do not reveal a God who knows the entirety of the future but One who knows that part of the future He has decided to control according to His purpose: "He foreknows that certain things are going to take place because he knows *his own purpose and intention* to bring these events about. As sovereign Lord of history, he has decided to settle *this much* about the future" (Boyd 2000, 30; emphasis Boyd's). When Isaiah records Yahweh's words that He declares "the end from the beginning," He supposedly speaks only of the settled portion of the future: "He declares that the future is settled to the extent that he is going to determine it, but nothing in the text requires that we believe that *everything* that will ever come to pass will do so according to his will and thus is settled ahead of time" (Boyd 2000, 30; emphasis Boyd's).

As to the prediction that Judas would betray Christ, Boyd claims that if Judas should not have chosen to betray Him, it is likely that Jesus could have found someone else. This is not as likely with Cyrus, since a limited number of kings was available to conquer Israel. To demonstrate his position, Boyd sets forth five categories of future events that God does know: (1) He knows His chosen people; (2) He knows individuals; (3) He knows Christ's ministry; (4) He knows the elect; and (5) He knows the end times (Boyd 2000, 25–29).

Boyd appears to confuse God's determination with direct causation. A person may know something without causing it in such a way as to take away any human self-determination, and so may God. If a person standing on the side of the road sees a car coming toward a person in the road, and then it hits that individual, he has not caused the accident.

Further, with twisted logic, Boyd believes that God expresses His sovereignty by not exercising control rather than by exercising it. He says,

> Indeed, God is so confident in his sovereignty, we hold, he does not need to micromanage everything. He could if he wanted to, but this would demean his sovereignty. So he chooses to leave some of the future open to possibilities, allowing them to be resolved by the decisions of free agents. It takes a greater God to steer a world populated with free agents than it does to steer a world of preprogrammed automatons. (Boyd 2000, 31)

This seems to be an equivocation: God is so much in control that He is not in control? But then, Boyd says that God is in control in some sense, steering the world. If controlling *all* of the future would be demeaning, why would being in total control of *some* of the future not also be demeaning? One can easily be dizzied by such antinomies, on top of God's limited omniscience and limited infinitude.

What is more, according to neotheists, in a number of things of the future God has definite intentions and so truly knows them ahead of time, but in most other things He does not. Unless Scripture specifically mentions that God knows something, it is relegated to the side as things that He does not know with certainty. Using this logic and interpretative method, the Bible specifies that the very hairs of our head are numbered, so God does not know the number of hairs on our arms. God knows the birds of the air who fall to the ground, but He must not know when an airliner falls from the sky. Surely, Matthew 10:29–30 and Luke 12:6–7 make precisely the point that these are examples of the infinite knowledge of the God in whom we can place trust.

It is difficult to take Scripture seriously and not hear its clear teaching that God determines all things and thus knows all things that He has determined. In this determination, He has chosen to be proactive to accomplish His will at times but generally to refrain from acting, preserving the free acts of men consistent with their natures, and thus accomplish His will in reference to these acts.

Predictions Based on Character

Boyd argues that God can predict with great accuracy without infallible foreknowledge, based on His knowledge of the character of those performing the acts. He says,

> Our omniscient Creator knows us perfectly, far better than we even know ourselves. Hence, we can assume that he is able to predict our behavior far more extensively and accurately than we could predict it ourselves. This does not mean that everything we will ever do is predictable, for our present character doesn't determine all of our future. But it does mean that our behavior is predictable to the extent that our character is solidified and future circumstances that will affect us are in place. (Boyd 2000, 35)

To illustrate his view, he discusses Peter and Judas. Boyd says that absolute knowledge of the future was not necessary for Jesus to predict that Peter would deny the Lord three times (Matt. 26:33–35):

Contrary to the assumption of many, we do not need to believe that the future is exhaustively settled to explain this prediction. We only need to believe that God the Father knew and revealed to Jesus one very predictable aspect of Peter's character. Anyone who knew Peter's character perfectly could have predicted that under certain highly pressured circumstances (that God could easily orchestrate), he would act just the way he did. (Boyd 2000, 35)

Boyd's view supposes that a person's character may inevitably lead to a particular action that may be certainly known by God. When presented with the circumstances we will choose to act in a certain way without fail. How is this not a form of determinism? If Peter genuinely has the right to self-determination, sometimes called free will, then no matter what the circumstances, he can make the choice he desires. But other problems loom over Boyd's view.

It should be observed that even perfect knowledge of character could not predict what God did in Peter's case. How does knowledge of character not only reveal that he would deny Christ, but that he would deny Jesus three times? Not one, two, or four, but exactly three! Now Boyd may respond that God sent three different people to Peter to ensure that it would be specifically three times to fulfill the prophecy, but must Peter fail at each with certainty? And how could God, in open theism, ensure that someone else would not also tempt Peter and thus contradict the prophecy, or maybe be an encourager and move him from this course?

Further, not only was the prediction that Peter would deny Christ, and do it three times, but that it would be before the rooster crowed. Boyd merely says before morning, but there is more than morning involved. The denials occurred immediately before a rooster crowed. How would God, in an open view, anticipate this chain of events? Boyd's view is incredible.

What is more, knowledge of character, no matter how accurate, cannot predict events with certainty. Yet the New

Testament reveals that such events as Jesus' betrayal and death were determined with certainty before they happened (cf. John 6:64; Acts 2:23). In a libertarian view of freedom, innumerable choices could always have thwarted God's plan.

Judas's Freedom in God's Plan

Boyd believes that Judas's betrayal was not determined in eternity. In fact, any of the disciples could have been the betrayer, for determining that Judas would betray Jesus would violate free action. He supports his argument in three ways:

First, he questions that John 6:64 teaches that Jesus knew in eternity or even early in His ministry that Judas would betray him. He claims that the word *archē* used here does not imply that Jesus knew who would betray Him from a time before the person decided in his heart to betray Him. As in Philippians 4:15, the word can mean "early on." This verse, thus, suggests that Jesus knew who would betray Him from the moment this person resolved to betray Him, or from the time Jesus chose him to be a disciple, but not from eternity (Boyd 2000, 37).

Second, Boyd disclaims that the statement "son of perdition" (NASB) relates specifically to Judas in John 17:12:

> Many assume that when Jesus referred to Judas as one who was "destined to be lost," he meant that Judas was damned from the beginning of time (John 17:12). However, the verse simply doesn't say this. The Greek translated as "destined to be lost" [NRSV] literally says "son of perdition," with no indication as to *when* Judas had become this. We only know that by the time Jesus said this, Judas had, of his own free will, made himself into a person fit for destruction. (Boyd 2000, 37)

Third, Boyd argues that Judas did fulfill prophecy, but it was not necessary that he be the one who would fulfill Scripture. Boyd says that "we have every reason to suppose that Judas could have (and should have) chosen a different path for his

life, but as a free moral agent, Judas tragically chose a path of
. . . self-destruction. If he had made himself into a different
kind of person, he would not have been a candidate for fulfilling
the prophecy of the Lord's betrayal. In this case, the Lord
simply would have found someone else to fill this role" (Boyd
2000, 38).

Another neotheist, John Sanders, weighs in on the betrayal
of the Christ, arguing that Jesus did not know that Judas would
do so up until he actually did. Sanders argues that when Jesus
announced at the Passover meal that one of the disciples
would betray Him—hand him over (*paradidōmi*) to the temple
authorities—we would be wrong to believe that Judas in fact
betrayed Jesus. Relying on the work of William Klassen,
Sanders argues that none of the disciples considered Judas
to be the betrayer at the Last Supper, and that Judas was on
friendly terms with Jesus. He says that "hand over"
(*paradidōmi*) does not mean betray in John 13:21. Instead,
Judas was attempting to get Jesus to confront the high priest
and resolve their differences. When Jesus sent Judas from the
supper (John 13:27), it was not to betray Him, for this would
be for Jesus to tell a fellow Jew to go and deliberately commit
a sin. Rather, He reaches out to Judas trying to get him to
decide what sort of Messiah he expected Jesus to be (Sanders
1998, 98–99).

Boyd's argument seems to be that Jesus did not have a prior
knowledge of Judas's intent to betray Jesus when He chose him
as a disciple. Jesus only discovered this at the time of Judas's
actual decision to do so later, or at the exact time He selected
Judas as a disciple. One wonders why God's unfailing anticipation
of character, as argued earlier in reference to Peter, is not used
here? Under the neotheist hermeneutic rubric, this would not
require the absolute knowledge of the future. Nonetheless, the
text reveals that Jesus knew who believed Him and specifically
who would betray Him. This text does not speak of a later time
in His ministry or even necessarily to His choosing of Judas.
Nothing in the sixth chapter of John would indicate this.

John applies the word *archē* both to eternity (John 1:1-2; 8:44) and to the beginning of Jesus' ministry with the twelve (John 6:64; 8:25; 15:27; 16:4). The text does not say which should be understood here, but the context suggests that eternity is in view. Note that the verse following this pronouncement in 6:64 has the conclusionary "for this reason": "And He was saying, 'For this reason I have said to you, that no one can come to Me unless it has been granted to him from the Father'" (John 6:65 NASB). The reason Jesus had knowledge of who would believe and who would betray related to God's election, which is eternal.

Second, in response to Boyd's rejection of "destined to be lost" for "son of perdition," we agree that the phrase does not need to be translated "destined to be lost." Moreover, we do not dispute that humans are lost because they fit themselves for destruction, as taught by Paul in Romans 9:22.

But we must disagree with Boyd's point that Judas's betrayal was not a specific fulfillment of Scripture, and that someone else could have betrayed Jesus as a fulfillment of Scripture. First, though Boyd believes that God would have found someone else to fill this role if Judas had not betrayed Jesus, it is not so simple to find one to betray Jesus and thus fulfill Scripture. Maybe no one would, if we grant the complete freedom neotheists espouse. For another thing, Boyd's comment that Jesus does not say that Judas had to fulfill Scripture misses the point. For while Jesus did not say his, Peter did say this. Note his words to the 120 in the upper room: "Men and brethren, this Scripture *had to be fulfilled*, which the Holy Spirit spoke before by the mouth of David concerning Judas. . . . For it is written in the book of Psalms: 'Let his dwelling place be desolate, And let no one live in it'; and 'Let another take his office'" (Acts 1:16-20). It is here that Boyd's evaluation of the evidence directly contradicts the literal meaning of the text.

Sanders's interpretation of the betrayal of Jesus by Judas stretches interpretation to the breaking point. John 13:11, spoken on the night of Jesus' betrayal in the upper room, clearly says, "For he knew would betray him; therefore he said, "You are not all clean'" (Sanders 1998, 99). In his excellent review of Sanders's book, A. B. Canedy says Sanders's discussion of "hand over" (*paradidōmi*) commits the *root fallacy* and the *prescriptive fallacy*. In the root fallacy, he presumes that the etymology of the word establishes the meaning, and he prescribes the one root meaning of "hand over" to every occurrence (Caneday 1999, 131–63). Sanders fails to learn from the arguments of James Barr in the early 1960s in his important work, *The Semantics of Biblical Language*, that words rely on context, not etymology, for meaning (Barr 1961, 217–18).[22]

Additionally, though Sanders avers that Jesus dipping His bread in the bowl and giving it to Judas was an act of friendship, not a sign that he was the betrayer, this is opposed to the words of Scripture which indicates that He dipped into the bowl specifically to identify Judas as the betrayer, quelling the unease of at least two of the disciples regarding His announcement of a betrayer among them. After the dipping, the text indicates that Satan entered into Judas to do his dastardly deed (John 13:21–27). It is special pleading to argue that when Judas seeks to hand over Jesus to the authorities it is not a breaking of trust and thus not a betrayal.

God's Regrets

Neotheists claim that, not only does God have limited knowledge, but He also makes bad or unwise decisions. Boyd writes:

> Now some may object that if God regretted a decision he made, he must not be perfectly wise. Wouldn't God be admitting to making a mistake? . . . It is better to allow

---

22. Barr says, "The error that arises, when the 'meaning' of a word (understood as the total series of relations in which it is used in the literature) is read into a particular case as its sense and implication there, may be called 'illegitimate identity transfer'" (p. 218).

> Scripture to inform us regarding the nature of divine wisdom than to reinterpret an entire motif in order to square it with our preconceptions of divine wisdom. If God says he regretted a decision, and if Scripture elsewhere tells us that God is perfectly wise, then we should simply conclude that one can be perfectly wise and still regret a decision. Even if this is a mystery to us, it is better to allow the mystery to stand than to assume that we know what God's wisdom is like and conclude on this basis that God can't mean what he clearly says. (Boyd 2000, 56–57)

This kind of interpretation is hard to reconcile with the all-wise God of Scripture. Foremost, it is at odds with the clear teaching of the Bible that God's knowledge is limitless (Ps. 147:5), that He knows the end from the beginning (Isa. 46:10) and that His Wisdom is the basis of all human wisdom aimed at avoiding bad decisions like that (Proverbs). How can God be the source, foundation, and repository of all wisdom (Prov. 1:7; Col. 2:3) and be so foolish?

Further, the neotheist view undermines the biblical teaching that God is absolutely perfect. The psalmist wrote, "The law of the LORD is perfect, converting the soul; the testimony of the LORD is sure, making wise the simple" (Ps. 19:7). Job added, "Do you know how the clouds are balanced, those wondrous works of Him who is perfect in knowledge?" (Job 37:16). But how can God be perfect in knowledge and wisdom and yet make such mistakes?

It is unnecessary to take these anthropomorphic expressions as literal. Even neotheists admit that the Bible is filled with anthropomorphic references to God's eyes, ears, arms, legs, and even wings. Why, then, should these expressions not be understood anthropomorphically?

NEOTHEISTS' THEOLOGICAL OBJECTIONS

In addition to lacking biblical and historical support for their belief in limited omniscience, neotheists fail to provide compelling theological support for their doctrine. The arguments they offer are easily explained in terms of classical theism.

Knowledge of Future Free Acts

At the heart of the view of limited omniscience is this reasoning:

1. God knows infallibly whatever is possible to know.
2. It is not possible to know infallibly future free acts.
3. Therefore, God does not know future free acts infallibly.

Sanders states that, "though God's knowledge is coextensive with reality in that God knows all that can be known, the future free actions of free creatures are not yet reality, and so there is nothing to be known" (Sanders 1998, 198). This is often called *qualified* or *limited omniscience*, in contrast to classical omniscience, which is unlimited.

Thus, according to neotheism, God's knowledge of future free acts is fallible. So states Sanders: "Nonetheless, this [the gaps in God's knowledge of the future] does leave open the possibility that God might be 'mistaken' about some points, as the biblical record acknowledges" (Sanders 1998, 132). Sanders does not say that God's will is not good—only that it is not certain. With regard to free choices, God can only prognosticate based on His vast knowledge of human character, events, and tendencies what free creatures are likely to do. He cannot be absolutely sure what they will do. "Given the depth and breadth of God's knowledge of the present situation, God forecasts what he thinks will happen," Sanders theorizes. "In this regard, God is the consummate social scientist predicting what will happen" (Sanders 1998, 131). Neotheists, however, make one important proviso. Anything God wishes to know absolutely and control completely about the future, so as to accomplish His ultimate plan, He can know by divine intervention. He can tamper with human freedom, if necessary and on occasion, so as to determine the final outcome of things. Ordinarily God does not do this, hence, creatures are free to do what even God Himself does not know infallibly they will do, according to Boyd (Boyd 2000, 34).

> Many prophecies pertaining to individuals can be understood as examples of the Lord establishing particular parameters ahead of time. The two most impressive examples of this are Josiah and Cyrus. As a supernatural sign to his people, God named Josiah ("the Lord strengthens") and Cyrus and declared their accomplishments before they were born. This decree obviously set strict parameters around the freedom of the parents in naming these individuals (see also Luke 1:11–23). It also restricted the scope of freedom these individuals could exercise *as it pertained to particular foreordained activities*. In other respects, however, these two individuals and their parents remained self-determining agents. (Boyd 2000, 34)

Classical theists have no difficulty with the logical form of this basic argument about God's omniscience. Of course, God cannot know the impossible. The disagreement is with the content of the second premise: "It is not possible to know infallibly any future free acts." Traditional theists contend that the defense given for this premise is lacking. An examination of each of the arguments will reveal why.

The Nature of Free Choice

According to neotheist reasoning,

1. Free acts are those that could have been otherwise.
2. God's infallible knowledge of events means they cannot be otherwise (for if they could then God would have been mistaken and not infallible in His knowledge).
3. Hence, infallible knowledge of free acts is impossible.

This conclusion can be challenged in two ways. First, it assumes
a particular view of free choice called "libertarianism" that not
all theists accept. Many, particularly in the strong Calvinist
tradition of Jonathan Edwards, argue that free acts are actions
in which one simply does what one desires.[23] God gives free
agents the desires He decrees. Hence, future free acts in the sense
described by Edwards can be free and yet determined. Since they
are determined, they can be infallibly known in advance.

Second, other classical theists, such as Augustine, Anselm,
and Thomas Aquinas, point out that there is no contradiction
in claiming both that a future free act is determined as it relates
to God's infallible foreknowledge and that it is free as it relates
to the individual's power to do otherwise. Thus, infallible
foreknowledge and free choice are not contradictory. The law
of noncontradiction demands that, to be contradictory, two
propositions must affirm and deny the same thing in the same
sense and in the same relationship. But in this case, an event
is determined in one relationship (God's knowledge) but not
determined in a different relationship (free choice).

The Nature of Truth

According to neotheists,

1. Future events have not yet occurred.
2. A true statement is what corresponds to what has
   occurred.

---

23. Edwards defined freedom thus: "The plain and obvious meaning of the
    words Freedom and Liberty, in common speech, is power, opportunity
    or advantage, that any one has, to do as he pleases" (*Jonathan Edwards:
    Selections*, 279, cf. 311). Of course, he goes on to argue that it is God
    alone who gives the desire to do good to His creatures. So, fallen hu-
    mans are not free to do what they decide (with the power of contrary
    choice), but only what they desire as God gives the desire to do good or
    to do evil as their own fallen nature demands. Edwards has no explana-
    tion as to why unfallen creatures as Lucifer and Adam could desire to
    choose evil, since God surely did not give them this desire, and they
    had no fallen nature.

3. Hence, no statements about the future can be true (since the future has not yet occurred).

That is to say, it makes no sense to talk about knowing something as true in advance, since it cannot be true until it actually happens.

This seeks to prove more than the neotheist would wish. If nothing can be known to be true before it occurs, God could not know anything in advance—even necessary events—since they have not yet happened. But neotheists admit that God has infallible foreknowledge of necessary events. Therefore, they cannot object to the possibility of God knowing future free events on the basis of the nature of truth.

Also, the logical problem evaporates when one simply phrases the proposition that the truth God knows in advance is that the event will occur later. At best, the neotheist argument only works if the classical theist said that God knows something to be an accomplished fact at this moment that will not be an accomplished fact until some future point in history. There is no difficulty with saying that God can know something is going to occur, and that is all that is necessary to defend the classical view of omniscience.

Finally, the problem is a nonissue for a classical theist since God is eternal (see ch. 3). There are no time indicators on His knowledge. An eternal God does not *fore-see*. He simply sees from all eternity all that from a temporal stand point was, is, and will be. All future events are present to Him in His eternal now. So God knows what we know, but He does not know it the way we know it. We know things as past, present, or future. But God knows our past, present, and future in His eternal present. In order to demonstrate that it is impossible for an omniscient God to know the future, the neotheist must prove that God is temporal, that is, not eternal. No such proof has been given.

The Unreality of the Future

In his book *The God Who Risks*, Sanders argues that God cannot know the unreal future. He writes: "Though God's knowledge is coextensive with reality in that God knows all that can be known, the future actions of free creatures are not yet reality, and so there is nothing to be known" (Sanders 1998, 198). In other words,

1. The future is not real because it has not yet happened.
2. God can only know what is real.
3. Hence, God cannot know the future.

Sanders anticipates two objections. First, "it cannot be an imperfection not to know what is not in itself knowable, i.e., the future, the not yet real, at least in its free or not yet determined aspects." Second, this view is no more an "attenuated" or "limited" understanding of omniscience than is that of Aquinas. Aquinas defined omnipotence as the ability to do all that is logically possible, and knowing what is not real is not logically possible (Sanders 1998, 199).

Aquinas responded to this objection nearly 800 years earlier by noting that the future is real, since reality is made up of the actual and the potential. Only the impossible is not real. The future is a potentiality. It has not yet happened, but it can occur and it will yet occur. So in knowing the future, God is knowing what is real, namely what is really possible.

Further, for the classical theist the future preexists in God, who is its ultimate Cause. Since the future preexists in God, God can and does know it in Himself as one of the things He will cause to occur, and there is no contradiction in affirming that an omnipotent Being can know everything that exists in Himself.

As Aquinas noted, it would be an imperfection for an omniscient Being not to know everything, since everything He knows is known in and through His own nature. And since His nature is absolutely perfect, it follows that everything God knows, including both His own nature and all ways any creature can participate in His perfections, must be known perfectly.

Not to know some ways some creatures can (and will) participate in those perfections would be an imperfection in God's knowledge.

The Possibility of Action in Foreknowledge

Nontheists argue that God cannot intervene in what He foresees:

1. What is infallibly foreseen is determined.
2. If God foresees what will actually occur, then He cannot intervene to change it.
3. Therefore, God cannot interfere in a world He foreknows will occur.

Sanders claims, "The problem arises because of the fact that what God previsions is what will *actually* occur. Divine foreknowledge, by definition, is always correct. If what will actually happen is, for example, the Holocaust, then God knows it is going to happen and cannot prevent it from happening, since his foreknowledge is never mistaken" (Sanders 1998, 201).

Moreover, he says, "If what God has foreseen is the entire human history *at once,* then the difficulty is to somehow allow for God's intervention into that history. This raises a serious problem. Does simple foreknowledge imply that God previsions his own decisions and actions?" That is to say, if God has infallible foreknowledge of what He Himself will do, can foreknowledge be the basis for His actions (Sanders 1998, 201)?

Citing another author with approval, he explains that "it is impossible that God should use a foreknowledge derived from the actual occurrence of future events to determine his own prior actions in the providential governance of the world. Such a deity would then know what he is going to do before deciding what to do." Such a God would "be unable to plan, anticipate, or decide—he would simply know. This seems to call the divine freedom into question, making God a prisoner of his own omniprescience, lacking perfect freedom" (Sanders 1998, 201).

It is important to observe that this objection poses a problem for Molinists but not for other classical theists. Molinists insist that God's decisions are based on what He foreknows will actually occur, should He choose to create that kind of world (Craig 1987, 127–52). However, classical theists hold that God does not have *fore-knowledge* as in sequential time. He simply knows in one eternal *Now*. God's knowledge is not based on anything outside Himself. God's knowledge of all things is based on knowing Himself and all other things as they preexist in Him as their Primary Cause.

The basic argument in favor of the classical theist's view goes like this:

1. God is an independent Being.
2. But God's knowledge is identical to His Being (since He is simple).
3. Hence, God's knowledge is independent.

If this is so, then the belief that God has dependent knowledge (as in Molinism) is false. All His knowledge must be part of His independent Being. That is, He must know everything in and through Himself and not through anything that is contingent.

The Freedom of God

For the same reasons just given, neotheists argue that it is impossible for a God who knows the future infallibly to be truly free. For if God knows the future infallibly, it must occur the way He knows it, or else He would be wrong in what He knows about it. But if it must occur that way, then God is not free to change it. Hence, a God who knows the future infallibly is not really free to act otherwise. The argument can be stated this way: "If God knows already what will happen in the future, then God's knowing this is part of the past and is now fixed, impossible to change." And "since God is infallible, it is completely impossible that things will turn out differently than God expects them to." But "if God knows that a person is going to perform it, then it is impossible that the person fail to perform it—so one does not have a free choice whether or not to perform it" (Pinnock et al. 1994, 147).

Of course, God could be free in the nonlibertarian sense of doing what He desires. This view is open to Calvinists in the Edwards tradition. However, another alternative is possible for those who accept a libertarian concept of freedom. As Anselm noted (see ch. 8), there is a difference between antecedent and consequent necessity. If God wills the future to be a certain way, then by consequent necessity it must be that way. But God is free not to will it that way. Hence, He has antecedent freedom with regard to what the future will be. God could have chosen to create a different world. But when God decides to make a certain world His omniscience knows it will be that way by consequent necessity.

Being a simple Being, God's will and knowledge are coordinate. He knows what He wills and wills what He knows. In fact, He knows eternally what He wills eternally, and He wills eternally what He knows eternally. One is not subsequent to the other chronologically (since He is not temporal) or logically (since He knows intuitively, not sequentially).

The neotheist argument also assumes wrongly that God knows the way we know and wills as we do. But an eternal Being does not foreknow anything as future; He knows it in His eternal present.

Further, a completely independent Being does not react to what he knows, since He is not dependent on anything outside His Being in order to decide or act. He does not react but simply acts from eternity prior to any event happening.

NEOTHEISTIC HISTORICAL ARGUMENTS

Neotheists search in vain to find representatives of their view among any of the orthodox Fathers of the Church. Only a few heretical voices, most of whom are late, even venture to contradict the virtually unanimous teaching that God has infallible foreknowledge of all future events, including free ones.

As for neotheist arguments that the orthodox view of God is based in Greek thought, not the Bible, two things are worthy of mention. First, this can be refuted by a careful examination of the biblical text (see above). Isaiah's God proclaimed "the end from the beginning" (Isa. 46:10) and the psalmist's God was one whose understanding is infinite (Ps. 147:5). Second, there simply is no foundation for asserting that the orthodox Christian view of God is based on Greek philosophy (see chs. 2–3). Who has found omniscience in the finite god of Plato, Aristotle, or any other ancient philosopher? Any Greek conception of God is opposed to the God of Christian theism.

CONCLUSION

The classical theism that has dominated the orthodox Christian church from the very beginning need not be set aside in favor of a Johnny-come-lately view. Neotheism has no adequate biblical or theological grounds. Indeed, there are good reasons biblically, historically, theologically, and philosophically to retain orthodox theism. The neotheistic view capitulates to process theology, which seriously undermines historic Christianity.

Neotheists have created a dangerous paradigm of God, based on anthropomorphism and speculative inferences. These inferences have been borrowed largely from contemporary process theology.

Certainly a person's overall view of God guides their interpretation of truth. Classical theists understand statements about God's eyes, ears, and hands to be metaphors that illustrate how He acts. Similarly, we understand as metaphors the references in Scripture to God repenting, forgetting, or changing His mind. Some biblical language shows God from below and some shows Him from above. Anyone who interprets these anthropomorphic texts literally inevitably will create a finite God.

If the neotheist finds this God more satisfying to believe in, worship, pray to, or serve they must face the implications. By forfeiting God's sovereignty at the expense of a libertarian human freedom, neotheists may answer questions about foreknowledge and predetermination. They have done so, however, at the expense of the basis for orthodox theology as a whole. Denial of the infallible foreknowledge of God has serious ramifications, not the least of which is that it undermines the infallibility of Scripture. That is the lynchpin for all other orthodox teachings (see ch. 9).

CHAPTER THREE

Eternality

CLASSICAL THEISM AFFIRMS that God is above and beyond time. God has no past, present, or future. He simply has an enduring eternal present. This attribute of non-temporality is unanimously rejected by contemporary neotheists.

THE BIBLICAL AFFIRMATION OF ETERNALITY

The biblical basis for God's attribute of non-temporality is firm. Despite the frequent use of metaphors and anthropomorphism, Scripture clearly presents God as being above and beyond time. Regarding the biblical statements about a nontemporal God, there is a firm foundation in Scripture for the belief in a non-temporal God. The use of anthropmorphisms and figures of speech in no way diminishes what the Bible teaches.

From beginning to end, the Bible declares that God is beyond time. The Bible's very first verse testifies that God existed beyond time: "In the beginning God created the heavens and the earth" (Gen. 1:1).[1] If time does not begin until the universe does, this places God beyond time. Indeed, according to Hebrews, God created time. "In these last days He has spoken

---

1. In recent years, many Old Testament scholars have argued that the first verse of the Bible should be translated as a dependent clause. See Bruce K. Waltke, *Creation and Chaos,* for a discussion of the various options that have been posited for the first three verses of Genesis. We believe that the traditional interpretation is preferred, in conformity to the perspective of Jewish and Christian interpreters through the centuries, the translation of the LXX, and consistent with the grammar of Gen. 1:1-3.

by His Son . . . through whom He framed the ages" (Heb. 1:2 auth. trans.). The word *ages* (Gk: *aiōnes*; Heb: *ʿÔlām*) is not a reference to the material nature of the universe (for which would be used the Gk: *kosmos*) but to its unfolding temporal periods.[2] This sense of *aiōn* is explained by James Orr when

---

2. Henry Liddell and Robert Scott, *A Greek-English Lexicon*, speaks of the term *age* primarily in reference to time, rather than matter: αἰών, ῶνος, ὁ, poët. ἡ· apocop. acc. αἰῶ (properly αἰ ών, cf. *aevum*, *v.* αἰ εἱ):—*period of existence:*
   1. one's lifetime, life, Hom. and Att. Poets.
   2. an age, generation, Aesch.; ὁ μέλλων αἰών *posterity*, Dem.
   3. a long space of time, an age, ἀπ᾽ αἰῶνος *of old*, for ages, Hes., N.T.; τὸν δι᾽ αἰῶνος χρόνον *for ever*, Aesch.; ἅπαντα τὸν αἱ. Lycurg.
   4. a definite space of time, an era, epoch, age, period, ὁ αἰών οὗτος this present world, opp. to ὁ μέλλων, N.T.:—hence its usage in pl., εἰς τοὺς αἰῶνας for ever, Ib.

   An Intermediate Greek-English Lexicon founded upon Liddell and Scott's *Greek-English Lexicon7*. Oxford, Clarendon, 1889. Electronic version © Harvard College and the Corporation for Public Broadcasting, 1996. Used by permission of Yale University Press. Electronic text hypertexted and prepared by OakTree Software, Inc. Version 1.1.

   In contrast, *Theological Dictionary of the New Testament* considers αἰῶνας in Heb. 1:2 to be spatial in meaning: "The plural αἰῶνες shares the change of meaning. Hence the αἰῶνες of Hb. 1:2 (δι᾽ οὗ καὶ ἐποίησεν τοὺς αἰῶνας) and 11:3 (κατηρτίσθαι τοὺς αἰῶνας ῥήματι θεοῦ) are to be understood spatially as 'worlds' or 'spheres.'" *TDNT* compares this use with some Rabbinic texts: "For Rabbinic examples of עוֹלָמִים in the same sense, v. Str.-B., III, 671 f.). It is often said that God has created the עָלְמָא עוֹלָם cf. Hb. 11:3; Tg. Dt. 33:28: בְּמִימְרֵיה אִתְעֲבֵיד עָלְמָא ('by his word is the world made'). There is even reference to the creation of more worlds (עָלְמוֹת). Thus it is said in Gn. r., 3 on 1:5 that the Holy One, before He created the present world, created others (בְּרָא עָלְמוֹת), but then destroyed them again because He took no pleasure in them." Gerhard Kittel and Gerhard Friedrich, eds., *Theological Dictionary of the New Testament*, trans. and abr. G. W. Bromiley (Grand Rapids: Eerdmans, 1985).

   Similarly, Louw and Nida discount the nonmaterial sense of αἰών in Heb 1:2: "1.2 αἰών b, ῶνος m (always occurring in the plural): the universe, perhaps with some associated meaning of 'eon' or 'age' in the sense of the transitory nature of the universe (but this is doubtful in the contexts of He 1:2 and He 11:3) — 'universe.' δι᾽ οὗ καὶ ἐποίησεν τοὺς 'through whom (God) made the universe' He 1:2." *BDAG* also lists αἰών in Heb 1:2 as a reference to a spatial concept but admits at the end of the paragraph that "many of these pass. may belong under 2." *BDAG*,

he says that the term *eternal* or *everlasting*, when referring to
God "describes Him as filling, or enduring through, the 'ages'
of time. It is only thus that we can symbolically represent
eternity."

Some neotheists speak of God as being everlasting, that is,
dwelling in time but simply not aging. Orr's discussion reveals
much more about God's eternal existence, namely, that it is "not
simply His filling of ever-flowing 'ages,' but rather that . . . He is
above time; for which time . . . does not exist; to which the terms
past, present and future do not apply. Yet, while God is not in
time (rather holds time in Himself), time-sequence, as the form
of existence of the world, is a reality for God" (*ISBE:* "Eternity").

God dwells in eternity and from eternity brings time and space
into being. The psalmist declares in exuberant praise, "Before
the mountains were brought forth, or ever You had formed the
earth and the world, even from everlasting to everlasting, You

---

33. Section 2 speaks of "a segment of time as a particular unit of history." W. Bauer, F. W. Danker, W. F. Arndt, and F. W. Gingrich, *Greek-
English Lexicon of the New Testament and Other Early Christian Literature*,
3d ed. (Chicago: University of Chicago Press, 1999), 32.

Commentators divided on whether one should understand this pas-
sage to refer to the creation of the universe, including space, (Paul
Ellingworth, *Commentary on Hebrews*. New International Greek Testa-
ment Commentary [Grand Rapids: Eerdmans, 1993, 96]) or whether
the reference is to the creation of epochs or period of time (Brooke
Foss Westcott, *The Epistle to the Hebrews: The Greek Text with Notes and
Essays* [1903; repr. ed. London: Macmillan, 1920, 8]; George Wesley
Buchanan, *To the Hebrews*. The Anchor Bible [Garden City, N.Y.:
Doubleday, 1972], 5-6). See Westcott, *Epistle to the Hebrews*, and Henry
Alford, *The Greek Testament*, Vol 4: *Hebrews-Revelation*. [London:
Rivingtons, 1871–74], 4.5-6 for presentation of alternate views). Cer-
tainly we see elsewhere that the Son created the universe (John 1:3).
Even if the less restrictive undertanding is to be seen in this text, it
includes both space and time (F. F. Bruce, *The Epistle to the Hebrews*.
New International Commentary on the New Testament, rev. ed. [Grand
Rapids: Eerdmans, 1990], 4), not in any way nullifying the point made
here.

are God (Ps. 90:2). Psalm 90:2 expresses the same ideas as "from the ages to the ages" indicating the beginning of time to the end of time as boundary points within which God has acted; He was ontologically prior to this creation, thus not in time. This idea is also given in Isa. 44:6 where Yahweh is called the First and the Last. Yahweh encompasses time, thus is not in time. Note the words of the prophet in Isaiah 57:15, "For thus says the High and Lofty One Who inhabits eternity."

Boundaries of Time

In Exodus 3:14a "God said to Moses, 'I AM WHO I AM.'"[3] In contrast to contemporary linguists who are heavily influenced by process thought, this is best taken as a reference to God's self-existence. Jesus sanctioned this meaning when He said, "Before Abraham was, I AM" (in John 8:58b). It would have made no sense to say "Before Abraham was, I will become what I will become," as many current scholars would like to translate Exodus 3:14. But as the self-existent One before anything else existed, God is prior to time or non-temporal.

In Jesus' great high priestly prayer in John 17:5, He declared: "And now, O Father, glorify me with Yourself, with the glory which I had with You before the world was." But before the world began is before time began. Thus, Jesus is proclaiming God's timelessness. This same concept is emphasized in John 1:3, where

---

3. The traditional understanding of the Hebrew in Exod. 3:14 is "I AM WHO I AM" or "I AM THAT WHICH I AM" (Heb.: *ehyeh asher ehyeh*). Some innovative translations translate the Hebrew phrase as "I will be-there howsoever I will be-there," seeking to reflect the idea that the term is not God's name but a statement of God's immediate presence (*The Schocken Bible*: Vol. 1, *The Five Books of Moses*). Others leave it untranslated (*The Tanakh*); or translate the phrase "The Sovereign God" (*Living Bible*), which seems to totally miss the sense of the Hebrew. Alternate translations that retain the sense of the original include "I am the eternal God" (cev); "I AM THE ONE WHO ALWAYS IS" (nlt) which is close to the *egō eimi ho ōn* of the Septuagint. The Vulgate reads, consistent with the Hebrew, *ego sum qui sum*.

John tells us that "all things were created by Him," the One who was "in the beginning facing God" (John 1:1 auth. trans.).

The apostle Paul, writing to Timothy, said it clearly: "He chose us in Him before the foundation of the world" (Eph. 1:4a). Here again, time began with the universe. According to modern science, time, space, and matter all came into existence at the moment of the Big Bang. Before that, there was no time. If this is so, then the God who existed before the universe did, must have been beyond time.

Elsewhere Paul declared that God is before time in just those words. He wrote Timothy of God's "grace which was given to us in Christ Jesus before time began" (2 Tim. 1:9c). The word *time* (Gk.: *chronos*) is time as we experience it, that is, a succession of moments forming a past, a present, and a future. But Christ is said to be before all of this. He is literally *e-ternal* (not-temporal).[4] Rather, He brought the temporal world into existence (John 1:3; Col. 1:16).

Near the end of Scripture, Jude proclaimed God's eternality in these words: "to the only God our Savior be glory, majesty, power and authority, through Jesus Christ our Lord, before all ages [πρὸ παντὸς τοῦ αἰῶνος], now and forevermore! Amen" (Jude 25 NIV). The ASV more clearly translates the verse, "to the only God our Saviour, through Jesus Christ our Lord, be glory, majesty, dominion and power, before all time, and now, and for evermore. Amen." God not only created the ages, but He was before the ages. But to be before time and to have made time is not to be in time. Hence, the Bible teaches that it was not a creation *in* time but a creation *of* time that God accomplished at the beginning. Hence, the Creator of time can be no more temporal than the Creator of the contingent can be contingent or the Creator of all effect can be an effect.

---

4. The Latin term from which eternal comes is *aeternus* meaning without beginning or end. Charlton T. Lewis and Charles Short, *A Latin Dictionary* (Oxford: Clarendon, 1879), 63.

Anthropomorphism and Figures of Speech

The Bible speaks of God in temporal terms from a human point of view. God is said to "foreknow" (Rom. 8:29), as though He were standing at one moment of time and looking forward to the future. However, these expressions are anthropomorphic, speaking of God in human terms, and are no more to be taken literally than when the biblical text says God has wings (Exod. 19:4), arms (Num. 11:23), or eyes (Heb. 4:13). Likewise, God's repenting (Gen. 6:6) is no more to be taken literally than God's forgetting (Isa. 43:25; Boyd 2000, 118–20). There are no objective criteria by which one can accept one of these as literal and the other as anthropomorphic.

Neotheist Gregory Boyd offers ridiculousness as a criterion for determining what is figurative.[5] But this is not an objective criterion. What is ridiculous to one person from one perspective is not ridiculous to another person from another perspective. Certainly, one is hard pressed to take God's repenting as any less ridiculous if taken literally than his forgetting (Isa. 43:25). This is particularly true since the Bible says God "is not a man, that he should change his mind" (1 Sam. 15:29 cf. Num. 23:19). If this is taken literally, then it is ridiculous to say that God does repent.

Further, if one takes literally God's statement to Adam "Where are you?" (Gen. 3:9), then we are forced to the startling conclusion that God is neither omniscient nor omnipresent if He could not see Adam hiding from Him in the Garden. But by their own logic, neotheists would be forced to conclude that God is finite in His knowledge of things that do not involve free will. Further, God would not be omnipresent, since He was walking in the Garden (Gen. 3:8), which would mean He is limited to one place at a time. Suddenly, by their own logic, a cluster of traditional attributes of God tumbles, laying bare a finite God. Yet they claim to believe in an infinite God.

---

5. See chapter two on the nature of God's knowledge and chapter four on God's immutability.

THE THEOLOGICAL BASIS FOR ETERNALITY

In addition to the strong biblical support for God's eternality, there are strong arguments connected to other attributes of God, some of which neotheists claim to embrace.

God as an Uncaused Cause

The Bible declares and logic demands that God is the First, Uncaused Cause of everything else that exists. This means that God existed before and beyond the space-time universe. But the Creator of time cannot be in time, that is, temporal. Hence, God must be nontemporal by nature.

To argue, as some, that God became temporal at creation makes no sense. If He was nontemporal by nature before creation, then He would still be nontemporal by nature after creation. The act of creation no more makes God temporal than it makes Him a creature because He made creatures, or finite because He formed a finite world. Creation brought about a difference in relationship, not in essence. Prior to creation, the Creator had no relationship with creation. But that no more makes a change in His nature than putting a person next to a pillar changes the nature of a pillar.

God's Infinity

All theists affirm that God is infinite in His Being. However, an infinite Being has no limits. Temporal beings do have limits. Hence, God is not a temporal being. If He were, then He would be limited in being, which He is not.

A temporal being experiences a succession of moments. But, as the Kalam argument for God shows, an infinite number of finite moments before today is impossible. For the present moment is the end of moments before it, but an infinite series of moments has no end.[6] Hence, a temporal God would have a beginning. But whatever has a beginning must have a cause.

---

6. See Craig, *Kalam Cosmological Argument*, 1979.

Hence a temporal "God" would not be God at all, but only a creature that needed a Creator.

God, Space, and Matter

According to the prevailing view in modern science, space and time are correlative. That is, there is never time without space or space without time. If this is so, then any temporal being is also spatial. Likewise, if God is not spatial, then He cannot be temporal. What is more, whatever is in space and time is material. If God is spatial, He is material. But both theists and neotheists believe that God is pure Spirit (John 4:24). If this is the case, then God cannot be temporal either.

Finally, something that is temporal, spatial, and material is subject to the Second Law of Thermodynamics, which declares that it is running out of useable energy. And whatever is running down must have had a beginning. But all theists agree that God did not have a beginning. Therefore, God cannot be temporal.

Immutability

According to the Bible, God is immutable or unchangeable (see ch. 4). Malachi declared: "I the LORD do not change" (Mal. 3:6). He is the One "who does not change like shifting shadows" (James 1:17). The universe changes, but God remains the same, for the writer of Hebrews affirms, "You will roll them up like a robe; like a garment they will be changed. But you remain the same, and your years will never end" (Heb. 1:12). However, if God cannot change, then He cannot be temporal. For whatever is temporal changes. Time itself is a form of measurement based on change from one moment to another. Hence, an unchanging Being cannot be temporal.

Pure Actuality

God is Pure Actuality. He *is* Being; everything else merely *has* being. When we say "God is Being," we are not saying that being is God. In the same manner, when we say "God is good," we do not mean that everything good is God. He is the great I AM, the Self-Existent One (see ch. 1). But what is Pure Actuality has no potentiality in its Being. And what has no potentiality cannot change, since change is a passing from a state of potentiality to a change of actuality or from actuality to potentiality.

Hence, God cannot change. As shown above, time is a form of change. Therefore, God cannot be temporal. From these theological arguments emerge a powerful case for the eternality (nontemporality of God). To deny God's nontemporality tampers with a whole cluster of divine attributes, some of which neotheists claim to hold. Therefore, to deny God's eternality, as they do, is both inconsistent with their own beliefs and disastrous for other attributes of God that undergird orthodox theology.

HISTORICAL SUPPORT FOR ETERNALITY

In addition to the strong biblical arguments in favor of God's eternality, there is virtually universal historical support among the great orthodox fathers of the church for the traditional understanding of God's eternality as meaning non- or a-temporal.

The Early Fathers and Eternality

The early fathers of the church uniformly agree that God is an eternal Being, not subject to the passage of time. In fact, He is the Creator of time. In speaking of God, the early church fathers, and the prayers of early Christians, speak of "the eternal God."

Clement of Alexandria says that God is without beginning, and produces both the beginning and the ending (Clement of Alexandria. *Stromata* 5.14). For example, Tertullian refers to God's eternality in his discussion of fasting: "If the eternal God will not hunger, as He testifies through Isaiah (Ps. 40:28, LXX), this will be the time for man to be made equal with God, when he lives without food" (Tertullian, *On Fasting* 8.6). Peter, the bishop of Alexandria (d. 311), says, "For then, as they say, our eternal God also, the Maker and Creator of all things, framed all things" (Tertullian, *Fragments* ANF 5.1.1). Also, various prayers of thanksgiving, prayers over the dead, and other forms of prayers are often made to God addressing Him as the "eternal God" (*Constitutions of the Holy Apostles* 8.2.5, 8.2.9, 8.2.12, 8.3.20, 8.3.22, 8.4.38).

In his response to Hermogenes, who claims that God created all things from pre-existing matter, making it somehow eternal with God, though inferior, Tertullian says, "since this [eternity] is the property of God, it will belong to God alone, whose property it is—of course on this ground, that if it can be ascribed to any other being, it will no longer be the property of God, but will belong, along with Him, to that being also to which it is ascribed" (Tertullian, *Against Hermogenes* 3).

Dionysius the Great (c. 200–264) taught,

> Now this word "I am" [in John 8:58] expresses His eternal subsistence. For if He is the reflection of the eternal light, He must also be eternal Himself. . . . God is eternal light, having neither beginning nor end. And along with Him there is the reflection, also without beginning, and everlasting. The Father, then, being eternal, the Son is also eternal, being light of light; and if God is the light, Christ is the reflection. (*On John* 8)

Alcuin (c. 735–804), wrote that the Word of God, which "is coeternal with God the Father, was before all time" (Aquinas, *Catena Aurea*, John 11). Cyril of Jerusalem (c. 315–387), said, "God is Alone, alone unbegotten, without beginning, change, or variation; neither begotten of another, nor having another to succeed Him in His life; who neither began to live in time, nor endeth ever" (*Catechetical Lectures* 2.7, 4.4). The fact that God stands outside of time and is the Creator of it places these fathers squarely in line with the testimony that we have seen in the Hebrew Scriptures.

Ignatius declared that Jesus Christ, as the only-begotten Son and Word, existed "before time began, but who afterwards became also man, of Mary the virgin. For 'the Word was made flesh.' Being incorporeal, He was in the body; being impassible, He was in a passible body; being immortal, He was in a mortal body; being life, He became subject to corruption, that He might free our souls from death and corruption." Ignatius says that the Son of God "was begotten before time began, and established all things according to the will of the Father" (Ignatius, *To the Ephesians* 7).

Hilary of Poitiers (c. 315–387) asserted, "His [Christ's] nature forbids us to say that He ever began to be, for His birth lies beyond the beginnings of time. But while we confess Him existent before all ages, we do not hesitate to pronounce Him born in timeless eternity, for we believe His birth, though we know it never had a beginning" (*On the Trinity* 9.57 in *NPNF2* 9.482). He added, "Whatever . . . is created is made in the beginning, . . . [but] the Word was what it is, and is not bounded by any time, nor commenced therein, seeing It was not made in the beginning, but was" (*On the Trinity* 100.13 in *NPNF2* 9.482).[7]

Although things future, insofar as they are to be created, are as yet unmade, to God they have already been made. For Him, nothing is new or sudden in creation. "There is a dispensation of times for their creation, and in the prescient working of the divine power they have already been made" (*On the Trinity.* 12.39 in *NPNF2* 12.227–28).

Concerning Christ, Cyril of Jerusalem reasoned,

> Two fathers He hath: one, David, according to the flesh, and one, God, His Father in a Divine manner. As the Son of David, He is subject to time, and to handling, and to genealogical descent: but as Son according to the Godhead, He is subject neither to time nor to place, nor to genealogical

---

7. See Aquinas, *Catena Aurea*, St. John 7–8.

descent: for His generation who shall declare? God is a Spirit.
. . . [For] the Son Himself says of the Father, The Lord said
unto Me, Thou art My Son, to-day have I begotten Thee. Now
this today is not recent, but eternal: a timeless today, before
all ages. From the womb, before the morning star, have I
begotten Thee. (*First Catechetical Lecture of Our Holy Father
Cyril* 11.5 in *NPNF2* 7.208)

John Chrysostom (c. 344–407) speaking of Christ in John
6:6, said, "But are not made and was, altogether different? For
in like manner as the word is, when spoken of man, signifies
the present only, but when applied to God, that which always
and eternally is; so too was, predicated of our nature, signifies
the past, but predicated of God, eternity" (*Catena Aurea*, St.
John, 7).

Historical theologian Thomas Oden explains the meaning
of the early fathers regarding God and time: God is the "giver
of time, the divine essence, is in itself absolutely independent
of time permitting time as wholly contingent upon the divine
will" (Oden, *Systematic Theology* 1.63). God who chooses "to
create the temporal world and to enter into relationships with
creatures, freely wills to participate in time, and orders and
guides the temporal process, not as if it were necessary to God's
essential Being, but as contingent upon the divine giving"
(Oden, *Systematic Theology* 1.63).

The Medieval View of God's Eternality

From the fourth to the thirteenth century and beyond, there
was virtually unanimous consent on the nature of God as an a-
temporal Being.

Augustine

Augustine set the stage in extensive references to God's
eternality. According to Augustine, God possesses eternality
because He possesses aseity (self-existence), as God told Moses
in Exodus 3:14 (*Exposition on the Book of Psalms* 121.5). "God

always is, nor has He been and is not, nor is but has not been, but as He never will not be; so He never was not" (*On the Trinity* 14.15). Time can be distinguished from eternity in that time does not exist without movement and change, while in the latter there is no change at all.

God did not create in time, Augustine reasoned, for there was no time before He created a changing world: "At no time, therefore, hadst Thou not made anything, because Thou hadst made time itself. And no times are co-eternal with Thee, because Thou remainest for ever" (*Confessions* 11.14). So "the world was made not in time but together with time. For, what is made in time is made after one period of time and before another, namely, after a past and before a future time" (*City of God* 1983 ET, 11.6).[8]

God's eternity is qualitatively different from time. We must "by degrees catch the glory of that ever-standing eternity, and compare it with the times which never stand, and see that it is incomparable." For "in the Eternal nothing passeth away, but that the whole is present; but no time is wholly present; and let him see that . . . both past and future, is created and issues from that which is always present" (*Confessions* 11.11).

What God does in time He willed from eternity. "Thou callest us, therefore, to understand the Word, God with Thee, God, which is spoken eternally, and by it are all things spoken eternally. For what was spoken was not finished, and another spoken until all were spoken; but all things at once and for ever. For otherwise have we time and change, and not a true eternity nor a true immortality" (*Confessions* 11.7).

Thus, God created time from eternity. Augustine asks, "For whence could innumerable ages pass by which Thou didst not

---

8. For Augustine, time is a measure of change, and change involves the coming to be or the ceasing to be of something. However, since God does not come to be nor cease to be, there is no immanent movement to be measured, and given that God is omnipresent, there is no transient movement. Therefore, God cannot be measured by time.

make, since Thou art the Author and Creator of all ages?" But "if before heaven and earth there was no time, why is it asked, What didst Thou then? For there was no 'then' when time was not" (*Confessions* 11.13).

Further, God's decision to create was unchangeable. For a temporal creation "is compatible with the immutability of God's decision. This being so, they should also believe that the world could be made in time without God who made it having to change the eternal decision of His will" (*City of God* 1983 ET, 11.4).

According to Augustine, "God does not see things in time." God declared, "O man, that which My Scripture saith, I say; and yet doth that speak in time; but time has no reference to My Word, because My Word existeth in equal eternity with Myself. . . . And so when ye see those things in time, I see them not in time; as when ye speak them in time, I speak them not in time" (*Confessions* 13.29).

What is more, God's knowledge is independent of time. "Neither does His attention pass from thought to thought, for His knowledge embraces everything in a single spiritual contuition. His knowledge of what happens in time, like His movement of what changes in time, is completely independent of time" (*City of God* 1983 ET, 11.21).

Anselm

Anselm argued that "it is evident that this supreme Substance is without beginning and without end; that it has neither past, nor future, nor the temporal, that is, transient present in which we live; since its age, or eternity, which is nothing else that itself, is immutable and without parts" (Anselm 1962 ET, 83). Thus, "He exists before all things and transcends all things. . . . The eternity of God is present as a whole with him: while other things have not yet that part of their eternity which is still to be and have no longer that part which is past" (Anselm 1962 ET, 26). God "does not exist finitely, at some place or time, [He] must exist everywhere and always, that is, in every place and at every time" (Anselm 1962 ET, 73).

For Anselm, true eternity can belong only to uncreated substance, since true eternity must be free from the limits of beginning and end. Every created thing is bounded by a beginning (Anselm 1962 ET, 83).

> A thing's existence in time is so different from its existence in eternity that at a given moment something may not be present in time which is present in eternity, or something may not be present in time which is present in eternity, or something may be past in time without being past in eternity, or may be future in time without being future in eternity. . . . When we realize this, we have no basis for denying that something can be mutable in time while being immutable in eternity. (Anselm 1970 ET, 163)

God sees all of time at once. "This is due to the very nature of eternity, which encompasses all time and everything whatsoever that exists at any time" (Anselm 1970 ET, 164). "For yesterday and today and tomorrow have no existence, except in time; but thou, although nothing exists without thee, nevertheless dost not exist in space or time, but all things exist in thee" (Aquinas 1962 ET, 25).

Thomas Aquinas

According to Thomas Aquinas, God is not temporal (*Summa Theologica* 1a.10.1). Thomas offers several arguments in support of his conclusion that God is beyond time. A central thought is that whatever exists in time can be computed according to befores and afters. However, a changeless Being has no befores or afters; it is always the same. Consequently, God must be timeless. Time is a measure of befores and afters. But God has no before or after, since He is changeless. It follows, then, that He must be timeless. If He were in time, He could be measured according to a before and after, implying change.

God's eternity also follows from immutability. It begins with the premise that whatever is immutable has no succession.

Whatever is in time has successive states, so nothing immutable is temporal. If whatever is temporal has successive states, one after the other, God has no changing states, so God cannot be temporal (*Summa Theologica* 1a.10.2). Not only is God eternal but He alone is eternal (*Summa Theologica* 1a.10.3). God alone is essentially immutable, since all creatures can cease to exist. But as eternity necessarily follows from immutability, God alone is essentially eternal.

Aquinas distinguishes eternity from endless time for several reasons (*Summa Theologica* 1a.10.4).[9] First, whatever is essentially whole is essentially different from what has parts. Eternity differs from time in this way. Eternity is a *now*; time has *now* and *then*. Hence, eternity is essentially different from time. God's eternity is not divided; it is all present to Him in His eternal *now*, so it must be essentially different from time, which comes only in successive moments.

Second, endless time is not eternity: it is just more of time. Eternity differs in essence, not merely accidentally in quantity. Endless time is only an elongation of time. More of the same thing is essentially the same thing. Third, an eternal Being cannot change, whereas time involves measurable changes in befores and afters. Endless time can be computed according to before and afters. The eternal is changeless, but that which can be computed by its before and after has changed, so eternity must be qualitatively different.

Fourth, there is a crucial difference between the "now" of time and the "now" of eternity (*Summa Theologica* 1a.10.4,ad.2). The "now" of time moves; the "now" of eternity does not move in any way. The eternal "now" is unchanging, but the now of time is ever changing. There is analogy between time and eternity, but there is no identity between the two. God's *now* has no past or future; time's *now* does.

Some have mistakenly concluded that Aquinas does not

---

9. See Norman L. Geisler, *Thomas Aquinas: An Evangelical Appraisal* (Grand Rapids: Baker, 1991), ch. 8.

believe in God's duration because He rejects temporality in God. Aquinas explicitly argued that duration occurs as long as actuality exists. *Eternity* (God) endures without any potentiality. *Aeviternity* (Angels) endure with completely actualized potentiality. Their changes are not essential but accidental. Time endures with progressive actualized potentiality. It follows, therefore that the essential difference comes from the condition of the actuality that is measured.

Eternality from the Reformation

Martin Luther

Martin Luther is consistent with the views of earlier orthodox theologians. God "does not see time lengthwise but obliquely, just as you look crosswise at a long tree that lies before you. Then you can bring into the range of your vision both ends at once. This you are unable to do if you look at it lengthwise. By our reason we are able to look at time only according to its duration (*nach der Länge*)." We must count one year after another from Adam to history's last day. But to God all is at one point (*auf einem Haufen*)" (Luther 1959, 542).

Luther explains that God does not count time in sequence or consecutively, one year before another.

> God grasps everything in a moment, the beginning, the middle, and the end of the entire human race and of all time. And what we consider and measure according to the sequence of time as a very long, extended tapeline, He sees in its entirety, as though wound together into a ball. And so both the life and the death of the last and the first human being are no farther apart for Him than a single moment. (Luther 1959, 542)

John Calvin

John Calvin anticipates panentheistic thought similar to that which influenced neotheism. He speaks of Isaiah's charges against worshippers of false gods in his day (Isa. 40:21): "The idea that God is the soul of the world, though the most tolerable that philosophers have suggested, is absurd" (*Institutes* 1.14.1).

Calvin contrasts such a view with that of biblical history on which the "faith of the Church might lean without seeking any other God than Him whom Moses sets forth as the Creator and Architect of the world." He then says that this history may be contrasted with the fables of the ancient world "as a means of giving a clearer manifestation of the eternity of God as contrasted with the birth of creation, and thereby inspiring us with higher admiration" (*Institutes* 1.14.1).

Calvin encourages his readers to withhold skepticism regarding God's working in eternity and time. He also in another place wisely reminds us that it is just as improper to raise questions about infinite periods of time as about infinite space. However wide the circuit of the heavens may be, it is of some definite extent (*Institutes* 1.14.1).

The eternal existence that Calvin recognizes to be the domain of the eternal God is shared with the eternal Son, the Word of God: "We necessarily understand that the Word was begotten of the Father before all ages. [The apostles] tell us that the worlds were created by the Son, and that he sustains all things by his mighty word (Heb. 1:2). For we here see that *word* is used for the nod or command of the Son, who is himself the eternal and essential Word of the Father" (*Institutes* 1.13.7).

Jacobus Arminius

Jacobus Arminius affirms the traditional belief that God is eternal in his analysis of Acts 15:18. "God does nothing in time which He has not decreed from all eternity to do, this vocation is likewise instituted and administered according to God's eternal decree." Arminius extends this eternal nature to the issue of predestination: "So that what man soever is called in time, was from all eternity predestinated to be called, and to be called in that state, time, place, mode, and with that efficacy, in and with which he was predestinated (Ephes. iii, 5, 6, 9-11;

James i, 17, 18; 2 Tim. i, 9.)" (Arminius, *Disputation* 16.15). He
adds the evidence of Acts 15:18 and Ephesians 1:4 that God's
decrees are from the beginning of the world. "If it were
otherwise, God might be charged with mutability" (Arminius,
Disputation 16.15).

Francis Turretin

Francis Turretin attaches the eternity of God to God's
infinitude, to which nothing can be added (Turretin 1992 ET
171). In response to the Socinian arguments regarding God's
infinity, Turretin says, "The infinity of God follows his simplicity
and is equally diffused through the other attributes of God,
and by it the divine nature is conceived as free from all limit in
imperfection: as to essence (by incomprehensibility) and as to
duration (by eternity) and as to circumscription, in reference
to place (by immensity)" (Turretin 1992 ET 1.3.9.19).

The concept of eternity is related to the immenseness of
God's Being: "After the infinity of God with respect to essence,
the same is to be considered with respect to place and time by
which he is conceived as uncircumscribed by any limits
(*aperigraptos*) of place or time. The former is called immensity,
the latter eternity" (Turretin 1992 ET 3.8.1, 1.196–7).

The three aspects to the eternity of God, according to
Turretin, are that it is without beginning, without end, and
without succession. The latter is especially important to
interaction with neotheists, even as it was to Turretin as he faced
the protounitarian Fausto Socinus (1539–1604) and his Dutch
champion, Conradus Vorstius (1569–1622). Turretin correctly
discerns that the question is not whether God is without
beginning or end. Socinus and Vorstius could not deny these
aspects without denying the clear testimonies of Scripture
(Turretin 1992 ET 1.3.9.19).

Rather, the misunderstanding was whether the eternal God
is within time—whether God experiences a succession of
moments or events. Turretin says, "We maintain that God is
free from every difference of time, and no less from succession

than from beginning and end" (Turretin 1992 ET, 1.3.10.1).
Elsewhere he elaborates:

> The eternity of God cannot have succession because his
> essence, with which it is really identified, admits none. This
> is so both because it is perfectly simple and immutable (and
> therefore rejects the change of former into latter, of past into
> present, of present into future, which succession involves),
> and because it is unmeasurable, as being the first and
> independent. However that which continues by succession
> can in some way be measured. (Turretin 1992 ET, 1.3.10.5)

Jonathan Edwards

Jonathan Edwards calls God the "Eternal Spirit," who as the
eternal God of Deuteronomy 33:27 may be trusted to provide
care and goodness (Edwards 1987 ET, 1.1743).[10] To deny the
necessary eternal existence of an All-comprehending Mind is
a major contradiction (*Memoirs,* append. 4). Edwards regards
it as absurd, given the nature of things, to suppose that there
is no God or to deny being in general or to deny the eternal
infinity of the most perfect Being who created all things
(Edwards 1987 ET, "A Careful and Strict Inquiry"). God's
eternality relates to the fact that He "comprehends all entity,
and all excellence, in his own essence. The eternal and infinite
being, is in effect, being in general; and comprehends universal
existence" (Edwards 1987 ET, "The End for Which God Created
the World").

John Wesley (1703–1791) believed that God is eternal. He
wrote, "In the evening I published the great decree of God,
eternal, unchangeable . . ." (*Complete Works,* 336).

God's timelessness has been the consistent and virtually
unanimous affirmation of the orthodox fathers of the church
from the earliest to modern times.

---

10. See also Jonathan Edwards, *Memoirs of Jonathan Edwards,* appendix 2.
Ages Library System.

NEOTHEISTS' OBJECTIONS FROM THE BIBLE

The classical view of God's eternality is under strong attack from both process theology and the kindred openness of God view. This challenge is primarily on biblical and theological grounds, though there is a concerted effort to undermine the historical argument by alleging a source for the concept of eternality in Greek philosophy.

Neotheists offer many objections to God's attribute of nontemporality based on the Bible. The following objections are typical.

The Need for a Temporal Creator

Neotheist Clark Pinnock asks, "How can a timeless God be the Creator of a temporal world?" (Pinnock, et al. 1994, 120). He poses what he believes are many difficulties with a timeless God. First, we cannot know what timelessness means, since we are temporally conditioned. Second, it creates problems for biblical history since we see God planning and acting in history. Third, it undermines worship, since Christians praise God for His redemption in time, not because He is beyond time and change. Fourth, if God did not experience events as they happen, He would not know the world as it actually is (Pinnock et al. 1994, 120).

Pinnock asserts that we cannot know what timelessness is. We cannot fully understand what it means that God is spaceless or without matter, either, but orthodox Christians have never disbelieved those doctrines as a result.

Pinnock's argument that a timeless Being cannot be the creator of a temporal world is self-refuting. Actually, only an eternal Being could create time, for if He were in time at any point, even endless, it would be everlastingly existent with Him, so He could not be its Creator. Scripture teaches that the Logos created "all things," which includes "time and space," and that He is "before all things" (Col. 1:17).[11]

---

11. See ch. 4 for further discussion from Charnock and the early fathers of the church against the inability of an unchangeable God creating the world.

That God acts in history is seen by Pinnock as an indication that God exists in time. Moreover God is said to do His planning in history. But, though God certainly does "act" in time and "interact" with humans in time, His decisions are made from all eternity, not through discursive thinking in time. Isaiah 46:9–10 tells us that God makes His declarations from the beginning. Ephesians 1:4 says that we were chosen in Christ by the Father before the universe began. God the Father made Christ the satisfaction for sins before time began (Rev. 13:8). Even though He knows and decides from eternity, He acts in time, bringing out the fulfillment of His will in a manner in which the will of humans are not coerced (see Acts 17:30–31; Gal. 4:4–5).

Pinnock contends that believers praise God because He has redeemed us, not because He is beyond time and change. If neotheists praise God only for redemption, most Christians through history have magnified God for His matchless Being and attributes as well. Even the wonderful doxology of the apostle Paul in Romans 11:33–36 belies such a perspective. Note the words of the hymnodist Isaac Watts (1674–1748):

> The gospel bears my spirit up;
> A faithful and unchanging God
> Lays the foundation for my hope
> In oaths, and promises, and blood.
> (*Hymns and Spiritual Songs*, 1707)

Eternity Is Just Endless Time

Pinnock defines *eternity* as endless time, not timelessness: "The God of the Bible is not timeless. His eternity means that there has never been and never will be a time when God does not exist. Timelessness limits God." If he were timeless, "God would be unable to work salvation in history, would be cut off from the world, have no real relationship with people and would be completely static. God is not temporal as creatures are, however, but can enter into time and relate to sequence and history" (Pinnock et al. 1994, 121).

Pinnock bases his rejection of God's timelessness on an eternal God's inability to work in time but then he says that God is not temporal, as we are, and so can enter into time. There are only two options regarding God's Being. Either God exists in time or He exists in eternity. He cannot exist in both. However, God can exist in eternity but work in time. If God is truly infinite, infinity cannot exist within the finite. Pinnock claims, "I do not mean that God is exhaustively in time," but if God has endless time, which is seemingly what neotheists are saying, He nonetheless is in time, so how is it that He has created it, as Pinnock says (Pinnock et al. 1994, 121)?

There is serious confusion in the use of terms in Pinnock's statements. By definition, something temporal relates to time, as opposed to eternity. Temporality relates to the sequence of time or to a particular point in the continuum of time.

Timelessness Is Not Taught in the Bible

William Hasker, a neotheist, says that timelessness is not taught in Scripture. He elaborates that "it is clear that the doctrine of divine timelessness is not taught in the Bible and does not reflect the way the biblical writers understood God. In spite of appeals by defenders of the doctrine to texts such as Exodus 3:14, John 8:58 and 2 Peter 3:8, there simply is no trace in the Scripture of the elaborate metaphysical and conceptual apparatus that is required to make sense of divine timelessness" (Pinnock et al. 1994, 128).

Hasker is not correct in saying that Scripture does not teach that God is not in but beyond time; this is what is meant by timelessness. Time relates not to something that has a beginning and an end, but to a succession of moments in one's own being. God has no such movement in His Being but is unchangeable (see ch. 4) in His essence.

From a human perspective the Hebrew and Greek Scriptures speak of something being "forever" when in fact only a long time is meant (e.g. Exod. 12:24). As well, Christians are said to have eternal life, when what is meant is from the point of justification onwards. This concept does not mean that we never had a beginning nor that our everlasting life is not dependent on God's life. Though we will live forever, we still have motion and relationship to matter, and exist in time (cf. Rev. 21:23, 25; 22:2). God was before time, and created it (Gen. 1:1; Pss. 90:2; 102:27; Col. 1:16; Heb. 1:2). He is the beginning and the ending, so that time is present before Him in eternity (Rev. 1:8; cf. 4:8). Hasker rejects the teaching of Exodus 3:14 and John 8:58 regarding the eternal nature of God, but offers no better explanation of the texts. Moreover, the teaching of Psalm 90:4 and 2 Peter 3:8 shows that how we view time is but a moment from God's perspective. God sees the world from outside of time and declares the end from the beginning (Isa. 46:9–10).

NEOTHEISTS' OBJECTIONS FROM HISTORY

Neotheists admit that up to modern times there is scant historical support for their view. In response, however, they insist that this is a result of the early and lasting influence of Greek philosophy on Christian thought.

According to neotheists, the Jewish philosopher Philo, who was known for his allegorical interpretative philosophy and Platonic leanings, misunderstood Exodus 3:14 to mean "My nature is to be, not to be described by a name" (Pinnock et al. 1994, 74). Later, Origen is responsible for passing this view on to Christian theism, and the other early fathers joined him (Pinnock et al. 1994, 69).

Neotheists argue that "Greek philosphers were looking for that which was stable and reliable in contrast to the earthly world of chance. . . . This leads to the distinction between being and becoming or reality and appearance" (Pinnock et al. 1994, 68). Thus, in the Greek translation of the Old Testament, "the dynamic 'I AM' of the Hebrew text became the impersonal 'Being who is there'" (Pinnock et al. 1994, 106). This set the stage for a static view of God in terms of an eternal and unchangeable Being.

Close analysis of this argument from Greek philosophy

exposes its serious flaws. Christian theologians of every age have
been influenced to some degree by the prevailing philosophies.
Nor are neotheistic thinkers immune from this. They show
much influence of process theology. This in itself does not make
their view wrong. Likewise, to be influenced by Greek
philosophy does not make the classical view of God wrong. The
issue is whether the influence was healthy or unhealthy. Are
there biblical and rational grounds for the theory? Rejecting a
view because of its source is the genetic fallacy. It is not a matter
of whether the reason is Greek but whether it is correct.

The early Fathers stressed biblical support for their view over
philosophical arguments. They quoted the New Testament
alone more than thirty-six thousand times, omitting from all
reference only eleven verses.[12]

While not always successful, the church fathers made a
conscious effort to weed out unacceptable aspects of Greek
thought. They rejected any prebirth life for the human soul,
for example, as well as the eternity of the universe and the
denial of a physical resurrection of Christ. This effort to exorcise
Hellenic heresy marked their views of God and the Ultimate.
They kept their view of God distinct from polytheism and
impersonal metaphysical principles.

On the other hand, neotheists accept views from Greek
philosophy. Their ideas of process are rooted in Heraclitus (c.
540–c. 480 B.C.), who said that "no man steps into the same
river twice." Likewise, neotheistic philosophers and theologians
use logic that owes its formal structure to the Greek philosopher
Aristotle (384–c. 322 B.C.). They also carry on the tradition of
Plato (428–348 B.C.) by their belief in an eternal world of
properties (forms) from Plato. Indeed, the father of process
theology, Alfred North Whitehead, commented that Western
thought is largely "a series of footnotes to Plato" (Whitehead
1979, 63).

---

12. See Norman L. Geisler and William E. Nix, *General Introduction to the
    Bible* (Chicago: Moody, 1986), 431.

Fifth, there are many things about the traditional Christian view of God that are contrary to Greek thought, including the concept of a Trinity of one essence and three Persons. Nor did the Greeks ever identify their god(s) with their ultimate metaphysical principle. The ultimate in Plato's system was not God (the *Demiurgos*) but the Good (the *Agathos*). Likewise, Aristotle never considered his many unmoved movers to be the object of worship but simply to be the explanation for movement in the universe. The unique, but not Greek, contribution of Christian thinkers was to identify their ultimate metaphysical principle with the God they worshiped.[13]

So the argument from Greek philosophy cuts both ways. Formally, it is a genetic fallacy. Actually, it is groundless. And substantially it boils down, not to whether the reasoning behind the classical view of God is Hellenic, but to whether it is authentic. And this must be determined by further investigation.

NEOTHEISTS' OBJECTIONS FROM THEOLOGY

Neotheists offer many theological reasons for rejecting the traditional view of God. Virtually all of these were refuted some eight hundred years in advance by Thomas Aquinas, and none of their objections is conclusive.

God's Actions in Time

One argument for the new theism is that acting in time makes God temporal, since:

1. God acts in time.
2. All acts in time are tainted by time in that they have a before and an after.
3. Therefore, a God who acts in time is tainted by time (i.e., is temporal).

---

13. See Etienne Gilson, *God and Philosophy* (London: Oxford, 1941), 40–41.

In this argument there is confusion between the eternal *Actor* (God) and His temporal *actions*. The neotheist assumes that the cause of any temporal act must itself be temporal. But no proof is offered that this must be the case. The argument merely proves that the effect must be temporal, not the Cause.

Classical theists have gone to great length to demonstrate that this cannot be the case in both the Kalam original-cause and in the Thomistic current-cause arguments. In either case, there is absolutely no reason to suppose that the cause of an effect in time must be temporal as the effect is. In the Kalam argument the whole point is that the universe must have had a beginning, but the Cause did not. In the Thomistic argument the point is that the Cause of a contingent being cannot itself be contingent but is a Necessary Being.

Another way to state the problem is to note that process and neotheist thinkers who use this argument confuse God's *attributes* and His *acts*. His acts are in time, but His attributes are beyond time. There is no reason why the Eternal cannot act in the temporal world. Just as all the radii of a circle are many and the center from which they come is one, even so God can have multiple acts in a temporal sequence without being multiple Himself. Likewise, just as spokes move faster at the circumference, more slowly near the center, and not at all at the mathematical point in the center of the hub, even so God's actions can occur in a moving temporal world without any movement in Him. There is nothing logically incoherent about a timeless God acting in a temporal world.

What is interesting to note is that at times the proponents of neotheism come very close to recognizing this or a similar distinction. They claim that, while God changes, His "essential nature" remains unchanged (Pinnock et al. 1994, 28). What then is changing? At times they say it is His "will," and at other times they imply that it is part of His nature, a nonessential part. Since the former suggestion will be discussed later, the latter will be addressed here. If God has "part" of His essence that can change and another "part" that cannot, then God is not an indivisible Being. He must have at least two "parts" or poles, one that is changing and another that is unchanging (see ch. 5). But this view is not theism but the heart of bipolar panentheism—the very theology from which neotheism would distance itself.

Or, to put the objection another way, if God is necessary in the unchanging part (pole) and not necessary (i.e., contingent) in the changing part (pole), this raises a whole nest of metaphysical problems. Which attributes of God are necessary and which are not? How do we know which are which? How do we know God's moral attributes (love, purity, truthfulness, etc.) are part of His unchanging nature? Further, if God is contingent in one part, this part of God has the possibility not to be. Only a Necessary Being has no possibility not to be. But as Aristotle pointed out and good reasoning supports, no mere potentiality for existence can actualize itself. It cannot be in a state of actuality and potentiality at the same time. The potentiality to be cannot actualize anything. Only what actually exists can actualize anything.

God's Knowledge of the Temporal World

Another argument moves from God's knowledge of temporal events:

1. God knows temporal events.
2. The truth value of temporal events changes with time (e.g., Luther is not now tacking up his 95 Theses).
3. Hence, God cannot know temporal events without His knowledge changing.

Again there is a confusion of categories. An infinite, eternal God knows *what* we know, but He does not know it in the *way* we know it. As an eternal Being, God knows eternally. As a temporal being, we know temporally. Each being must know in accordance with its own nature. For instance, neotheists believe that God is infinite. But as such He must know infinitely.

But we are finite beings and, hence, we know only finitely. Hence, while God knows *what* we know, He does not know it the *way* we know it.

Further, since neotheists believe in *ex nihilo* creation, they must admit that at least before creation God was eternal and knew what He knew eternally. This is logically necessary, since time had not yet been created, so He could not know in a temporal way. Further, God cannot be temporal before He created a temporal world, since He had no beginning, and an infinite number of temporal moments is impossible. An infinite number of moments cannot be traversed before creation or else the world would never have come into existence. But creation did occur. Hence, God must have been nontemporal before creation.

Statements About a Nontemporal God

According to neotheist reasoning, no references from our temporal perspective can be made to a nontemporal Being, for:

1. All statements made by a temporal being are temporal.
2. But God is nontemporal.
3. Therefore, none of our statements about God can really apply to Him.

According to John Sanders, "God knows how to use language. . . . This requires us to presuppose a shared context between God and the creation. By context, I mean the conditions of our existence, including our language, history, and spatiotemporal world. . . . Entering into our context, God makes use of human ways of knowing and speaking to communicate with us" (Sanders 1998, 24).

What neotheists fail to see is that this is not really an argument against all talk about God but only why talking about Him in temporal terms is not possible. Further, rather than eliminate all God-talk, it calls for analogous God-talk. It points out that temporal language does not fit a nontemporal Being.

But it does not follow that no language is appropriately used of a nontemporal God.

Of course temporal statements cannot be applied to God univocally. If they could, then God would have to be temporal. On the other hand, unless we are willing to accept the total (self-defeating) agnostic view that no statements can be applied to an eternal God (including this statement), then we must accept some form of analogy. This is precisely what classical theists argue: All finite and limited temporal conditions must be removed from a term before it applies to God. Hence, if we say God is good, He cannot be good in any temporal or changing sense of the term. He can only be eternally and unchangeably good (Geisler 1999: "Analogy, Principle of").

Creation of a Temporal World

Unlike process theology, neotheism maintains that "the triune God is Creator of the world out of nothing. This means that God does not simply influence preexisting matter but that everything depends on God for its existence. . . . It also implies that God has the power to intervene in the world, interrupting (if need be) the normal causal sequences" (Pinnock et al. 1994, 109). But if God can act in time, then neotheists argue that God must be temporal. For whatever acts in the temporal world is part of the temporal process. And the temporal process involves a past, present, and future. So when God acted in bringing Israel from Egypt, there was a time before that redemptive act and a time after it. Thus God is tainted with time by His action in time.

It should be pointed out that there is a difference between saying God created *in time* and that He is the Creator *of time*. There was no time before God made the temporal world. Time began with the temporal world. Hebrews 1:2 can be rendered that God "framed the ages" (cf. John 17:5). So God was ontologically prior to time but not chronologically prior to it. Hence, this is no impediment to God's creating a world in time without Himself being temporal. No temporal continuum existed before He created the world. Hence, it was not necessary for Him to choose a moment in time in which to create. Rather, from all eternity God chose to create the temporal continuum itself, which has a beginning.

It is equally incoherent to speak of God being eternal before creation and temporal after creation.[14] For a theist, creating the world does not change the nature of God. The world is not created *ex Deo* (out of God); that is pantheism. For theism, the world is created *ex nihilo*, out of nothing. Hence, God does not change "internally," that is, in His essence, by creating something else. The only thing that changes is "external," the relationship of the world to Him. Prior to creation, the world had no relationship to God, since it did not exist. At creation and after, God became "Creator" for the first time. It is not possible that God was a Creator until He created something. Prior to creation He was God but not Creator. At creation, God gained a new relationship but not new attributes. He did not change in His essence but in His external activity. There is no change in what God is but in what He has done. The change is only in the effect, not the Cause, since God caused from eternity all that was later to be effected in time. Failure to make this distinction leads to the neotheistic confusion of speaking of God changing in His nonessential nature.

The objection that God was temporal when He made a temporal world makes the same errors that were noted regarding the previous objection. Neotheists assume that to act in time is to be temporal. Creation does not demonstrate that the Actor is temporal, but only that His acts are temporal.

---

14. William Craig wrote: "We have thus concluded to a personal Creator of the universe who exists changelessly and independently prior to creation and in time subsequent to creation" (Craig, *Kalam Cosmological Argument* 1979, 152). If this means God is temporal in His Being after creation, then it is difficult to make any sense of it. For how can a God who is changeless in His Being change in His Being? If it simply means that God is nontemporal in His essence but can create a temporal world that is related to Him after it is created, then this is what Aquinas meant.

Classical theists do not deny that God's actions are temporal. They only insist that God's attributes are not temporal. God cannot have a "nonessential" nature. "Nonessential" means something God has but does not need to have, but "nature" is what is essential to a thing. For example, human nature is essential to humans. Without it we would not be human. So, a nonessential nature is a contradiction in terms. Since nature means essence, it would be a *nonessential essence*, which is nonsense.

Even neotheists recognize that there is a real difference between an uncreated Creator and a created world. One has no beginning, and the other does. One has no temporal starting point, and the other does. In the same way, classical theists insist that God is beyond time even though He made time. This should not be difficult to understand. After all, every creator is beyond his creation the way an artist is beyond his painting or a composer is beyond his composition.

Incarnation into a Temporal World

The Bible declares that Jesus is God, and that He entered the temporal world (John 1:1, 14). By simple logic it would seem to follow that in Christ God lived a temporal life. To deny this would appear to be a denial of the deity of Christ. Neotheists insist that this indicates that God is a temporal being. So states Richard Rice: "The fundamental claim here is not simply that God revealed himself in Jesus, but that God revealed himself in Jesus *as nowhere else*. . . . From a Christian standpoint it is appropriate to say not only that *Jesus is God,* but that *God is Jesus"* (Pinnock et al. 1994, 39; italics his).

This argument seems stronger than the previous one from creation, since a Creator is beyond His creation, but here the Creator became part of His creation. It would appear that the Incarnation of God in human flesh is evidence that God, at least in Christ, became a temporal being. In fact, the premises seem to be true (according to orthodox Christianity), and the conclusion is validly drawn:

1. God became human in the incarnation of Christ.
2. Human beings are by nature temporal beings.
3. Therefore, God by nature became a temporal being in the Incarnation.

As persuasive as this argument may seem, it is based on the unorthodox assumption that the divine nature became human in the Incarnation. The eternal did not become temporal. Nor did the divine nature become human, any more than the human nature became divine. As a matter of fact, this is the Monophysite heresy condemned at the Council of Chalcedon in A.D. 454. It is a confusion of the two natures of Christ. In the Incarnation the divine nature did not become a human nature or vice versa. The divine person—the second person of the Trinity—became human, that is, assumed a human nature in addition to His divine nature. Notice carefully the words of Scripture. "The Word was God. . . . And the *Word* became flesh and dwelt among us" (John 1:1c, 14a). It does not say that *God* became flesh. It is as impossible for God to become man as it is for an infinite to become a finite or an uncreated to become created.

As Athanasius would say, the Incarnation was not the substraction of deity but the addition of humanity. God the Son did not change His divine nature. Rather, he added a distinct human nature. So, the plausibility of the neotheist's argument is based on heresy. Once one rejects the Monophysite-like error, this argument fails.

Tensed Verbs

Another objection comes from the use of tensed verbs used of God in the Bible. Boyd asks: "Doesn't every page of the Bible paint a portrait of a God who experiences things, thinks things, and responds to things *sequentially?* Every verb applied to God in the Bible testifies to this" (Boyd 2000, 131–32; italics his).

At the outset, it should be noted that any tense proposition can be made tenseless by the addition of a date (Craig 1987, 63–65). For example, "World War I occurred in 1914" can be made tenseless by rephrasing the proposition: "In 1914, World War I is occurring." So, the neotheist presupposition is flawed in its assumption that whatever is represented by a tensed verb cannot be timeless.

This argument also is based on the false assumption that language *determines* reality. But language only *describes* reality. And it is perfectly appropriate to describe a tenseless reality in tensed terms from a human perspective. Even neotheists admit that the Bible often speaks anthropomorphically, describing God from a human perspective.

If we apply the neotheist hermeneutic, 2 Chronicles 16:9a says that the "eyes of the Lord run to and fro throughout the whole earth." Does this imply that God's physical eyes pop out of His head and go roaming throughout the earth? Furthermore, in Genesis 3:9, God asks, "Where are you?" By neotheist reckoning, God does not know the present, and He is not omnipresent. In Genesis 3:11, God asks Adam, "Who told you that you were naked?" According to the neotheist hermeneutic, God does not know the past.

Neotheist theological arguments fall short of the mark. All are answerable from a classical theistic perspective. They either beg the question or miss the point. Hence, there is no reason to forsake the theologically sound position that God is a timeless Being, the time-honored view of Christian theology down through the ages.

CONCLUSION

The attribute of God's eternality in the nontemporal, timeless sense is firmly grounded biblically, historically, and theologically. Neotheists have not offered any unanswerable arguments to reject any one of these pillars for the classical attribute of God. On the contrary, the neotheistic view is virtually without significant biblical, historical, or theological basis. There is no reason to reject the classical view of God, based on the arguments set forth. To do so is to swim against the whole stream of orthodoxy from the earliest time.

CHAPTER FOUR

Immutability

IN A CHANGING WORLD, the unchangeableness of God is a comfort. The Scriptures declare that God is the same yesterday, today, and forever (Heb. 13:8). In what way that is so is the subject of controversy between those who hold to the historic faith of Christianity and those who support neotheism.

THE BIBLICAL BASIS FOR GOD'S IMMUTABILITY

The Scripture rings out loudly and clearly that our God is unchangeable. Our trust is based on this immutability. Whereas the world around us vacillates, we know that God will remain the same in His character, and standards. While we may change, and thus receive grace or judgment, He is consistent.

God's Character Does Not Change Internally

God does not change within His nature. As a simple Being (see ch. 5), all of His attributes are in perfect harmony and do not modify to fit external circumstances (James 1:17). In contrast to the changing world, He remains the same: "They will perish, but You will endure; Yes, all of them will grow old like a garment; like a cloak You will change them, and they will be changed. But You are the same, and Your years will have no end" (Ps. 102:26–27). The writer to the Hebrews refers to this psalm when speaking of Jesus Christ, declaring the divine Christ to be unchangeable (Heb. 1:10–12).

God's immutable essence allows Scripture to make descriptive statements. The most important is God's self-identification, which He gives to Moses at the burning bush (Exod. 3:14), "I am Who [or That] I am." This statement identifies God in terms of His immutable and eternal Being.[1] Wolfhart Pannenberg compares this manner of speaking by Yahweh with the cultural practice of early Near Eastern communities. In this culture, knowledge of one's name assumed some measure of control. The name in Exodus 3, Pannenberg writes, "points to the self-identity of God. He will show himself in his historical acts and will not come under any human influence" (Pannenberg 1991 ET, 1.205).

Moreover, the references to Jesus in the Revelation of John as the "Alpha and the Omega," the "first and the last," and the "beginning and the end" (1:8, 17; 21:6; 22:13) fit well with the depiction of God in the Hebrew Scriptures (Isa. 44:6; 48:12), and the implications of immutability found in Paul's references to God's eternal Being (Rom. 1:23; 1 Tim. 1:17; 6:16).

God Does Not Change in Relation to Creation

In contrast to the created order, in which there is change and decay, the immutable God stays the same. He is not altered by relationship to what He has created. Some have thought that

---

1. The Hebrew is אֶהְיֶה אֲשֶׁר אֶהְיֶה, (*ehyeh asher ehyeh*). The LXX translates the statement in an absolute sense of being (Ἐγώ εἰμι ὁ ὤν; but the *Vg ego sum qui sum*), and this is the manner in which the New Testament refers to the Exodus passage in the words of Jesus in John 8:58, I AM (ἐγώ; εἰμί). The present force of the verbal clause is borne out in the comments of John I. Durham, אֶהְיֶה אֲשֶׁר אֶהְיֶה, 'I AM that I AM,' replies God. The verbs are first person common qal imperfects of the verb hyh 'to be,' connoting continuing, unfinished action: 'I am being that I am being,' or 'I am the Is-ing One,' that is, 'the One Who Always Is.' Not conceptual being, being in the abstract, but active being, is the intent of this reply. It is a reply that suggests that it is inappropriate to refer to God as 'was' or as 'will be,' for the reality of this active existence can be suggested only by the present: 'is' or 'is-ing,' 'Always Is,' or 'Am'" (*Word Biblical Commentary*, Exodus, 3.14).

creation requires some change in God (*ISBE*: "Unchangeable").[2]
Orthodox Christians acknowledge that God in eternity willed
to create. Since this creation had a temporal beginning, has
this not in some sense made God mutable? Puritan theologian
Stephen Charnock (1628–1680) answers this charge:

> There was no change in God by the act of creation, because
> there was . . . no new act of his will which was not before.
> The creation began in time, but the will of creating was from
> eternity. The work was new, but the decree whence that new
> work sprung was as ancient as the Ancient of days. . . .
> whatsoever God willed to be now done, he willed from
> eternity to be done; but he willed also that is should not be
> done till such an instant of time, and that it should not exist
> before such a time. (Charnock 1971 ET, 121–22)

Charnock explains how this relates to God's unchangeability:

> If God had willed the creation of the world only at that time
> when the world was produced, and not before, then, indeed,
> God had been changeable. But though God spake that word
> which he had not spoke before, whereby the world was
> brought into act, yet he did not will that will he willed not
> before. God did not create by a new counsel or new will, but
> by that which was from eternity, Eph i:9. (Charnock 1971 ET,
> 122)

---

2. Pieper speaks of this perspective, "It has been said that the creation of
the world and the incarnation of the Son imply a change in God. The
first objection can be raised only by theosophical pantheists, who view
the world as an emanation from God and a part of God's Being and
deny the *creatio ex nihilo*. Indeed, the creation of the world implies a
change, a change, however, not in God, but in relation to the creature.
And the second objection can be made only by the kenotics. Scripture
teaches that the Son of God without any change in His deity has assumed into His Person the human nature from the Virgin Mary." (Franz
August Pieper, *Christian Dogmatics*. ET, 4 vols. [St. Louis: Concordia,
1950–57], I.441).

God Does not Change in Relation to His People

God's unchangeableness of character provides great solace, but also caution for His creatures—solace for the obedient, and caution for the disobedient. The Bible indicates that God is faithful to His promises, that He expresses love and mercy toward the repentant, but wrath and judgment on the wicked and unrepentant. Scripture also tells us that certain things are true of God's nature, which never changes. He never lies and whatever He plans in eternity He will in fact do in time. What many understand as change in God is only God's manner of interaction with His creation in time. For example, He may decide to judge, based on His eternal and unchanging standard of holiness. In time His creatures change their ways. Consequently, God in applying His standard, does not punish the repentant, but now exercises His unchanging attitude toward the repentant.

God Does not Change in Relation to His Promises

The writer of the Kings rejoices in the faithfulness of God in His promises toward His people when he says, "There has not failed one word of all His good promise, which He promised through His servant Moses" (1 Kings 8:56). Paul affirms the confidence that believers may have in the consistent and unchanging God: "For no matter how many promises God has made, they are 'Yes' in Christ. And so through him the 'Amen' is spoken by us to the glory of God" (2 Cor. 1:20).

In revealing His name, God showed His trustworthiness. When Moses asked the name of God, that He might know His character, God said that He was the I AM, the eternally Immutable One (Exod. 3:14).[3] He had come down to deliver His people and had never strayed from His promise to Abraham

---

3. One's name in the Near Eastern world was a statement of character, so that when circumstances changed in a person's life, often the name would change. This is certainly true with Abram becoming Abraham, and Jacob becoming Israel, but also in the culture at large (*ISBE*, 4.2116–17).

(Gen. 15:13–16). As He stated to Moses, "Thus you shall say to the children of Israel: 'The LORD God of your fathers, the God of Abraham, the God of Isaac, and the God of Jacob, has sent me to you'" (Exod. 3:15a). God was extending His covenant with their fathers to these Hebrew slaves in Egypt. The unconditional promise to Abraham regarding seed, land, and kingdom could be trusted because He was the unchanging God.

This unchangeableness provides a shelter for God's people. As Caspar Hodge says, "Because He is unchangeably true to His promises, He is the secure object of religious faith and trust, upon whom alone we can rely in the midst of human change and decay" (*ISBE*, 3035).

God Does Not Change in Love and Mercy

The immutability of God assures us who fear Him that God will always be there with outstretched arms of love and forgiveness. The Psalmist speaks of the love of Yahweh, using the Hebrew word *ḥesed* (חֶסֶד), meaning loyal or steadfast love.[4] "Yahweh's faithful love [וְחֶסֶד יְהוָה] for those who fear him is from eternity and for ever; And his saving justice for their children's children. As long as they keep His covenant, And carefully obey His precepts" (Ps. 103:17–18 NJB).

God Does Not Change in Justice

The unchanging nature of God acts in relation to changes in our character or actions. In his encounter with God, Abraham seems to test (or maybe to confirm his understanding) whether the God he has come to know is consistent (Gen. 18:25). In verse 19, Yahweh has established a standard to which He will hold Abraham and his descendants so that they may

---

4. This word has been translated a number of ways, including mercy (*Die Heilige Schrift des Alten und Neuen Testaments*, 1749 [*die Gnade*]; KJV, NKJV), kindness (*Nouvelle Version Segond Rvise*, 1978 [*la bienveillance*]; *New American Bible*, 1970), lovingkindness (ASV, NASB), steadfast love (TANAKH, RSV, NRSV), and faithful love (NJB), the latter bringing out the richer meaning of *ḥesed* on loyalty and fidelity.

fulfill what He has spoken. Now Abraham questions God's judgment of wicked Sodom, given that some within the city may be righteous. Does God have a different yardstick for this city? Though Abraham clearly considers this differentiation to be part of Yahweh's own righteous judging, the narrative reveals that God adheres to the standard of His own nature (see Isa. 28:17). How man changes, then, reveals how God will apply His absolute standards of love, goodness, wrath, and judgment.[5]

God Does Not Change in Will and Knowledge

Although some of His actions occur within time, God remains consistent in His eternal nature as He responds to acts and attitudes of His creatures. His eternal will and decrees do not change. Yahweh is depicted by Isaiah as immutable in His decrees, "The LORD of hosts has sworn, saying, 'Surely, as I have thought, so it shall come to pass, and as I have purposed, so it shall stand'" (Isa. 14:24). This changelessness in respect to His eternal decrees is given by God Himself as a sign of His deity. Through this aspect of His Being, He shows that He cannot be compared to those who are not God (Isa. 46:9–10).

Since human decisions often collide with what God wills to do, neotheism maintains that God's will and plan must be changeable. Otherwise, there would be no integrity in human decision-making. Yet Scripture declares that although people scheme, God's decisions are not altered: "There are many plans in a man's heart, nevertheless the LORD's counsel—that will stand" (Prov. 19:21). If God did anything other than what He has eternally determined, then this would be a moral failing tantamount to a lie. That is the assumption of Numbers 23:19: "God is not a man, that He should lie, nor a son of man, that He should repent. Has He said and will He not do it? Or has He spoken, and will He not make it good?" Though God appears to change His mind in time in response to the situation,

---

5. See John Miley, *Systematic Theology* (Cincinnati: Jennings & Pye, 1892–94), 1.221.

the repeated emphasis of Holy Scripture is that for God to alter
His course in eternity would be a sin:

- "The Strength of Israel will not lie nor relent. For He is
  not a man, that He should relent" (1 Sam. 15:29).
- "Paul, a servant of God and an apostle of Jesus Christ,
  according to the faith of God's elect and the acknowledgment
  of the truth which is according to godliness, in hope of eternal
  life which God, who cannot lie, promised before time began,
  but has in due time manifested His word through preaching,
  which was committed to me according to the commandment
  of God our Savior . . ." (Titus 1:1–3).
- "Thus God determined to show more abundantly to the
  heirs of promise the immutability of His counsel,
  confirmed it by an oath, that by two immutable things, in
  which it is impossible for God to lie, we might have strong
  consolation, who have fled for refuge to lay hold of the
  hope set before us" (Heb. 6:17–18).

Immutability, but Not Immobility

The meaning of immutability has been obscured somewhat
due to certain writers failing to differentiate adequately between
God's immutability and the idea of immobility. Some
theologians, in defining the immutability of God, have
presented a rather stilted view of God, in which because He is
unchanging in His essential Being in eternity, He must,
therefore, be disinterested in the creatures He has created. His
relation to the world, which correctly does not alter His own
eternal nature nor purpose, is nonetheless portrayed as closer
to Deism than to the loving heavenly Father shown to us by
Christ.

One should be cautious in defining immutability in a manner
that might be understood to exclude God's interaction with
His world, particularly His people. The scholastic view, as
Richard Muller explains, should not be seen as immobile but
unmoved: "This is, doubtless, the Aristotelian conception of

an 'unmoved Mover,' but it is not a conception which in and of itself implies statis or incapability of relation with externals. Rather it indicates a being who has not been 'moved' or brought into being by another" ("Incarnation, Immutability, and the Case for Classical Theism" 1983).

God's nature in eternity is settled, with no possibility of change, but His actions in the world are predetermined in accord with how humans relate to God's immutable nature. God initiates relationships with changing people. For there to be a real relationship, an unchangeable God must have changing relations, yet remain unchangeable in character and purpose.[6]

For example, God deals differently with people before their justification than He does after it. Also, the God who cannot "repent" (Num. 23:19) is described as repenting because He changes His dealings with a group when they move from or to wickedness (Gen. 6:6; Exod. 32:14; Jer. 18:7–11; Joel 2:13; Jonah 3:10; Thiessen 1949, 83).[7]

Thomas Oden observes that "The biblical witness views God not as immobile or static, but as consistent with his own nature, congruent with the depths of his own personal being, stable, not woodenly predictable. If God promises forgiveness, 'He is just, and may be trusted to forgive our sins' (1 John 1:9), because the character of God is dependable" (*Systematic Theology,* 1:112). God's immutability is not an issue, for as Oden points out, "Classical Christianty's deepest objection to Arianism was its notion that 'the Son of God is variable or changeable' and therefore less than God" (*Systematic Theology,* 1.111).[8]

---

6. Cf. Henry C. Thiessen, *Introductory Lectures in Systematic Theology* (Grand Rapids: Eerdmans, 1949), 83.

7. A more complete explanation of what is meant in Scripture by God repenting or changing His mind will be found in the response portion of the chapter below.

8. Oden cites Nicene, NPNF 2.14, p. 3. *Against the Arians*, Victorinus Afer, one of the founders of Western trinitarianism, demonstrated "that whereas all change is an activity, not all activity is a change. God, said Victorinus, is eternally active, eternally and without alteration begetting and proceeding in the divine essence itself. Since the divine activity is

The unchangeableness of God is central to a biblical view of who God is. If God is not immutable, there can be little reason to trust that what He has revealed in His Word will occur. Nor can we know that He will be reliable in our times of difficulty. This view is the biblical view, and it was accepted by virtually all early theologians.

THE THEOLOGICAL BASIS FOR IMMUTABILITY

Solid arguments have been set forth for God's immutability by the great doctors of the church, especially Thomas Aquinas. Several will be briefly summarized here.

The Argument from Pure Actuality

Aquinas offered three basic arguments in favor of God's unchangeability (*Summa Theologica* 1a.13.7). The first argument is based on the fact that a God of Pure Actuality ("I Am-ness") has no potentiality. For everything that changes has potential to change. But there can be no such potential in God. It follows that God cannot change.

The Argument from Simplicity

The second argument follows from His simplicity (see ch. 5). Everything that changes is composed of what changes and what does not change. But there can be no composition in God. He is an absolutely simple Being. Hence, God cannot change.

The Argument from Perfection

The third argument for God's unchangeability reasons from His absolute perfection. Whatever changes acquires something new. But God cannot acquire anything new, since He is

---

constant and continuous it implies no change in God: it is an immutable activity." See *Marii Victorini rhetoris urbis Romae ad Candidum Arrianum*, in Marius Victorinus, *Tratés théologiques sur la Trinité*, ed. P. Henry and P. Hadot, *Sources chrétiennes* 68 (Paris: Cerf., 1960), 170. Cited by Müller, 28–29.

absolutely perfect; He could not be more complete or find improvement. Therefore, God cannot change.

The Argument from Infinity

Of course, neotheists reject the prior three attributes from which was argued God's immutability. However, the attribute of God's infinity, which is accepted by neotheists, also is evidence for immutability. An infinite Being has no parts. If it did, it could not be infinite, since an infinite number of parts is impossible. Regardless of how many parts one has, it is always possible to add one more. But there cannot be more than an infinite number of parts. Hence, it is not possible for an infinite Being to have parts. But what has no parts cannot change. For change involves the loss or gain of parts. Hence, an infinite Being cannot change.

The Argument from Necessity

Both classical theists and neotheists accept God's necessity. But a Necessary Being cannot change in its being. For the being that it has, it has necessarily. If it did not have being necessarily, then it would not be a Necessary Being. It follows, therefore, that a Necessary Being cannot change.

Of course, it could be argued that God may have Being necessarily, but that there are other characteristics that He has only accidentally. This can be rejected on two grounds. First, God is simple and cannot have parts (see ch. 5). Second, even if God had accidents (unnecessary parts to His Being), He would still be necessary in His basic Being, for that is within the definition of a Necessary Being. And if God is necessary in His Being, then He must be unchanging in His Being, as the above argument shows.

The Argument of Change from an Unchanging Cause

Aquinas argued that whatever changes passes from a state of potential change to a state of actual change (*Summa Theologica* 1.2.3). But no potentiality for being can actualize itself. For example, pigments and canvas have the potential to be a great painting, but they cannot actualize themselves. It takes a cause (artist) outside of that potential to actualize it. The potential that something changeable will change cannot itself account for the change. There must be an actualizer outside the potential. At the end of the chain of actualizers of change, there must be an Actualizer without the potential for change who is the First Cause. There cannot be an infinite regress of causes, since there would be nothing to do the actualizing. Every cause would be actualized, but none would be the needed first actualizer. Hence, there must be an unchangeable First Actualizer of all change.

THE HISTORICAL BASIS FOR GOD'S IMMUTABILITY

From earliest times, orthodox Christian theologians have all accepted God's immutability. This is evident from numerous citations.

The Patristic View of Immutability

Early fathers maintained that the true God was unchangeable in character. They did not deny that God altered His actions in time, so that humans might see God ostensibly changing His mind. But from all eternity, these supposed changes were in fact settled. Changes within time are for the benefit of the succession of events to be understood by finite beings.

God is immutable in His essential Being, according to Novatian (c. 200–258). In his discussion of the Trinity, Novatian embraces the view that God does not change in essential Being. He illustrates his perspective by averring that God's nature does not permit Him to be both good and evil or to be the originator of good and evil. Novatian says that God never changes "Himself into any forms, lest by change He should appear to be mortal. . . . Thus there is never in Him any accession or increase of any part or honour, lest anything should appear to have ever been wanting to His perfection, nor is any loss sustained in Him, lest a degree of mortality should appear to have been suffered by Him" (*Concerning the Trinity, ANF* 4).

This immutability, to Novatian, is because "what He is, He always is; and who He is, He is always Himself; and what character He has, He always has. . . . And therefore He says, 'I am God, I change not;' in that, what is not born cannot suffer change, holding His condition always. For whatever it be in Him which constitutes Divinity, must necessarily exist always, maintaining itself by its own powers, so that He should always be God" (*Concerning the Trinity, ANF* 4).

The attribute of simplicity is directly related to immutability. God's attributes are not independent of each other, and they interact without any alteration in their exercise: "He is therefore also both immortal and incorruptible, neither conscious of any kind of loss nor ending. For because He is incorruptible, He is therefore immortal; and because He is immortal, He is certainly also incorruptible, each being involved by turns in the other, with itself and in itself, by a mutual connection, and prolonged by a vicarious concatenation to the condition of eternity; immortality arising from incorruption, as well as incorruption coming from immortality" (*Concerning the Trinity, ANF* 4).

Mutability also would make God less than Deity, Novatian argued. For God to experience change is to cease to be God: "Because if He does not contain all that is, whatever it is—seeing that what is found in that whereby it is contained is found to be less than that whereby it is contained—He will cease to be God. Being reduced into the power of another, in whose greatness He, being smaller, shall have been included. And therefore what contained Him would then rather claim to be God" (*Concerning the Trinity, ANF* 4).

Aristides (2d cent.) distinguishes immutability as an evidence that someone truly is a god. He speaks of those who are "not gods, but a created thing, liable to ruin and change, which is of the same nature as man; whereas God is imperishable and unvarying [immutable], and invisible, while yet He sees, and overrules, and transforms all things" (*Apology, ANF* 4).

Melito of Sardis (c. 170) has a similar standard, as did

Clement of Alexandria. He chides individuals for serving what does not really exist, in contrast to the true God, "He, I say, really exists, and by His power doth everything subsist. This being is in no sense made, nor did He ever come into being; but He has existed from eternity, and will continue to exist for ever and ever. He changeth not, while everything else changes" (*Philosopher, Remains of the Second and Third Century, ANF* 8.751).

Gregory Thaumaturgus says that normal human passions of grief and distress are not properties "of the immutable Divinity." The incarnate Word "exhibited in Himself the exercise of the affections and susceptibilities proper to us, having endued Himself with our passibility, even as it is written, that 'He hath borne our griefs, and carried our sorrows'" (*Twelve Topics on the Faith* 5, *ANF* 6.11).[9]

Alexander, Bishop of Alexandria (d. 328) also affirms that the immutability of God is the belief of the Apostolic Church, in contrast to the heretical teachings of Arianism, when he says, "Concerning whom we thus believe, even as the Apostolic Church believes, in one Father unbegotten, who has from no one the cause of His Being, who is unchangeable and immutable, who is always the same, and admits of no increase or diminution." Moreover, the Son, as of the essence of the Father, is also immutable: "He is equally with the Father unchangeable and immutable, wanting in nothing" (*Epistles on the Arian Heresy* 12).

The Medieval View of Immutability

Augustine

Augustine held that "Whatever hath in it the possibility of change, being changed is not what it was." Just "think on God and thou wilt find 'is' where 'has been' and 'will be' cannot

---

9. David W. Bercot says that the work attributed to Gregory Thaumaturgus in *ANF* vol. 6 is in reality a post-Nicene work by another. (Bercot,ed, DECB, xii). Nonetheless, if it in fact is by another than Gregory, it still reflects early Christian thinking regarding the matter of the immutability of God.

be" (*On the Gospel of John* 38.10). God is the unchanging Is, the I AM of Exodus 3:14.

God's immutability follows from His supremacy. "Since God is supreme being, that is, since He supremely is and, therefore, is immutable, it follows that He gave being to all that He created out of nothing; not, however, absolute being" (*City of God* 1983 ET 12.2).

Immutability also follows from simplicity. For "there is a Good which alone is simple and, therefore, which alone is unchangeable and this is God." And "This Good has created all goods; but these are not simple and, therefore, they are mutable" (*City of God* 1983 ET 11.1).

Augustine affirmed that only God is immutable, for "no created nature can be immutable. Every such nature is made, indeed, by God, the supreme and immutable Good who made all things" (*City of God* 1983 ET 22.1). "Thus, there can be no unchangeable good except our one, true, and blessed God. All things which He has made are good because made by Him, but they are subject to change because they were made, not out of Him, but out of nothing" (*City of God* 1983 ET 12.1).

According to Augustine, God's immutability can be proven from the judgments we make about form and beauty in the world. For "it is the mind that makes this judgment. This means that there must be within the mind a superior form, one that is immaterial and independent of sound and space and time." However, "the mind itself is not immutable, for, if it were, all minds would judge alike concerning sensible forms" (*City of God* 1983 ET 8.6).

Augustine argued that "anything susceptible of degrees is mutable, and for this reason, the most able, learned and experienced philosophers readily concluded that the first form of all could not be in any of these things in which the form was clearly mutable" (*City of God* 1983 ET 8.6).

Even God's will is immutable and eternal:

> Truth tells me in my inner ear, concerning the very eternity
> of the Creator, that His substance is in no wise changed by

> time, nor that His will is separate from His substance? . . .
> He willeth not one thing now, another anon, but once and
> for ever He willeth all things that He willeth; not again and
> again, nor now this, now that; nor willeth afterwards what
> He willeth not before, nor willeth not what before He willed.
> . . . Such a will is mutable, and no mutable thing is eternal;
> but our God is eternal. (*Confessions* 12.15)

God's mind cannot change. For "all thought which is thus
varied is mutable, and nothing mutable is eternal; but our God
is eternal" (*Confessions* 12.15). But "not in our way does God
look forward to the future, see the present, and look back upon
the past, but in a manner remotely and profoundly unlike our
way of thinking" (*City of God* 11.21).

> God's mind does not pass from one thought to another His vision
> is utterly unchangeable. Thus, He comprehends all that takes
> place in time—the not-yet existing future, the existing present,
> and the no-longer-existing past in an immutable and eternal
> present. . . . [Neither] is there any then, now, and afterwards in
> His knowledge, for, unlike ours, it suffers no change with triple
> time present, past, and future. With Him, there is no change,
> nor shadow of alteration. (*City of God* 1983 ET, 11.21)

The divine mind and will cannot change because they are
identical with His unchangeable essence. God's will can be
associated with His very substance, and God's substance cannot
change or it would not be eternal (*Confessions* 11.10). So God is
forever identical with Himself. "What then is, the same, save
that which is? What is that which is? That which is everlasting.
. . . Behold The Same: I AM THAT I AM" (*Expositions on the
Book of Psalms* 122.5).

Anselm

Anselm rooted God's absolute unchangeability in His
perfection, simplicity, supremacy, and His unique immateriality.

One of Anselm's proofs for God's existence is the argument from degrees of perfection in the world:

1. Some beings are more nearly perfect than others.
2. But things cannot be more or less perfect unless there is something wholly perfect by which they can be compared and judged to be more or less perfect than it.
3. Therefore, there must be a most perfect Being which we call God. But if God is absolutely perfect He cannot change, since any change would be for the worst, and He would then not be perfect.[10]

Anselm also based immutability on God's simplicity. "Supreme Nature is in no wise composite, but is supremely simple, supremely immutable" (Anselm of Canterbury 1962 ET, 77). For Anselm God's immutability follows from His unique immateriality. "But, seeing that one spirit has not any parts, and there cannot be more spirits than one of this kind, it must, by all means, be an indivisible spirit" (Anselm of Canterbury 1962 ET, 87).

Immutability is the basis for God's eternality, "whether God's willing and causing are understood in terms of the immutable present of eternity or in terms of the temporal order. According to the former, nothing is past or future, but everything exists together without any change" (Anselm of Canterbury 1970 ET, 159). This supreme Substance must be eternal, without beginning or end; it has no temporal transience, being immutable and without parts (Anselm of Canterbury 1962 ET, 83).

Immutability also leads to infallible foreknowledge. God cannot be deceived, for He sees only what is true; whether that truth is necessary or related to human free will makes no difference. He established in Himself something that seems alterable from the human perspective before it comes to pass (Anselm of Canterbury 1970 ET, 161). Therefore, "God's

---

10. See Anselm, *Monologion* 2.

essence is always, in every way, substantially identical with itself; and is never in any way different from itself, even accidentally" (Anselm of Canterbury 1962 ET, 85). He cannot change in His nature, since He is perfect, unique, spiritual, and supreme. Further, this immutability is the basis for God's nontemporality and His infallible ability to foresee the future.

Thomas Aquinas

In his epic *Summa Theologica*, Aquinas offers three basic arguments in favor of God's unchangeability. The first argument is that a God of Pure Actuality ("I Am-ness") has no potential to be other than what He is, while change can only come from potential to be something other than what one is (*Summa Theologica* 1a.13.7).

The second argument relates to simplicity. Everything that changes is composed of what changes and what does not. But God is without parts, so He cannot change. The reasoning is that only something that does not change attaches to self-identity. If everything about a being changed, it would not be the same being. That would not be a change, but the annihilation of one thing and creation of something entirely new. An absolutely simple Being, then can only remain absolutely the same or go out of existence and become something else. Neither way can it change.[11]

The third argument extends from absolute perfection. Whatever changes acquires something new. But an absolutely complete Being cannot acquire anything new. He is perfect. Therefore, God cannot change. God is by His very nature and absolutely perfect Being. If there were any perfection that He lacked, then He would not be God. However, in order to change, one must gain something new. But to gain a new perfection is to have lacked it to begin with. Hence, God cannot change. If He did change, He would not be God but a being lacking in some perfection.

---

11. That is to say it would not be an accidental change.

Aquinas also argues that God alone is immutable (*Summa Theologica* 1.13.7). This is necessary because all creatures exist only because of the will of the Creator. It was His power that brought them into existence, and it is His power that keeps them in existence. Therefore, if He withdrew His power, they would cease to exist. Whatever can cease to exist is not immutable.[12] Therefore, God alone is immutable; everything else could cease to exist.

IMMUTABILITY FROM THE REFORMATION

Martin Luther

Martin Luther, in discussing the wrath of God against the false "attrition" of the unbelieving, bases the "lively faith" of those with a contrite heart "on the immutable truth of God . . . so that the truth of God's threatening is the cause of contrition, and the truth of His promise the cause of consolation, if it be believed" (Luther 1955–86, 3.178).

Though there is some truth in his opponents' contention that contrition is attained by recollection and contemplation of sins, Luther says, "yet their teaching is perilous and perverse so long as they do not teach first of all the beginning and cause of contrition—the immutable truth of God's threatening and promise, to the awakening of faith—so that men may learn to pay more heed to the truth of God" (Luther 1955–86, 3.178).

Luther also says that "God is not magnified by us so far as His nature is concerned—He is unchangeable—but He is magnified in our knowledge and experience, when we greatly esteem Him and highly regard Him, especially as to His grace and goodness" (Luther 1955–86, 3.117).

John Calvin

John Calvin considers it a given in Christian theology that God is immutable. The immutability of the Word of God is inherent in the very essence of God according to Calvin, "For

---

12. Change in this context denotes substantial change.

John at once attributes to the Word a solid and abiding essence, and ascribes something uniquely His own, and clearly shows how God, by speaking, was Creator of the universe. . . . Unchangeable, the Word abides everlastingly one and the same with God, and is God himself" (Calvin 1960 ET 1.13).

God's unchangeableness is strategic to Calvin's ensuring that the attempt to thwart God fails. In discussing Psalm 110:1 he says, "Here [the psalmist] asserts that, no matter how many strong enemies plot to overthrow the church, they do not have sufficient strength to prevail over God's immutable decree by which he appointed his Son eternal King. Hence it follows that the devil, with all the resources of the world, can never destroy the church, founded as it is on the eternal throne of Christ" (Calvin 1960 ET 2.15).

Human curiosity about God's eternal and immutable decree is inappropriate, especially as it relates to the Incarnation. "It is not lawful to inquire further how Christ became our Redeemer and the partaker of our nature. For he who is tickled with desire to know something more, not content with God's unchangeable ordinance, also shows that he is not even content with this very Christ who was given to us as the price of our redemption" (Calvin 1960 ET 2.12).

Calvin explains prayer in relation to God's changelessness by drawing on Augustine, quoting him that Christians "pray according to his will, not that hidden and unchangeable will but the will that he inspires in them, that he may hearken to them in another way, as he wisely decides'" (Calvin 1960 ET 3.20). Calvin sought to hold God's immutable counsel in tension with personal freedom to sin: "When it is narrated of Eli's sons that they did not heed his wholesome admonitions, 'for it was the will of the Lord to slay them' [1 Samuel 2:25], it is not denied that their stubbornness arose out of their own wickedness; but at the same time it is noted why they were left in their stubbornness, even though the Lord could have softened their hearts—because his immutable decree had once for all destined them to destruction" (Calvin 1960 ET 3.24).

Jacobus Arminius

Immutability is inherent in the very nature of God in the thought of Jacobus Arminius, and is integral with God's other attributes. He says, "The life of God is his essence itself, and his very being; because the Divine Essence is in every respect simple, as well as infinite, and therefore, eternal and immutable (Arminius 1853 ET 1.1.4.28).

Arminius includes immutability among the things that make God superior to His creation:

> He is the greatest Being, and the only great One; for he is able to subdue to his sway even nothing itself, that it may become capable of divine good by the communication of himself. . . . The whole of this system of heaven and earth appears scarcely equal to a point "before him, whose center is every where, but whose circumference is no where." He is immutable, always the same, and endureth forever; "his years have no end (Psalm 102). (Arminius 1853 ET 1.2.43–44)

The immutability of God is an attribute for which believers should glorify God: "Nothing can be added to him, and nothing can be taken from him; with him "is no variableness, neither shadow of turning (James i, 17). Whatsoever obtains stability for a single moment, borrows it from him, and receives it of mere grace. Pleasant, therefore, and most delightful is it to contemplate him, on account of his goodness; it is glorious in consideration of his greatness; and it is sure, in reference to his immutability" (Arminius 1853 ET 1.2.44).

Francis Turretin

Francis Turretin affirms that God's unchangeableness is Scripture's explicit teaching in Malachi 3:6; Psalm 102:26; and James 1:17. He notes that in James "not only change is denied of him, but even the shadow of change. . . . Immutability of the divine will and counsel in particular is often asserted," as in Numbers 23:19 (Turretin 1992 ET 1.11.3.205). That God is a necessary and independent Being requires that He be immutable, just as created beings must be mutable: "Reason confirms it for He is Jehovah, and so a necessary and independent being that can be changed by no one" (*Dialogus contra Manichaeos* 68 PG 94.1568). God is immutable because He is from Himself and recognizes no cause above Himself. He can neither be changed for the better (because He is the best) nor for the worse (because He would cease to be the most perfect) (Turretin 1992 ET 1.11.4.205).

The double-point here is that God's creation of the world does not bring change to Him, but it does bring change to creatures, who pass from nonexistence to existence. "When God became the Creator, He was not changed in Himself (for nothing new happened to Him, for from eternity He had the efficacious will of creating the world in time), but only in order to the creature (because a new relation took place with it)" (Turretin 1992 ET 1.11.5.205).

In the Incarnation, Turretin says, God was not changed. "The Word (*logos*) was made flesh, not by a conversion of the Word (*tou logou*) into flesh, but by an assumption of the flesh to the hypostasis of the Word (*logou*)" (Turretin 1992 ET 1.11.6.205). Likewise,

> it is one thing to change the will; another to will the change of anything. God can will the change of various things (as the institution and abrogation of the Levitical worship) without prejudice to the immutability of his will because even from eternity he had decreed such a change. . . . [So] from eternity he decreed to create the world and preserve it until a certain time, but afterwards to destroy it with a flood. In the same manner, we must reason concerning his knowledge. The knowledge of God does not change with the thing known because God who knew it not only knew that this change would take place, but even decreed it. (Turretin 1992 ET 1.11.7.205–6)

Turretin, in speaking about God not changing His mind, says, "Repentance is attributed to God after the manner of men (*anthropopathos*) but must be understood after the manner of God (*theoprepos*): not with respect to his counsel, but to the event; not in reference to his will, but to the thing willed; not to affection and internal grief, but to the effect and external work because he does what a penitent man usually does" (Turretin 1992 ET 1.12.11.206).

That God did not fulfill some promises and threatenings does not mean He changed, Turretin said, for these predictions were conditional, not absolute (see Jer. 18:7–8). "Although the condition may not often be expressed, it must be understood as tacit and implied" (Turretin 1992 ET 1.12.12.206). For example, in Isaiah 38:1–8, Isaiah predicted the death of Hezekiah, then God granted the king fifteen more years. Turretin notices, "There was not a declaration of what would happen according to the will of GOD, but of what (according to the nature of second causes) would happen unless GOD interposed" (Turretin 1992 ET 1.12.12.206).

Jonathan Edwards

Jonathan Edwards, in interacting with those arguing for God's mutability, shows the futility of a mutable God: "From this notion, . . . as God is liable to be continually repenting what he has done, so he must be exposed to be constantly changing his mind and intentions as to his future conduct; altering his measures, relinquishing his old designs, and forming new schemes and projections" (*Freedom of the Will*, 2.11.4.111).

The consequences of God being this way is to put Him into divine perplexity and human insecurity:

> He must be continually putting his system to rights, as it gets out of order, through the contingence of the actions of moral agents: he must be a being, who, instead of being absolutely immutable, must necessarily be the subject of infinitely the most numerous acts of repentance and changes of intention, of any being whatsoever; for this plain reason, that his vastly

extensive charge comprehends an infinitely greater number of those things which are to him contingent and uncertain. . . . He must have little else to do but to mend broken titles as well as he can, and be rectifying his disjointed frame, and disordered movements, in the best manner the case will allow. (*Freedom of the Will*, 2.11.4.111)

A mutable God provides little help:

The supreme Lord of all things must needs be under great and miserable disadvantages, in governing the world which he has made, and has the care of, through his being utterly unable to find out things of chief importance which hereafter shall befall his system, which, if he did but know, he might make seasonable provision for. . . . It is in the power of man, on these principles, by his devices, purposes, and actions, thus to disappoint God, break his measures, make him continually to change his mind, subject him to vexation, and bring him into confusion. (*Freedom of the Will*, 2.11.4.111)

John Wesley

John Wesley (1703–1791) believed that God is eternal. He says, "In the evening I published the great decree of God, eternal unchangeable . . ." (*Works* 1984 ET, 336).

It is evident that God's immutability was affirmed by the early church fathers, by medieval theologians, by the Reformers, and by Arminians.

OBJECTIONS TO GOD'S IMMUTABILITY FROM THE BIBLE

Neotheists contend that God may be so affected by human actions that He alters His intentions and decisions. He may change His mind and will, dependent on what humans do.

God's Extension of Hezekiah's Life

Gregory Boyd gives examples from Scripture seeking to prove that God, in fact, makes one decision on what He will do, then changes that decision. We shall look at one example to which Boyd gives special consideration, the lengthening of King Hezekiah's life. Similar reasoning applies to Boyd's other examples. Boyd argues,

> Now, if we accept the classical view of foreknowledge and suppose that the Lord was certain that he would *not* let Hezekiah die, wasn't he being duplicitous when he initially told Hezekiah that he would not recover? . . . If we suppose that the Lord was certain all along that Hezekiah would, in fact, live fifteen years after this episode, wasn't it misleading for God to tell him that he was adding fifteen years to his life? Wouldn't Jeremiah [Jer. 26:19] also be mistaken in announcing that God *changed his mind* when he reversed his stated intentions to Hezekiah—if, in fact, God's mind never really changes? (Boyd 2000, 82; italics his)

From a theist's perspective, there is a better interpretation than Boyd's: God does not change His mind in eternity but changes His acts towards humans in accordance with His foreknowledge of their acts and attitudes. He keeps His word, but He predicts human actions and attitudes. Thus, God acts and interacts with human free choices, but He is proactive and not reactive.

Boyd fails to recognize that God's communication gives genuine respect to human decision and the sequential process of human reason and emotions. Within the temporal and spatial revelation of God to Hezekiah, God is genuinely interacting with Hezekiah's prayer. Wayne Grudem stresses that interpreters of Scripture should understand such Scripture to reflect accurately God's intent in relation to a situation. This does not keep God from knowing infallibly that the situation will change and a change in His immediate intent will be appropriate. "This is just saying that God responds differently to different situations," he writes (Grudem 1994, 164).

One logical aspect of the story seems to escape Boyd: How

can God truthfully tell Hezekiah that he will have fifteen more years if he doesn't know the future where it interacts with human free will? And why should God not know a future that He controls, since Scripture says He gives and takes life, which is the issue in the passage (e.g., Deut. 32:39; Job 33:4; John 5:21; Acts 17:25; 1 Tim. 6:13)? How long Hezekiah would live was God's decision.

Moreover, interpretive analogy demands that we interpret texts about God changing His mind in a similar way to texts about God forgetting. To apply the same interpretive strategy neotheists use here, we must assume that God has some form of divine Alzheimer's disease? Why should we take God changing His mind literally here and elsewhere but insist that His forgetfulness is merely metaphorical?

Finally, since neotheists often attempt to pit Calvinists against Arminians, we shall cite Arminian theologians to help clarify the controversy that Boyd, and other neotheists, have fomented. Oden, a contemporary Arminian scholar, has written: "What may appear to be a change of God's mind may upon closer inspection be a different phase of the unfolding of the divine plan. God's sovereign freedom is able to will changes within the contingencies of history. This is not a contradiction of the divine reliability. Rather, the execution of the divine purpose is firm precisely because it is responsive to temporal contingencies" (*Systematic Theology*, 1.113).

Nineteenth-century Arminian scholar John Miley's comments still fit: "Sacred history discloses a changing frame-work of expedience in the older dispensations of revealed religion, and a great change from the elaborate ceremonials of Judaism into the simple forms of Christianity, but the same moral principles abide through all these economies." Miley believed that those unchanging moral principles and change in response to a situation in applying those principles are both consistent with immutability. "That he regards the same person now with reprehensive displeasure, and again with approving love, is not only consistent with his immutability, but a requirement of it

in view of the moral change in the object of his changed results"
(Miley 1892–94, 1.221).

Humans May Thwart the Will of God

John Sanders, responding to Christopher Hall in *Christianity
Today*, seeks to mute Hall's argument of God's omniscience
in Isaiah 41:21–24 by encouraging Hall to read 46:9–10 and
48:3–5. He says, "The glory of Yahweh is not that he simply
knows what is going to happen. Rather, it is that he can declare
what will happen and bring it about—that it does, in fact occur.
Isaiah is not touting foreknowledge but contrasting Yahweh's
power with the importance of the other gods" (Sanders 2001,
255). Further, "according to openness and Arminianism, yes,
we can sometimes thwart God's will." Thus, "the only way to
guarantee that God's will is never thwarted is for God to
micromanage everything, and this is the position of classical
theism. Arminianism and openness, however, believe that God
grants us free will, and so it is possible that we can go against
God's will" (Sanders 2001, 255).

Certainly Isaiah 41:21–24 is about more than foreknowledge,
but foreknowledge must be included. Other passages do not
negate God's exhaustive knowledge of all things (past, present,
future, real and potential); they buttress this attribute by declaring
God's sovereign determination of a future that He knows.

Numerous texts make it clear that nothing can thwart the
sovereign will of God (see ch. 8). Job confessed to God: "I know
that you can do everything, and that no purpose of Yours can
be withheld from you" (Job 42:2). The psalmist added, "But
our God is in heaven; He does whatever He pleases" (Ps. 115:3).
In another psalm extolling the providential government of the
Lord, the psalmist says, "Whatever the LORD pleases He does,
in heaven and in earth, in the seas and in all deep places" (Ps.
135:6).

Since the Scriptures do not contradict themselves, any
unclear passage should be understood in the light of clear ones.
These and other texts seem clear.

It is interesting that Sanders attempts to identify neotheism with Arminianism. A. B. Caneday notes this strategy: "Evidently the 'open theists' initially drew the circle too small when they first circumscribed their views. . . . Sanders attempts to soften distinctions between 'open theism' and the Arminian segment of classical theism, he exaggerates theological differences within classical theism between Arminianism and Calvinism" ("Putting God at Risk" 1999). Although Sanders, Boyd, and other neotheists may seek to divide and conquer the evangelical wing of Christianity, Arminians and Calvinists (and those drawing from both traditions) stand together on God's control of His world and His exhaustive knowledge of all time (past, present, and future) and on His infinite and unchanging nature.

God's "Conditioning" by the World

Pinnock argued that "God is unchanging in nature and essence but not in experience, knowledge and action." He explains that "when I say that God is subject to change, I am referring to a uniquely divine kind of changeability. I do not mean that God is subject to change involuntarily, which would make God a contingent being, but that God allows the world to touch him, while being transcendent over it" (Pinnock et al. 1994, 118).

Certainly orthodox Christians of all ages have affirmed that God is reliable and loving, and that God responds to the "changing needs" of His children. The problem is that Pinnock and other neotheists believe that God does this in such a manner that He could make a mistake and have to correct it, and that the world can change this changeless God. They do so because they refuse to accept the eternal aspects of God's knowledge, wisdom, nature, and immutability and reject the concept that God's "actions" (effect) are within time in concert with His unmovable nature (cause), which is outside of time, in which there is all knowledge, all-consistency, and genuine transcendence.

God is Put to the Test

In explaining the event of Abraham on Mount Moriah, Sanders says that God learned about Abraham's faith, of which He was unsure until the test, so that, in reality, the test was not really so much Abraham's, as it was Yahweh's. Sanders comments,

> God's statement, "now I know," raises serious theological problems regarding divine immutability and foreknowledge. Many commentators either pass over this verse in silence or dismiss it as mere anthropomorphism. It is often suggested that the test was for Abraham's benefit, not God's. It should be noted, however, that the only one in the text said to learn anything from the test is *God*. (Sanders 1998, 52)

He argues that "Abraham probably learned something in his relationship with God, but that is not the point of the text. If one presupposes that God already 'knew' the results of the test beforehand, then the text is at least worded poorly and at most simply false" (Sanders 1998, 52).

There are serious difficulties with Sanders' understanding of the account. First, in his analysis of the Abraham story, Sanders proves more than he intended, for was not Abraham's faith already real, and therefore knowable prior to this time, a present reality, not a future contingent? If it was a present reality, and God was simply trying to gauge it, then He does not even know all that is now knowable, so that "omniscience" is even more limited than free will theists admit.

Second, the emphasis on God learning ("Now I know. . . ."), as though He did not know in eternity what would occur is missing the infinite-finite/divine-human dynamic. The Hebrew word "know" in Genesis 22:12 is the *Qal* of ידע (*yada^c*; LXX γινώσκω, *ginōskō*), expressing "in the sense of confirming his knowledge" (Wenham 1994; Gen. 22:12).[13] The sense of "know"

---

13. See Ludwig Kohler and Walter Baumgartner, *The Hebrew and Aramaic Lexicon of the Old Testament.* Rev. W. Baumgartner and J. J. Stamm (Leiden: Brill, 1994), 390–91. In the *Qal* stem, [ידע means "to notice (someone), to

in this text does not mean that God has come to need information of which He, in eternity, was unaware. This is similar to its usage in Genesis 18:21 in which the omnipresent God had to "come down" to observe Sodom to determine if, by individually counting the people, the city should be destroyed ("and if not I will know"). As Gordon Wenham says of this passage, "It is not that God needs to go down to confirm what he knows, but that he is visiting it with a view to judgment" (Wenham, 1994, Gen. 18:21).

The anthropomorphic "come down" and "to know" stand in juxtaposition here. Both express the activities of the transcendent God in human terms. As Genesis 18 uses God's knowledge with a view to judgment, so Genesis 22 uses it with regard to blessing. Thus, there is nothing in this text to impel us to believe that God actually changes in His nature or will.

God's Admission of "Poor Decisions"

As already observed, neotheists believe that God knows the future in a very limited way, since essentially all free acts of men are outside of His certain knowledge. He knows only what He in specific instances will do (provided these "free" acts do not conflict with most of human activity). Thus, Boyd argues that God regrets decisions that He has made (Gen. 6:6): "For example, in the light of the depravity that characterized humanity prior to the flood, the Bible says that 'The LORD *was sorry* that he had made humankind on the earth, and it grieved him to his heart' (Gen. 6:6). . . . Now, if everything about world history were exhaustively settled and known by God as such before he created the world, God would have known with absolute certainly that humans would come to this wicked state,

---

hear or learn (by notification), to know (by observation), to take care of (someone), to know sexually, to conclude, to understand something, to have experienced something, to have understanding. The term γινώσκω may mean, come to know, to perceive, to recognize, to form a judgment, to acknowledge as true, to know carnally. J. Lust et al, comps., *Greek-English Lexicon of the Septuagint* (Stuttgart: Deutsche Bibelgesellschaft, 1992), I.90.

at just this time, before he created them." But "how, then, could he authentically regret having made humankind? Doesn't the fact that God regretted the way things turned out—to the point of starting over—suggest that it *wasn't* a foregone conclusion at the time God created human beings that they would fall into this state of wickedness?" (Boyd 2000, 55).

God is apparently not only not omniscient ("all-knowing"), but He is also not omnisapient ("all-wise"). The purpose of wisdom is to avoid life's mistakes, and in traditional Christian theology, God's judgments are perfect (Ps. 19:7), and only He is essentially wise (Rom. 16:27). Boyd writes:

> Now some may object that if God regretted a decision he made, he must not be perfectly wise. Wouldn't God be admitting to making a mistake? . . . First, it is better to allow Scripture to inform us regarding the nature of divine wisdom than to reinterpret an entire motif in order to square it with our preconceptions of divine wisdom. If God says he regretted a decision, and if Scripture elsewhere tells us that God is perfectly wise, then we should simply conclude that one can be perfectly wise and still regret a decision. Even if this is a mystery to us, it is better to allow the mystery to stand than to assume that we know what God's wisdom is like and conclude on this basis that God can't mean what he clearly says. (Boyd 2000, 56–57)

Boyd avers that we cannot know what God's wisdom is like. However, this is self-defeating because in order to make this assertion, Boyd must know what God's wisdom is like. Also, since we are admonished to conclude what God clearly says in Scripture, we must remember that the Bible clearly teaches God's omniscience (cf. 1 Sam. 15:29; Isa. 44:6, 7; 46:9, 10; see ch. 2). God knows the future like the past and "the end from the beginning." His knowledge is "infinite" (Ps. 147:5). Likewise, since God is all-good, He must be all-wise. He must know the best means to the best ends.

Further, if the fall of humanity in Genesis 3, and the subsequent wickedness of man in later chapters of Genesis, was not already known by God from all eternity, as Boyd indicates, then how do we deal with the statement that Jesus was the lamb slain from the foundation of the world (Acts 2:23; Eph. 1:4; Rev. 13:8)? How would we be chosen in Him for redemption from the foundation of the world? This all presupposes God's eternal knowledge that humanity would fall into sin and need redemption.[14]

In reference to human sin in God's omniscience, one wonders whatever happened to God's capacity for anticipation that Boyd makes much of in reference to Peter and Judas (Boyd 2000, 35–38). Aside from this, God's pronouncement (in Gen. 6:6) occurred long after the creation in which He said that it was very good (Gen. 1:31). God is responding to the current state of man in his sin, not His original creation of man as good. His sorrow is for what people became through their own devices (cf. Eccl. 7:29).

Moreover, lacking in the neotheist's analysis is recognition of the infinite nature. Indeed, other Scriptures affirm that in His omniscience God does not change His mind. First Samuel 15:29 declares: "The Strength of Israel will not lie or relent.

---

14. John Sanders (1998, 102) dismisses the traditional interpretation of 13:8 on two grounds. First, he states that the syntax is ambiguous, and therefore, the referent—"before the foundation of earth" is the "Lamb" or "the names written in the book"—is ambiguous. Regardless, if the referent is the "Lamb," God had eternally planned for the Lamb to die for our sins, and if the referent is those whose "names were written in the book," then God has elected individuals.

Both interpretations are contrary to neotheistic interpretation. Moreover, it may be the case that this is not an either/or situation. The lamb slain before the foundation of the world, and the election of the saint is from eternity, so the false dichotomy can be avoided. Second, Sanders states that no one interprets Rev. 13:8 literally. But we do interpret Rev. 13:8 in its literal sense by taking into account literary context and figures of speech such as metonymy. In a metonymy, one noun is switched to represent another. Here the metonym "Lamb" functions for the person of "Christ."

Lastly, behind figures of speech there is literal meaning.

For he is not a man, that he should relent." So, the fact that God is said to repent in Genesis 6:6 must be taken in nonliteral terms unless we are to have a contradiction with His nature in eternity, above time and space, and His infinite character. For Samuel informs us that God will not "regret," "repent," or "relent"—all possible translations for the verb נָחַם (nāḥam).[15]

Finally, Jeremiah 18 adds light on how God uses human actions to accomplish His plans: "If at any time I announce that a nation or kingdom is to be uprooted, torn down and destroyed, and if that nation I warned repents of its evil, then I will relent and not inflict on it the disaster I had planned" (vv. 7–8). On the other hand, God continues through the prophet, "if at another time I announce that a nation or kingdom is to be built up and planted, and if it does evil in my sight and does not obey me, then I will reconsider the good I had intended to do for it" (vv. 9–10).

THEOLOGICAL OBJECTIONS TO GOD'S IMMUTABILITY

Many arguments are offered by the "new theists" against the classical attribute of God's immutability. Each will be stated and responded to in the following discussion.

Fallacy of the "Perfect Being" Argument

One argument used by classical theists to establish the immutability of God is the argument from degrees of perfection in the world. We saw above that both Anselm and Aquinas used forms of this argument.

Neotheists reject the classical view of God's immutability because of what Clark Pinnock calls "the difficulties with a perfect being theology" (Pinnock et al. 1994, 132). Pinnock defines this theology as stating, "if God were to change, so the argument goes, then He would change either for the better or for the worse. But God cannot change for the better, since He is already perfect. And He cannot change for the worse, for

---

15. See BDB, "to be sorry, console oneself, suffer grief, be sorry, repent."

this would mean that He would no longer be perfect. So God cannot change" (Pinnock et al. 1994, 131).

Neotheists reject this argument, not because God is imperfect, but because "it rests on the assumption that all change is either for the better or for the worse, an assumption that is simply false" (Pinnock et al. 1994, 132). They offer the "immutable watch" as an example. It registers the same time day in and day out. By contrast, an "extremely accurate watch" always resisters the correct time even though it is constantly changing. However, when it changes, its change is not for the better or worse. It remains the same in its changes, namely, an extremely accurate watch.

This objection seems to contain a significant category mistake by comparing changing being with unchanging being. For it only shows how one changing thing (the watch) is not better when it changes in reference to another changing thing (time). But this begs the question in favor of a nonimmutable view of God. The clock illustration does not tick if one assumes that God does not change, for in that case anything that represented Him as changing would be inaccurate because it changes.

Further, even the neotheistic critique here implies that God does not really change. For they assert that whatever changes in God is "consistent with and/or required by a constant state of excellence" (Pinnock et al. 1994, 133). But what is this "constant state of excellence" but the equivalent of an unchanging nature?

In another way, their response reveals an underlying premise that God does not really change in His essence. They speak of the possibility of an unchanging God suffering from "imperfection" because a worshiper may become disappointed with worshiping a God who could not change (Pinnock et al. 1994, 132). But how could one know God was imperfect unless one presupposed an absolute, unchanging standard of Perfection (which theists claim God is)?

Finally, even if one were to grant the argument from perfection has difficulties, it is not the only argument for immutability in the theist's arsenal. First of all, there are numerous, clear, and emphatic biblical declarations that God cannot change (Num. 23:19; 1 Sam. 15:29; Ps. 102:25–27; Mal. 3:6; Titus 1:2; Heb. 1:11–13; 6:18). Neotheists give only passing and incomplete reference to, and no serious analysis of, the many verses supporting the unchangeableness of God (Pinnock et al. 1994, 47).

Further, other arguments are stated from simplicity, infinity, necessity, and pure actuality. Taken together, the biblical, historical, and theological arguments form a formidable defense of God's immutability.

God's Unrelatability to a Changing World

Another argument used by neotheists, which like most of their other philosophical arguments comes from panentheists, is that an eternal, immutable God cannot have a real relationship with a changing world. The essence of the argument is this:

1. All real relationships involve change.
2. But an unchanging God cannot change.
3. Hence, an unchanging God cannot have a real relationship with a changing world.

They cite Aquinas as saying that God's relationship to the world is not real but only ideal.

Aquinas anticipated this objection and treated it extensively and adequately. First, he argued that there is a real relationship between the changing world and the unchanging God (*Summa Theologica* 1a.13.7). He observed that there are three kinds of relations: (1) One where both terms are ideas (e.g., the same is the same as itself); (2) one where both terms are real (e.g., a small thing compared to a large thing); and (3) one where one term is real and the other is an idea (e.g. on the right side).

Since creatures are really dependent on God but God is not dependent on them, they are related as real to an idea. That is, God knows about the relationship of dependence but He does not have it. Only the creature has ontological dependence. Thus, when there is a change in the creature's dependence on God there is no change in God. Just as when a person changes his position from one side of the pillar to the other, the pillar does not change; only the person changes in relation to the pillar. So, while the relationship between God and creatures is real, God is in no sense dependent in that relationship.

It is important to note here that Aquinas is only denying a dependent relationship and not all real ones. He is denying that God changes in His relationship with the world, but not that there are no real changes in the world's relation to God. The person's relation to the pillar really changes when he moves, but the pillar does not change. But when the man moves, then there is no longer the same relationship to the pillar.

The neotheist misrepresents Aquinas's analogy insofar as their emphasis is on the impersonal nature of the pillar. For example, John Sanders states, "What he [Aquinas] meant by this is that the very being of God is not altered by the creation . . . . But it seems that when he [Aquinas] compares the divine-human relationship to that of stone-human relationship, it becomes difficult to think of the relationship in personal terms" (Sanders 1998, 152). However, Aquinas's emphasis is on the changing relationship of the creature and the immutability of God. The reason that the neotheists have difficulty with the analogy is that they presuppose that only that which is mutable can be personal.

Neotheists should have no difficulty grasping the Creator-creature distinction, since they believe in *ex nihilo* creation. God was not related to the world before it was created but was related to the world after creation. Yet God is independent of the world. Like a concrete floor on which the chair depends does not change when the chair is removed, so God remains independent on creation before and after creation. The fact that there is a change from there being no creation to there being a creation does not change the Creator.

Once creatures exist, God is related to them as their Creator. And creatures are related to God because He is their Creator. However, dependence is in the creature, but not in the Creator. Therefore, the relation of creatures to God is real and not merely ideal (*Summa Theologica* 1a.13.7 ad 5).

God's Inability to Know a Changing World
Neotheists state:

> If God is absolutely unchangeable, how can He know a changing world? According to classical theism, God's knowledge is identical to Himself. Yet He is said to be unchangeable. Hence, His knowledge would have to be unchangeable. But how can He have unchangeable knowledge of what changes. For example, when time changes, God's knowledge changes too; otherwise He would not know what time it is. And if He does not know what time it is, He is not all-knowing. Hence, it may seem that God cannot be omniscient and unchangeable and yet know a changing world. (Pinnock et al. 1994, 120)

God is unchanging and His knowledge is identical with His essence, but does this mean that God cannot know changing things? He knows the changing times, but not as we know them, in a changing way. God knows past, present, and future in one eternal now. Therefore, when time changes, God's knowledge does not change, since He knew it in advance. God knows the whole of time from the perspective of eternity, but He knows what is before and what is after the temporal now of human history (*Summa Theologica* 1.14.15). God looks on the whole calendar of time in which He sees which days are before and after others. But He is not standing on the present day of the calendar looking back at days just past and forward to days to come.

He has unchanging knowledge of the changing, and eternal knowledge of the temporal. Each being must know in accordance with its own mode of being. Temporal beings know in a temporal way, and an immutable Being knows in an immutable way.

Further, as the cause of all things, God knows all things as they preexist in Him.[16] So, His knowledge of time is not infected by time. He knows time from beyond time, not from within it. He knows the temporal in His eternal Self as the cause of it. Thus, He knows the changing world in His unchanging nature as an effect that can and will flow from it. By knowing Himself perfectly, God knows everything He will create, which one day will participate in the likeness of Himself. God does not have to "wait" for time to change before He can know it has. Rather, He knows all of time's changing sequences in His unchanging Self from all eternity.

God's Free Will

Another objection to God's unchanging nature is based on the classical theist's belief that, since God is simple (see ch. 5), God's will is identical to His nature. But if His nature is necessary, then His will must be necessary. And if it is necessary, then His will, which is identical to it, cannot be free. Hence, if God is free, then He cannot be an immutable Being.

Classical theists point out that what is willed freely can also be necessary. Antecedent necessity that would eliminate free will differs from consequent necessity. God's will has antecedent freedom. He could have done otherwise. However, once He wills something, it must occur in the way He willed it. There was no necessity that God will things as He did, but once He freely willed them, it is necessary that they happen.

As to how free will can be identical to God's unchangeable nature, it can be necessary to God's nature that He do certain things freely, such as create. Likewise, His will can be free but

---

16. Evil is not a thing with its own act of existence. Rather, it is a privation. Therefore, evil did not pre-exist in God, nor can God be called the cause of evil.

still immutable. What he freely wills is willed immutably. God made free but unchangeable decisions from all eternity that things would change in the manner and order in which they do. So change can be willed by an unchanging God.

Of course, God wills other things because of His goodness but not necessitated by it. For God can exist without willing other things. God needs only will His own goodness necessarily and other things contingently. Therefore, these other things need not be willed with absolute necessity. It is not necessary that God wills anything other than Himself. But God did will things other than Himself. God must have willed these other things voluntarily.[17] God's will is unchangeable because He is omniscient, so what He knows will be, will be. God's will is in perfect accord with His knowledge. Therefore, God's will is unchangeable. This does not mean that God does not will that some things change. It means that God's will does not change, even though He does will that other things change (*Summa Theologica* 1a.19.7). God's will includes intermediate causes such as human free choice. So God knows what the intermediate causes will choose to do. And His will is in accord with His unchangeable knowledge. Therefore, God's will never changes, since He knows that what He wills must happen.

The Nature of God as Love

Neotheists labor the point that God is love. Ironically, while clear statements about God not changing (just listed) are not taken literally, they have no difficulty viewing "God is love" as unquestionably literal. They confidently affirm: "The statement God is love is as close as the Bible comes to giving us a definition of the divine reality." Again, "Love is the essence of the divine reality, the basic source from which all of God's attributes arise" (Pinnock et al. 1994, 18, 21).

Their argument for the necessity of change in a God of love goes like this:

---

17. See Aquinas, *Summa Theologica* 1a.19.3, ad 3.

1. God is essentially love.
2. Love, of necessity, involves the possibility of change.
3. Therefore, God's love involves possible change.

The crucial second premise is supported by a raft of material showing that God's love is a dynamic, interactive activity, whereby God engages in give and take with His creatures. Love suffers with the loved one, hence, God cannot be impassible as traditional theism affirms (Pinnock et al. 1994, 46). Indeed, the cross is given as the prime example of the sympathetic, suffering, and changing love of God. Kenneth Leech is quoted with approval by Richard Rice in saying, "The Cross is a rejection of the apathetic God, the God who is incapable of suffering, and an assertion of the passionate God, the God in whose heart there is pain, the crucified God" (Pinnock et al. 1994, 46).

At the very start one notices something strange about this argument against God's unchangeableness—the very first premise begins with a God who cannot change. For God is "essentially" love. But if God by His very nature is love and cannot be otherwise, then God cannot change in His nature. Neotheists admit this when they affirm that "God's essential nature and his ultimate purpose did not change" (Pinnock et al. 1994, 28). But is the premise that "God cannot change in His essential nature as love" consistent with their conclusion from this premise that God must be able to change because He is love?

The second premise seems a classic example of the quip that God made man in His own image, and man returned the compliment. Who said God has to love the way we love? To be sure, human love is changing because human beings are changing beings. Theism affirms that God is an unchanging Being and, therefore, He must love in an unchanging way. God can do whatever good we can do, but He does not do it in the way we do it. He does it in an infinitely better way than we do—an unchanging way. Even neotheists admit that God is infinite, ontologically independent, uncreated, and transcendent. But granting that God is infinite demands that He is and does things differently than finite beings do. Hence, the argument against immutability from the nature of God's love fails to prove its point.

HISTORICAL OBJECTION TO GOD'S IMMUTABILITY

Neotheists make two attempts to counter the powerful argument from the history of orthodox theology. First, they scan the history of doctrine for isolated examples to support their view. Second, they attempt to undermine the virtually unanimous voice of the Fathers by poisoning the well with the claim that it is based in Greek philosophy.

The Doctrine and Greek Philosophy

The argument from Greek philosophy was answered in chapter 3. It is sufficient here to note that it involves a genetic fallacy of rejecting a view because of its source; it is inconsistent, since neotheists also get their ideas from philosophical sources, some of which are Greek. Further, it overlooks the unique biblical and Christian grounds on which the Christian concept of God is based. Greeks never had a personal, triune God who is identified with ultimate reality.

The Alleged Implication of the Church Fathers

Sanders acknowledges that all church fathers agree that God is immutable, yet he concludes that the church fathers in some sense thought that God was mutable in His foreknowledge (Sanders 1998, 142–58). Sanders's logic goes like this:

1. The church fathers affirmed that God is immutable.
2. The church fathers affirmed that God knows future free acts.
3. Therefore, God acquires knowledge atemporally, for the creature's free-will future acts condition him (Sanders 1998, 143).

This argument is invalid, for from the aforementioned premises one can conclude that the church fathers thought that God is immutable and God knows future free acts. Moreover, it follows that if God is immutable and God knows future free acts, then God immutably knows future free acts. However, what does not logically follow is what Sanders asserts—that God acquires knowledge atemporally for He is conditioned by the creature.

If time is comprised of "moments of before and afters," and God at one moment did not possess knowledge and at a subsequent moment possessed knowledge (i.e., acquired knowledge), then it is contradictory to say that God atemporally acquired knowledge.[18] "Atemporally aquired" is tantamount to saying "atemporally temporally." In order to acquire, there must be a moment in which that which was aquired was not possessed and a subsequent moment in which it was possessed; however, this is no longer atemporal, but temporal.

CONCLUSION

God's immutability is firmly grounded in Scripture, Church history, and sound reasoning. Contemporary attempts to undermine this fundamental teaching about God have failed to make their case. Other than the fallacious procedure of taking anthropomorphism literally, there is no real biblical support for a changing God. On the contrary, there are numerous affirmations that God does not and cannot change. Furthermore, in the whole history of the Christian Church until modern times, one looks in vain for any major orthodox teacher who affirmed that God can change in His nature. Indeed, there are solid philosophical arguments from God's pure actuality, simplicity, necessity, infinity, and perfection that God is unchangeable by nature.

Further, Oden has denounced open theism (what he calls reformists) with these words, "If 'reformists' insist on keeping

---

18. This would also apply to the Molinist position.

the boundaries of heresy open, however, then they must be resisted with charity. The fantasy that God is ignorant of the future is a heresy that must be rejected on scriptural grounds . . . as it has been in the history of exegesis of relevant passages. The issue was thoroughly discussed by patristic exegetes as early as Origen's *Against Celsus*" ("Real Reformers," 45–46).

CHAPTER FIVE

Simplicity

IF THE DOCTRINE OF God is "basic to the whole theological system," as theologian Millard Erickson asserts, the divine attribute of simplicity is foundational to the orthodox view of the nature of God (Erickson 1997, 87). However, neotheists challenge the classical view of God's simplicity in accord with their affinity with process theism. This is one reason that neotheism's revisionist approach to the classical view of God presents an upheaval in the historic, orthodox view of God.

The terms *simplicity* and absolute *unity* are used interchangeably to mean that God cannot be analyzed or divided. "He is the basic minimum of divinity as well as the maximum, the ultimate reality in himself," writes Gerald Bray (Bray 1993, 94). God is ontologically one Being, without dimensions, poles, or divisions.

THE BIBLICAL BASIS FOR SIMPLICITY

The biblical basis for God's simplicity is found throughout the Old and New Testaments, which speak of His immateriality, unity, and self-existence or Pure Actuality.

The Immaterial God

In Luke 24:36–37, the resurrected Christ appears to His disciples, but they are frightened because they perceive Him to be a spirit. Jesus explains to them that "a spirit does not have flesh and bones." If Jesus didn't have a physical body, the implication is that He would be strictly spiritual. His statement makes an important distinction between flesh and spirit, materiality and immateriality.

God is metaphysically a spirit, as John 4:24 indicates. Leon Morris explains that "here Jesus is not saying, 'God is one spirit among many'; rather his meaning is 'God's essential nature is spirit. . . .' We must not think of God as material, or bound in any way to places or things. The word order puts an emphasis on spirit. The statement is emphatic" (Morris 1995, 240). D. A. Carson gives a good explanation of this text when he writes,

> Jesus is not suggesting that God is one spirit amongst many, nor simply that he is incorporeal in the Stoic sense, nor that "spirit" completely defines his metaphysical properties. In this context "spirit" characterizes what God is like, in the same way that flesh, location, and corporeality characterize what human beings and their world are like. Compare the parallelism of Isaiah 31:3, "But the Egyptians are men and not God; their horses are flesh and not spirit." "God is spirit" means that God is invisible, divine as opposed to human, life-giving and unknowable to human beings unless he chooses to reveal himself. (Carson 1991, 225)

The Invisible God

As an immaterial spirit, God is invisible. According to John 1:18, God has never been seen by a human being. John evidently did not see a contradiction between what he was writing and the Old Testament record of theophanies. Metaphysically, God is an invisible Spirit, unseen by the physical, but this does not preclude Him from manifesting Himself. According to Paul in Romans 1:20, God's divine nature is invisible. This represents the sum of his divine Being. Two examples of such qualities are expressed later in the verse.[1]

---

1. See also 1 Tim. 1:17, Col. 1:15–16, Heb. 11:27. Ignatius, *Trall.* 5:2, speaks of the invisible God, a notion affirmed in Greek philosophy (Aristotle, *De mundo* 6.399b.20: "Being invisible to every mortal being, he is perceived through his very deeds.") and in Hellenistic Judaism (Philo, *De vita Mos.* 2.12.65; Josephus, *Works of Josephus* 7.8.7.346). See Joseph A. Fitzmyer, *Romans: The Anchor Bible* (New York: Doubleday, 1993), 280.

In Colossians 1:15 Paul speaks of Christ as the "image of the invisible God." According to James D. G. Dunn,

> Here it is important to note the description of God as "invisible." The adjective is used of God in four of the five New Testament occurrences (here and in Romans 1:20; 1 Timothy 1:17; Hebrews 11:27) and nowhere else in biblical Greek, but is common in Philo. It is a central Jewish *theologoumenon* that God cannot be seen. Hence the figure of "the angel of the Lord" in the patriarchal narratives and the importance of the commandment against idolatry. (Dunn 1996, 87)[2]

God in Absolute Unity

Moses affirmed the unity of God in Deuteronomy 6:4: "Hear, O Israel: The LORD our God, the LORD is one" (cf. Isa 37:16–20). Even though the Hebrew word for "one" (*'eḥād*) leaves room for a plurality of persons within a unity of substance, in the monotheistic and anti-polytheistic context in which it was used there is no implication of a plurality of beings or even parts within a being.[3] This would be tantamount to the polytheism that Jewish monotheism vehemently opposed from the very beginning, and was expressly forbidden by God as told to Israel though Moses: "You shall have no other gods before me" (Exod. 20:3; cf. Isa. 45:18).

In the New Testament Jesus Christ taught the unity of God (Mark 12:29; cf. Deut. 6:4), as did the apostle Paul (Rom. 3:30; Eph. 4:6; 1 Tim. 2:5). In 1 Corinthians 8:4–6, Paul confronts idolatry by contrasting error with the fact of the unique true God. This being the case, idols are nothing more than physical

---

2. *Theologoumenon* is a Greek word meaning a theological word about God.
3. While the doctrine of the Trinity is not explicitly taught in the Old Testament, as it is the New Testament (Matt. 3:15–17; 28:18–20; 2 Cor. 13:14), nonetheless, it is implicitly contained in the fact that two or more persons are identified as God and sometimes even speak to each other (e.g., Pss. 45:6; 110:1; Zech. 1:12 cf. Isa. 63:7–10).

representations of nonexistent deities. It is evident from these verses that there is absolutely only one God. It is also true that God is absolutely One. He cannot be divided into parts as matter can be. Combined with God's immateriality, this lends support to God's simplicity.

The Self-Existent God

Process protests to the contrary, the self-identity of God as the great "I AM" in Exodus 3:14 is a declaration of His self-existence, His Pure Actuality. When Moses asked for His name, "God said to Moses, 'I AM WHO I AM [אֶהְיֶה אֲשֶׁר אֶהְיֶה; LXX Ἐγώ εἰμί ὁ ὤν]. This is what you are to say to the Israelites: 'I AM has sent me to you.'"

The name Yahweh (*YHWH*), usually translated LORD in the Old Testament, is probably an imperfect form of the Hebrew word *hāyāh*:[4] "The theological importance of *hāyāh* stems from its derived nouns, which identify the personal name of deity, Yahweh, or its contractions. The tetragrammaton YHWH is not ordinarily written with its appropriate Hebrew vowels. But that the original pronunciation was YaHWeH seems probable, both from the corresponding verbal form, the imperfect of *hāyeh*, anciently yahweh, and from later representation of YHWH in Greek ιαουε or ιαβε" (Harris et al. 1980, 210, 484).[5]

Some have viewed Yahweh as a contraction, so not etymologically connected to *hawa*, for "I Am Who I Am." According to Old Testament commentator R. Alan Cole, "This pithy clause is clearly a reference to the name YHWH. Probably 'Yahweh' is regarded as a shortening of the whole phrase, and a running together of the clause into one word" (Cole 1973, 69). Even the *Theological Dictionary of the New Testament* (*TDNT*) acknowledges that "the name is generally thought to be a verbal form derived from the root הָיָה [*hāyāh*], "be at hand, exist, come

---

4. יְהֹוָה is from the Hebrew verb הוה, meaning to be, and even as אֶהְיֶה is a first person singular for I am, יְהֹוָה is a third person, "He is."

5. See Harris's discussion on an alternative derivation and pronunciation of Yahweh in *Theological Wordbook*, 210–11.

to pass" (Kittel and Friedrich 1985: "YHWH"). Arthur Preuss summed it up well:

> The more general and more ancient opinion among theologians favors the view that aseity constitutes the metaphysical essence of God. Hence, we shall act prudently in adopting this theory, especially since it is well founded in Holy Scripture and Tradition, and can be defended with solid philosophical arguments. . . . Sacred Scripture defines יְהֹוָה as ὁ ὤν, and it would seem, therefore, that this definition is entitled to universal acceptance." The prophet Isaiah describes God as the everlasting, self-sufficient creator of all things: "To whom, then, will you compare God? What image will you compare him to? . . . He sits enthroned above the circle of the earth. . . . Or who is my equal?" says the Holy One. Lift your eyes and look to the heavens: Who created all these? He who brings out the starry host one by one, and calls them each by name. Because of his great power and mighty strength, not one of them is missing. . . . Do you not know? Have you not heard? The LORD is the everlasting God, the Creator of the ends of the earth (Isaiah 40:15–28).
> (Preuss 1911, 172)

He is the uncreated Creator, the self-existent and incomparable One who has no equals.

Before the philosophers on Mars Hill (Acts 17:25), Paul juxtaposed false gods with the one true God. "And he is not served by human hands [whereas the idols are dependent upon those who care for them], as if he needed anything, because he himself gives all men life and breath and everything else." This is a God who gives life and existence to all but has it in and of Himself. "In him we live and move and have our being" (v. 28), but He has Being in and of Himself. We are His "offspring" (v. 29), but He is the offspring of none. He simply is and always was, the self-existent One. God not only created all things but sustains them in existence. Their existence is from Him, but His existence is simply in Him. He neither came into existence nor will go out of existence. He simply is. Hence, there is nothing by which He can be divided. And whatever cannot be divided is absolutely simple. Hence, God is absolutely simple.

God is Intrinsically Immortal (Incorruptibility)

In the New Testament numerous passages ascribe immortality to God (e.g., Rom. 1:23; 1 Tim. 1:17). God's immortality is intrinsic, for He "alone has immortality, dwelling in unapproachable light, whom no one has seen or can see, to whom be honor and everlasting power" (1 Tim. 6:16). Our immortality is derived from God as a gift (Rom. 2:7; 1 Cor. 15:52–54; 2 Tim. 1:10). God is not only absolutely One but is intrinsically and essentially immortal, spiritual, and incorruptible.

The doctrine of God's simplicity is based on all the verses supporting His immateriality, unity, pure actuality, and immortality. Everything else that merely has existence is from Him (John 1:3–4; Col. 1:16). All of these derived things are multiple, and destructible. But God cannot be any of these, since He is their cause. If God had these characteristics, He too would need a cause. Therefore, God must be immaterial, immortal, and also indivisible. Unlike His creatures, God has no potentiality. Whatever has no potential is indivisible, for there is nothing by which it can be divided.

THE THEOLOGICAL BASIS FOR SIMPLICITY

Based on other attributes grounded in Scripture, there are several theological reasons for accepting the classical doctrine of God's simplicity. A few will be listed here, with more explanation in the historical section on Thomas Aquinas, who has prepared the way for our discussion.

Simplicity and Infinity

Classical theists and neotheists agree that God is infinite in His Being. But an infinite Being cannot be divided. If it could, it would have to have parts. But there cannot be an infinite number of parts, since no matter how many parts there are, one more can always be added. But there cannot be one more than an infinite. Hence, an infinite Being cannot have parts. It is absolutely simple.[6] To put it another way, no amount of finite parts add up to an infinite. But God is infinite. Therefore, God cannot have any parts. He must be simple.

Simplicity and God as First Cause

Classical theists and neotheists accept that God is the uncaused Cause of all that exists. As the First Cause, God has no cause.[7] Every composite being has a cause, for things diverse in themselves cannot unite unless something causes them to unite. But since God is uncaused, He cannot have diverse elements in Himself.

In more contemporary terms, most evangelical thinkers, including neotheists, are proponents of some form of intelligent-design theory, even those who allow the process of evolution to be a result of this intelligent design.[8] Intelligent-design proponents point out that irreducible complexity, such as is found in the smallest living things, is evidence of an intelligent Designer.[9] If this is so, then God could not have complexity— or else He must have been designed by something beyond Himself. But neo- and classical theists agree that God is the

---

6. However, it may be argued that one need not have an infinite number of parts, but one may have a finite number of parts each of which is infinite. But this entails that each infinite part is equal to the infinite whole. And this is not possible because the whole is equal to the sum of its parts. Further, there cannot be two infinite Beings, since it is not possible to have two of exactly the same kind of being. For there to be two, they must differ. But they cannot differ by the very respect in which they are identical. Hence, there can be only one infinite Being.

7. And God cannot be self-caused, since a cause is prior to its effect in being, if not in time. But nothing can be prior to itself.

8. See Michael Behe, *Darwin's Black Box: The Biochemical Challenge to Evolution* (New York: Free Press, 1980).

9. See *Darwin's Black Box*.

First Cause and there is nothing beyond Him. It would follow, therefore, that God cannot be complex.

Simplicity and Pure Actuality

The God of Scripture is self-existent, having no potential for nonexistence (see ch. 3). But what has no potential for nonexistence cannot be divided, since it has no potential for division or destruction. And what cannot be divided is, by definition, indivisible, which means that it is simple. Pure Actuality is unlimited and unique. It is one of a kind. But what is absolutely one cannot be divided.

Another way of approaching simplicity is that no two beings of Pure Actuality can be entirely the same. For what is entirely the same is absolutely one Being. And what is absolutely one Being is simple. Hence, God is absolutely simple in His Being. For God is Pure Actuality, with no admixture of anything else. And such a Being must be simple because there is nothing in it by which distinctions can be made.

Further, the only two ways a being can differ is by either being or nonbeing. But to differ by nonbeing is to differ by nothing. And to differ by nothing is not to differ at all. Furthermore, there cannot be two Pure Beings that are absolutely the same, since to be two they must differ. But they cannot differ by being; since both are the same (namely, Pure Actuality), they cannot differ in their being. Therefore, it follows that a God of Pure Actuality, with no potentiality, must be absolutely one.

Simplicity and Immutability

God's unchangeability is solidly grounded in Scripture and good reason (see ch. 4), for God cannot change (Mal. 3:6; Heb. 1:12; James 1:17). But whatever cannot change, cannot be divided, since division is a form of change. When something changes there must be a division between what remains the same and what does not. Otherwise, there would be no change; it would remain the same.

To put it another way, what is unchangeable is indivisible. And God is unchangeable. Hence, God is indivisible. That simplicity flows from immutability poses problems:

- *How can God be simple and also tripersonal?* God has one indivisible essence but three persons who share that one essence. God is essentially one but relationally three.
- *How can God be simple and have many attributes?* God has many attributes in one being. These are not the same attributes, but the same God has all of them. A rock can be solid, grey, and round, yet it is one rock. God's attributes are coordinated in Him. For example, He is loving holiness and has a holy love. He is loving truth and true love.
- *How can God be absolutely one and yet do many things?* The many things God does all come from the one Being He is, as many radii come from one center.

THE HISTORICAL BASIS FOR SIMPLICITY

The argument for God's simplicity has an early, firm, and continuous support in the history of the church. This begins in the earliest Fathers.

The Patristic View of Simplicity

Several characteristics of God are associated with His simplicity, including His unity, immortality, immateriality, and invisibility.

Clement of Rome, speaking of the unity of God, wrote, "Have we not [all] one God and one Christ?" (*Epistle to the Corinthians* 46). Irenaeus concurs, stating that he had proven that there is but one God (*Against Heresies* 2.2). Clement of Alexandria went to great lengths to argue that the Greeks plagiarized from the Hebrews regarding the nature of God. He quotes approvingly the Athenian historian Xenophon (c. 431–c. 352), who taught that God is "one and incorporeal" (*Epistle to the Corinthians* 46). Hippolytus, while acknowledging the Trinity, spoke of the absolute unity of God's essence beneath this plurality of persons, that "He, while existing alone, yet existed in plurality" (*Against the Heresy of Noetus* 10). Patristics scholar G. L. Prestige quotes Apollinarius (310–390) as writing that the Trinity is one God (Prestige 1959, 11). "The divine spirit, says the pseudo-Caesarius (378; resp. 43), is one, of single form, single character, single substance, indivisible" (Prestige 1959, 10).

God's immortality or incorruptibility is based upon His simplicity. Theophilus (115–181) wrote, "And He is without beginning, because He is unbegotten; and He is unchangeable, because He is immortal" (*Theophilus to Autolycus* 2.4). Justin Martyr declared that "God alone is unbegotten and incorruptible, and therefore He is God, but all other things after Him are created and corruptible" (*Dialogue with Trypho* 5). Hippolytus added, "For there is one God in whom we must believe, but unoriginated, impassible, immortal, doing all things as He wills, in the way He wills, and when He wills" (*Against the Heresy of Noetus* 8). God is one, simple, indivisible, and incorruptible substance.

Since matter is divisible, the immaterial was considered indivisible. The fact that God is an immaterial spirit is not only supported by the biblical evidence, but by the fathers as well. Tatian writes, "God is a Spirit, not pervading matter, but the Maker of material spirits, and of the forms that are in matter" (*Address to the Greeks* ch. 4).

God's simplicity is also associated with His invisiblility. As immaterial and indivisible, God is also invisible. According to Theophilus, "God cannot indeed be seen by human eyes, but is beheld and perceived through His providence and works (*Epistle to Diognetus* 7). Mathetes (130) is the name for the anonymous author of a book in which God is described as "almighty, the Creator of all things, and invisible" (*Epistle of Mathetes to Diognetus*). Tatian says that "God alone is to be feared—He who is not visible to human eyes. . . . He is invisible, impalpable, being Himself the Father of both sensible and invisible things" (*Address to the Greeks* 4). One of the more prolific writers, Tertullian, argues that God is the Almighty and invisible (*Against Praexes* 16), as did his contemporary, Clement of Alexandria, who taught that God is invisible (*Stromata* 5.11). In the words of Cyril of Alexandria (d. 444), "God is spirit, and if spirit, not embodied nor in bodily form" (*Ad Calosyr,* 364 A).

A very explicit description of God's classical attributes is found in Athenagoras (177), who comments that "we are not atheists, therefore, seeing that we acknowledge one God, uncreated, eternal, invisible, impassible, incomprehensible, illimitable, who is apprehended by the understanding only and the reason, who is encompassed by light, and beauty, and spirit, and power ineffable" (*A Plea for the Christians* 10). A contemporary of the apostles, Ignatius, delineates a very precise theological view of God, who "is above all time, eternal and invisible, yet who became visible for our sakes" (*Epistle of Ignatius to Polycarp,* 33).

Gregory of Nyssa (335–395) believed and taught that both God the Father and God the Son are simple, which he understands to be "free from all compositeness" (*Answer to Eunomius* 2). Some of the early creeds also spoke of God's substance as not "divided" (see Appendix 2).

The Medieval View of Simplicity

The three great medieval theologians (with most other teachers of their time) were unanimous in teaching God's absolute simplicity.

Augustine

Augustine of Hippo affirmed that nothing "can have existence apart from Him whose existence is simple and indivisible. For, in God, being is not one thing and living another as though He could be and not be living." Nor, added Augustine, could God be and live, yet not understand, "for, in God, to live, to know, to be blessed is one and the same as to be" (*City of God* 1983 ET, 8.6).

However, even though God is absolutely one in essence, He is three in Persons. "For the Spirit is other than the Father and the Son because He is neither the Father nor the Son." Augustine hastens to add that these centers of personhood are so equal and interrelated that God remains undivided, simple, unchangeable, and co-eternal. "This Trinity is one God. And, although it is a Trinity, it is none the less simple." God's Being must be called "simple" in essence, though the Father, Son, and Holy Spirit stand in true interrelationship with one another (*City of God* 1983 ET, 11.10).

Even the angels "know this Word and the Father and their Holy Spirit, understanding that this Trinity is indivisible and that each of the Persons is substantial, although there are not three Gods but only one" (*City of God* 1983 ET, 11.29). Hence, "Let it not be supposed that in this Trinity there is any separation in respect of time or place, but that these Three are equal and co-eternal, and absolutely of one nature" (*Letters* 169.2).

Anselm

Like Augustine, Anselm affirmed God's absolute indivisibility, pointing out the implications of divine simplicity. If God exists in parts at any time or place, He would be composite in being. This would be alien to the sort of nature He has shown Himself to be (Anselm of Canterbury 1962 ET, 74).

Anselm, then, provides a caution for care in all of our considerations of the attributes of God. He applies the issue of simplicity of being to our view of the eternality of God. Eternity must be nothing else than timelessness, or else God will be partitioned by the divisions of time. No, it is not so, for the "supreme Nature is in no wise composite, but is supremely simple, supremely immutable" (Anselm of Canterbury 1962 ET, 76–77). He adds, "It is evident that this supreme Substance is without beginning and without end; that it has neither past, nor future, nor the temporal, that is, transient present in which we live; since its age, or eternity, which is nothing else than itself, is immutable and without parts" (Anselm of Canterbury 1962 ET, 83).

Thomas Aquinas

Aquinas gave an extended defense of the absolute simplicity of God, listing five arguments in *Summa Theologica* (1.3.7):[10]

1. Since there are no ways God could differ, God is in no way composite.
2. Every composite is posterior to its component parts, and is dependent on them, but God is the First Being.
3. Every composite has a cause, for diverse things cannot unite without help from outside their being. Hence, God is uncaused.
4. In every composite there must be potentiality and actuality, but God is Pure Actuality.
5. Since God is an absolute form or Being, He can be in no way composite. For absolute Being is identical to itself. But if He had parts, this could not be said of Him, since no part can be absolute.

Aquinas felt simplicity was such a crucial attribute of God that he listed it first in his *Summa*. Indeed, many of his arguments for other attributes of God depend on God's simplicity.

SIMPLICITY FROM THE REFORMATION

The Refomers were unanimous in following the fathers in affirming the simplicity of God.

Martin Luther

Martin Luther associated simplicity with immensity. If part of God cannot be in one place and another part in another

---

10. In *On the Power of God* 3.7.1.–3.10.4 Aquinas also has an extensive treatment of simplicity, but he rests his case on three basic arguments.

place, then God has no parts. Hence, all of God must be in every place. In his treatise on the body of Christ as it relates to the Lord's Supper, Luther discussed at great length what is meant by Christ ascending to the right hand of God. He dispels any notion that God is confined to a particular location. "God in his essence is present everywhere, in and through the whole creation in all its parts and in all places, and so the world is full of God and he fills it all, yet he is not limited or circumscribed by it" (Luther 1955–86, 37.59).

For Luther, simplicity is also implied in immutability. "When Christ, the Son of God, was to be conceived in his mother's womb and become incarnate, he certainly had to be already present in essence and in person in the virgin's womb, and had to assume humanity there. For the Godhead is immutable in itself and cannot pass from one place to another as creatures do" (Luther 1955–86, 37.62).

Luther strongly interrelates God's attributes: "This, therefore, is also essentially necessary and wholesome for Christians to know: that God foreknows nothing by contingency, but that He foresees, purposes, and does all things according to His immutable, eternal, and infallible will" (*Bondage of the Will* 9).

Finally, the doctrine of the Trinity implies the simplicity of God, for all three persons are united in one indivisible essence. According to Luther, "the sacred article of the Holy Trinity teaches us to believe and say that the Father, the Son, and the Holy Spirit are three distinct persons, yet each person is the one God. Here it is said of the one Godhead that it is threefold, being three persons" (Luther 1955–86, 37.297).

John Calvin

Calvin says, "God . . . has shown himself with complete clarity in the Father, the Son, and the Spirit. Hence it is quite clear that in God's essence reside three persons in whom one God is known" (Calvin 1960 ET, 1.16). He adds, "Therefore, let those who dearly love soberness, and who will be content with the measure of faith, receive in brief form what is useful to know: namely, that, when we profess to believe in one God, under the name of God is understood a single, simple essence, in which we comprehend three persons, or hypostases" (Calvin 1960 ET, 1.20).

Jacobus Arminius

Jacobus Arminius said that the "essence of God is devoid of all cause, from this circumstance arise, in the first place, simplicity and infinity of Being in the essence of God" (Arminius 1853 ET, 2.115). Indeed, simplicity is pivotal to the nature of God: "Simplicity is a pre-eminent mode of the essence of God, by which he is void of all composition, and of component parts, whether they belong to the senses or to the understanding. He is without composition, because without external cause; and He is without component parts, because without internal cause. The essence of God therefore neither consists of material, integral and quantitive parts, of matter and form, of kind and difference, of subject and accident, nor of form and the thing formed" (Arminius 1853 ET, 2.115).

Francis Turretin

Francis Turretin speaks of God's simplicity as

> his incommunicable attribute by which the divine nature is conceived by us not only as free from all composition and division, but also as incapable of composition and divisibility. This is proved to be a property of God: (1) from his independence, because composition is of the formal reason of a being originated and dependent (since nothing can be composed by itself, but whatever is composed must necessarily be composed by another; now God is the first and independent being, recognizing no other prior to himself); (2) from his unity, because he who is absolutely one, is also absolutely simple and therefore can neither be divided nor composed; (3) from his perfection, because composition

implies imperfection inasmuch as it supposes passive power, dependency and mutability; (4) from his activity, because God is a most pure act having no passive admixture and therefore rejecting all composition (because in God there is nothing which needs to be made perfect or can receive perfection from any other, but he is whatever can be and cannot be other than what he is). When he is usually described not only by concrete but also abstract names—life, light, truth, etc. (Turretin 1992 ET, 1.191–92)

Jonathan Edwards

In his treatise *Images of Divine Things,* Jonathan Edwards used the natural world as an object lesson in God's attributes and sovereignty. In one section he describes God's providence using the analogy of a river. "I need not run the parallel between this [the river] and the course of God's providence through all the ages, from the beginning to the end of the world, when all things shall have their final issue in God, the infinite, inexhaustible fountain whence all things come at first, as all the rivers come from the sea, and whither they all shall come at last: for of him and to him are all things, and he is the Alpha and Omega, the beginning and the end" (Edwards 1842 ed., 2.79).

Stephen Charnock

Stephen Charnock says,

God is the most simple being; for that which is first in nature, having nothing beyond it, cannot by any means be thought to be compounded; for whatsoever is so, depends upon the parts whereof it is compounded, and so is not the first being: now God being infinitely simple, hath nothing in Himself which is not Himself, and therefore cannot will any change in Himself, He being His own essence and existence. (Charnock 1971 ET, 333)

He also affirms, "Since, therefore, God is without all composition, His understanding is not distinct from His essence" (Charnock 1971 ET, 328).

BIBLICAL OBJECTIONS TO SIMPLICITY

Neotheists mount objections to God's simplicity based on the Bible, theology, and history. First, the biblical objections will be considered.

God's Timelessness in Exodus 3:14

Neotheists draw attention to the fact that "Biblical statements such as 'I AM WHO I AM' (Exod. 3:14) are understood [by classical theists] to express the true divine nature as atemporal and pure actuality, while statements that describe God as the 'one who is, was, and will be' (Rev. 1:4) are ignored or written off as figures of speech" (Pinnock et al. 1994, 99). Since God's simplicity is based on His Pure Actuality, this serves also to argue against simplicity.

Here is a diversionary "red herring" fallacy, for the issue is not what another text may mean but what this one affirms. The other text does not contradict Exodus 3:14. For to claim that God always "IS" does not imply that He did not exist in the past, present, and future. On the contrary, it declares that He always is. It simply affirms that God cannot grow old; He has no age. He ever Is. Or, to borrow from one of the neotheists, "though we wither and die, God abides and is not threatened or undone by time." That is, "God transcends our experience of time, is immune from the ravages of time" (Pinnock et al. 1994, 120). But this is at the heart of what theists affirm about aseity.

Suppose there were a strong tension between Exodus 3:14 and Revelation 1:8. Assuming, there is no contradiction in Scripture, the question is, which passages must be taken literally (metaphysically) and which not. Two hermeneutical clues indicate that God really is the "I AM," namely, the eternal, self-existent One.

First, in the Exodus passage it was specifically asked, "What is His Name [character, essence]?" (Exod. 3:13), whereas Revelation 1:4 is simply John's description of the God who from a temporal vantage point always was, is, and will be. Second, when God speaks in the Revelation 1:4 passage, He describes Himself as the "I am" (present tense) who nevertheless is the beginning and end. Indeed, He is in the past, in the present, and in the future. In fact, He always is. For it goes on to say He is the one "who is and who was and who is to come" (Rev. 1:8).

When two passages conflict, the one to be taken literally is the one that can best explain the other. For example, John 4:24 says "God is spirit." Yet God is described as having eyes, arms, legs, and as being a tower, a rock, and even a bird with wings. Now it is clear that God is literally a spirit and the other words must be understood figuratively. It makes no sense to say He is literally all these other things and figuratively a spirit. It is not an unusual practice to understand some things in the Bible figuratively. Even neotheist proponents admit that when there are conflicting texts, one must take one literally and the other figuratively (Pinnock et al. 1994, 17).

What neotheists have not done is provide a convincing case for why Exodus 3:14—a text claiming to give the very essence of who God is—should not be taken as a literal declaration of self-existence. The Septuagint (Greek OT translation) renders the Hebrew as the equivalent of "I Am He who is." The rendering "I will be who I will be," while grammatically possible, is contextually implausible and historically late, emerging in the wake of process theology. This linguistic possibility must be rejected. For one thing, the context opposes it, since God is asked to give his "Name" (character or essence). Two, the history of both Jewish and Christian interpretation of this text is overwhelmingly in favor of the classical interpretation. Neotheists reluctantly acknowledge this, combing through church history to find teachers who may agree with them. The truth is that nearly all the great patristic, medieval, and

Reformation theologians understood Exodus 3:14 as an affirmation of God's self-existence.

As we saw in the biblical teaching at the beginning of the chapter, Yahweh relates to the name "I AM WHO I AM," affirming the eternal God. This process and neotheistic understanding is contrary to Jesus' use of it in John 8:58: "Before Abraham was, I am." Notice Jesus did not affirm: "Before Abraham was, I will be who I will be," as He should have if the process understanding of this text were correct. For a follower of Christ, Jesus' understanding of this text should be definitive. Ironically, for those who claim classical theism was influenced by the (Greek) philosophy of their day, it turns out that their view is molded by the (process) philosophy of our day.

Finally, even if it could be proven that Exodus 3:14 does not support the claim of God for self-existence, there are plenty of other texts and good arguments that do. The very concept of God as uncreated Creator (Gen. 1:1) who brought all other things into existence (John 1:2–3; Col. 1:15–16; Heb. 1:2) is sufficient to prove His self-existence, for neotheists claim to believe in *ex nihilo* creation, affirming that "The triune God is the Creator of the world out of nothing" (Pinnock et al. 1994, 109). Reason demands that if God is Creator of all things, then He was uncreated. And if He did not get His existence from another, then He must exist in and of Himself (aseity).

Theological Objections to God's Simplicity

According to neotheists, the doctrine of divine simplicity should be rejected because the notion of divine simplicity is based on neo-platonic metaphysics (Pinnock et al. 1994, 129).

It is a genetic fallacy to reject the truth-value of a proposition due to its origin. Demons claimed that Jesus was the Son of God (Luke 4:41), yet we do not reject that claim because the claim was enunciated by demons. Also, the view that all things change can be traced to the Greek philosopher Heraclitus. Therefore, if the neotheists are to be consistent, they should reject their own position, for the basis of this notion is also grounded in Greek philosophy.

In the same vein, the neotheist does not reject the basic laws of logic though Aristotle discovered them. In fact, John Sanders argues that one should not appeal to antinomies or contradictions (Sanders 1998, 34–37). Neotheists appeal to Aristotle to justify the necessity of God. For example, Gregory Boyd states, "Sound philosophizing leads us to the same conclusion. Aristotle wisely taught that what is eternal cannot be other than it is. It is (as philosophers say) 'necessary'" (Boyd 2000, 137). Boyd quotes Aristotle, but he forgets that Aristotle also stated that whatever is necessary is simple and immutable. Aristotle wrote, "Hence what is necessary in the primary and proper sense is what is simple, for this cannot be in more ways than one" (*Metaphysics* 5:1015b9–15).

Nor do neotheists reject metaphysics *in toto*. Clark Pinnock states, "Christian theology, I am arguing, needs to reevaluate classical theism in light of a more relational metaphysics (not all philosophy is bad!)" (Pinnock et al. 1994, 100). Sanders states that we should have a trinitarian metaphysic where "relationality" is essential to God (Sanders 1998, 175). However, neotheists fail to show why neo-platonic metaphysics is wrong. They assert that it is wrong, and they suggest that we ought to try their new brand of metaphysics on for size. But how does one adjudicate between good and bad metaphysics? What compelling evidence does the neotheist offer that would cause one to embrace a relational metaphysics? If the neotheist responds that the Bible is the unchanging standard by which they are judging which metaphysic is good or bad, they are arguing in a circle. For the basis of their metaphysics is their interpretation of the Bible, and the basis of their interpretation of the Bible is their metaphysics.[11]

---

11. Though the same circular reasoning may be levied against the classical theist, the assertion does not follow because for the classical theist, the nature of reality is the basis of their metaphysics.

Furthermore, one cannot be a neotheist and consistently hold that the Bible is the objective basis for determining one's metaphysics. According to the neotheist, God *can* make mistakes, and according to the neotheist, the Bible records that God *has* made mistakes (Sanders 1998, 132–33). The neotheist would respond that God only makes mistakes if He tries to predict some future free will act and it did not come to pass (Sanders 1998, 132–33). However, this begs the question, for if God can be mistaken about future free will acts, it is possible that He is mistaken about other things as well, and if this is the case, it follows that the neotheist has no objective basis for determining whether his metaphysics is correct. If one carries the neotheistic notion of divine fallibility to its logical conclusion (without begging the question), it would follow that God may have made mistakes in inspiring the Scripture. In this case, the Scriptures, which the neotheist affirms attribute errors to God, may themselves be in error. Therefore, the neotheist has no way to determine truth from Scripture unless they beg the question by saying that God only errs in future free acts, or unless they affirm that God does not commit error at all.

In distinction, the classical theist affirms that God is ultimate reality and the Author of the rest of reality (all created things). Therefore, reality and God's word will never contradict each other, for the truth of metaphysics and the truths of the Bible are both grounded in the nature of God, who is Truth and who does not err in any respect.

Neotheists have not given us any reasons why we should reject any existing metaphysics, nor have they shown internal inconsistencies in an existential metaphysics. Instead, they themselves use "neo-platonic" metaphysics to justify certain attributes of God. They engage in circular reasoning to justify their metaphysics, and to affirm that God can be mistaken only about the future. The classical theist maintains that God cannot err at all and that metaphysical truths are derived from the nature of reality, which is grounded in the nature of God.[12] Moreover, the question is not whether the philosophy is neo-platonic, but whether it is true.

Simplicity Is Unintelligible

According to neotheists, the doctrine of divine simplicity should be rejected because it is not intelligible. William Hasker states, "divine timelessness is strongly dependent . . . on the doctrine of divine simplicity (whose intelligibility has been strongly challenged). Once this metaphysical taproot has been severed, the prospects for divine timelessness are not bright" (Pinnock et al. 1994, 129).

Divine simplicity cannot be unintelligible in an absolute sense, for the very fact that people are denying the doctrine of divine simplicity is evidence for the intelligibility of divine simplicity. Otherwise, those who deny the doctrine are denying what they do not understand.

Also, simply because something may not be *comprehended* (God's infinitude, eternality, immutability, or simplicity as examples), does not mean that it cannot be *apprehended*. Just because one cannot define *being* does not mean that he or she does not know that anything exists. Further, because something is not conceivable doesn't mean that it is not actual. God cannot be comprehended, yet He is actual. The doctrine of divine simplicity may not be comprehensible to us (though it is apprehendable to us), yet it could be actual.

Also, a thing may be unintelligible in one of two ways. It may be unintelligible in itself, for example a jumble of symbols chosen utterly at random. Or, it may be intelligible in itself, but not intelligible to someone unlearned in the corresponding

---

12. When we say that reality is grounded in God's nature, we are not es-pousing some form of emanation, which is found in Plotinus. Rather, we are affirming that reality resembles God insofar as His Mind is the exemplar cause of all that came to be. Moreover, insofar as a thing exists, it reflects God's nature, for it is of His essence to exist. In other words, God cannot come to be, nor can He cease to be in any sense.

meaning of the symbols (*Summa Theologica* 1.2.1). The Spanish "*A mi me gusta arroz con pollo*" can be translated into English as "I like rice and chicken." It is intelligible in itself, but not to those who do not read Spanish. The doctrine of divine simplicity is intelligible in itself. However, it may not be intelligible to some. Therefore, to say that divine simplicity is unintelligible does not demonstrate that it is unintelligible in itself. It merely demonstrates that it is unintelligible to those who are making the claim.

Infinity cannot be comprehended (though it can be apprehended) by a finite mind, yet the neotheist affirms that God is infinite. The consistent neotheist ought to deny that God is infinite because infinity is not comprehended by a finite mind. Or he should affirm that like infinity, simplicity cannot be comprehended but can be apprehended, or he should show why simplicity is unintelligible in itself. For example, a three-sided circle is unintelligible in itself because it is impossible for a circle to exist with only three sides and no sides simultaneously. In other words, he must show that it is actually impossible for God to be simple because it would entail God being and not-being in the same sense and in the same relationship, yet the neotheist has yet to demonstrate this.

HISTORICAL OBJECTIONS TO GOD'S SIMPLICITY

On the historical dimension of this debate neotheists defend their position in two ways. First, there is the standard argument that simplicity, like eternality and immutability, has roots in Greek philosophy and not in the Bible. Second, they contend that no church council addressed this matter. Hence, one is free to reject it without being vulnerable to a charge of heresy.

The Influence of Greek Philosophy

According to neotheists, the Jewish philosopher Philo of Alexandria (1st century), known for his Platonic leanings, is said to have understood Exodus 3:14 to mean "My nature is to be, not to be described by a name" (Pinnock et al. 1994, 69).

Later Origen is alleged to be responsible for passing this view on to the church fathers (Pinnock et al. 1994, 106). The root of this was the Greek translation of the Old Testament: "the dynamic 'I AM' of the Hebrew text became the impersonal 'Being who is'" (Pinnock et al. 1994, 106). This set the stage for a static view of God in terms of an eternal, unchangeable, and simple Being.

This charge is both ungrounded and double-edged, for neotheism itself is grounded in some respects in Greek philosophy. We already said that it is a "Genetic Fallacy" to reject something simply because of its source. If one rejects a view because of its antiquity, he has engaged in the "Fallacy of Chronological Snobbery." The truth of a view is not determined by its age. The question is not whether the view is based in some philosophy, ancient or modern, but whether it is true. In Christian evangelical theology the test for the truth of a position is determined by whether it is based in good exegesis of Scripture and sound reasoning, and truth is determined by propositions that correspond to reality.

Ecumenical Creedal Silence

Boyd concedes that the open view of God has been relatively rare in church history. However, he raises the question of how much weight should be given to church tradition, especially in light of the fact that he believes the church's theology was flawed from the start. He writes, "In my estimation . . . almost from the start the church's theology was significantly influenced by Plato's notion that God's perfection must mean that he is in every respect unchanging—including in his knowledge and experience" (Boyd 2000, 115). He goes on to say that no ecumenical creed has issued an article of faith on divine foreknowledge (Boyd 2000, 116). Presumably, the same argument could be pressed on simplicity too.

If we speak about silence, the rarity of the open view of God in church history serves as a warning to anyone who deviates from the established theological positions. Boyd admits that tradition properly makes orthodox Christians cautious of new positions. While classical theists do not "canonize" traditions of the church, theological prudence would certainly compel responsible theologians to reconsider any view that departs drastically from the historic Christian faith, as does open theism.

Second, Boyd contends that the reason neotheism has been rare in church history is due to the influence of Platonism. He implies that in the absence of Platonism, neotheism would have possibly developed. However, Boyd seems to underestimate the theological acumen of the early fathers, medieval scholastics, and Reformers. If neotheism has the solid biblical support Sanders, Rice, and other neotheists claim, should not the view have been more evident? It seems unreasonable to insinuate that the early church was so influenced by Hellenism that it couldn't accurately read and interpret the biblical text. This is particularly so since orthodox fathers made a conspicuous effort to base all beliefs in Scripture. Their extant writings cite the Bible more than thirty-six thousand times in the first few centuries. They conscientiously rejected many elements of Greek thought in favor of the biblical view, eschewing polytheism, pre-existence, reincarnation, an eternal universe, and all efforts to deny the reality of a physical resurrection.

Though the creeds do not make explicit statements regarding some of these issues, they do contain theological statements that contradict openness theology. The Nicene Creed begins by establishing the fact that there is only one true God: "We believe in one God, the Father All Governing, creator of all things visible and invisible" (Leith 1963, 30). Regarding Jesus Christ, the creed says He is "begotten not created, of the same essence as the Father." Here we find a strong statement on the unity and eternality of the Godhead, which is an aspect of simplicity. Especially noteworthy is the final portion of the Nicene Creed, which reads: "But, those who say, Once he was not, or he was not before his generation, or he came to be out of nothing, or who assert that he, the Son of God, is of a different hypostasis or *ousia*, or that he is a creature, or changeable, or mutable, the Catholic and Apostolic Church anathematizes them" (Leith 1963, 31).

The creeds do speak to the matter of simplicity. They refer to God's nature as "indivisible." For example, the Athanasian Creed declares "We worship one God . . . neither confounding the Persons nor dividing the substance [essence]" (Schaff 1877, 2.66).[13]

Finally, it begs the question to assume that only what the early creeds explicitly treat can be used as a test for orthodoxy. No ancient creed has anything to say about the divine authority of Holy Scripture. Yet surely in any short list of essential orthodox doctrines, this should be included. This reasoning is as fallacious as claiming that abortion is not an important moral issue because neither Jesus nor any New Testament writer explicitly refers to it.

The Cappadocian Father's Rejected Simplicity.

Sanders states that the Cappadocian fathers argued against Eunomius, who claimed that God was a simple essence (not composed of parts) and so the Son and the Spirit could not be fully God: God is devoid of internal relations. In response, the Cappadocians affirmed that there are relationships endemic in the Godhead. According to Sanders, this entails that *person* not *substance* was the ultimate metaphysical category (Sanders 1998, 145–46).

This is a "Strawman Fallacy." We have seen that classical theists do not deny relationships within the Godhead, yet they affirm simplicity.[14] That God is a Trinity does not argue for composition, for the persons in the Godhead may be considered in two ways. First, in reference to the divine

---

13. See appendix 1 for a chart on what the creeds affirmed concerning the attributes of God.
14. See list of creeds affirming the Trinity and simplicity of God, appendix 2.

essence, each person is identical to the essence. Second, in respect to each other, each person is mutually distinct. However, to undergo composition there must be a union of the elements, which are being united (Aquinas, *On the Power of God* 3.7.1). Therefore, the Trinity and simplicity are not contradictory.

For the classical theist, the relationships really existing in God are the same as His essence. It only differs in its mode of intelligibility to us (*Summa Theologica* 1.28.2). Moreover, there is real distinction in God, not according to essence, but according to what is relative—personhood. Therefore, relationality in God does not demand composition (*Summa Theologica* 1.28.3).

It does not follow that, because there are real relationships in the Godhead, God has real reciprocal dependent relationships with creation. His relation to creation can be real, without Him being dependant on creation.

Also, personhood cannot be the ultimate metaphysical principle, for the ultimate metaphysical principle is that which applies to all things. However, personhood does not apply to all things. Therefore, personhood cannot be the ultimate metaphysical principle.

CONCLUSION

The simplicity (indivisibility) of God is a fundamental attribute of classical theism. It undergirds not only many of the other crucial attributes of God but also all the other doctrines based on them. Despite its rejection by contemporary process theology and neotheism, confession of the simplicity and aseity of God has a venerable tradition. From the patristic and medieval theologians to modern Catholic and Protestant thinkers, those who have seriously studied Scripture have defended this doctrine. Although challenges continue, no one has demonstrated the philosophical incoherence of God's simplicity and indivisibility, nor has there been shown a faulty biblical and theological foundation.

Rather, there are strong reasons to reject the neotheistic challenge to God's simplicity and reaffirm its standing as vital to classical Christianity.

CHAPTER SIX

Impassibility

THE IMPASSIBILITY OF God is a hotly debated topic in the contemporary battle for God for two basic reasons. First, some mistakenly believe that an impassible God must feel nothing analogous to human emotions. Second, the correctly understood, historically orthodox view of God's impassibility still runs counter to the changing God of neotheism.

THE MEANING OF IMPASSIBILITY

Unlike other attributes of God examined in this volume, impassibility is widely misunderstood. The root meaning of the theological term is that God is "not passible," or subject to passion (*im* = not and *passible* = passion). That is, God cannot undergo passion or suffering. This is not to say that God has no emotional states, but simply that His feelings are *not the result of actions imposed on Him by others*. God's feelings are part of His own eternal and unchangeable nature.

William G. T. Shedd (1820–1894) framed a good definition: "Impassibility means that the divine nature cannot be caused to suffer from any external cause. Nothing in the created universe can make God feel pain or misery" (Shedd 1980, 2.387). G. L. Prestige adds that "impassibility means not that God is inactive or uninterested, not that He surveys existence with Epicurean [sic] impassivity from the shelter of a metaphysical insulation, but that His will is determined from within instead of being swayed from without" (Prestige 1959,

7). Prestige's definition clarifies the classical view regarding God's relationship to His creation, stressing that God is not without feelings. A view that God expresses no emotional states would be clearly contrary to the teachings of the Old and New Testaments.

But Scripture does teach that God cannot be acted upon by anything outside of Himself. Human actions cannot generate in God an emotional reaction that alters or terminates what He has determined to be. Prestige goes on to relate that,

> just as God is supreme in power and wisdom, so is He morally supreme, incapable of being diverted or overborne by forces and passions such as commonly hold sway in the creation and among mankind. . . . [The classical definition of God's impassibility] safeguards the truth that the impulse alike in providential order and in redemption and sanctification comes from the will of God. If it were possible to admit that the impulse was wrung from Him either by the needs or by the claims of His creation, and that thus whether by pity or by justice His hand was forced, He would no longer be represented as absolute; He would be dependent on the created universe and thus at best only in possession of concurrent power. (Prestige 1959, 7)

AMBIVALENCE TOWARD IMPASSIBILITY

This particular attribute of God has not received much attention in systematic theology, nor presumably in systematics classes in colleges and seminaries. Yet the doctrine is important within the context of the current crisis in the battle for God. Evangelical theologians have either rejected the doctrine altogether or sought to modify it to alleviate tensions or inconsistencies they believe are inherent within the classical view of God. Reformed philosopher Ronald Nash, for example, believes impassibility poses a problem for classical theologians, in particular those of the Thomist persuasion (Nash 1983, 114).

Inadequate formulations of the doctrine still contribute to

the reluctance of some evangelicals to embrace the classical view of impassibility. Neotheists are notorious for incorrectly explaining the meaning of such basic terms as *infinite, eternal, immutable,* and *impassible*. Richard Rice states that the classical view of *impassibility* describes God as "essentially unaffected by creaturely events and experiences. He is untouched by the disappointment, sorrow or suffering of his creatures" (Pinnock et al. 1994, 12). Clark Pinnock believes that "impassibility is the most dubious of the divine attributes discussed in classical theism, because it suggests that God does not experience sorrow, sadness or pain. It appears to deny that God is touched by the feelings of our infirmities, despite what the Bible eloquently says about his love and his sorrow" (Pinnock et al. 1994, 118).

The conclusions reached by such orthodox scholars as Nash and such neotheists as Pinnock and Rice do not reflect the classical view. No responsible classical theist would argue that God is emotionally detached from human events. A *prima facie* reading of the biblical text would not sustain such an extreme view.

THE BIBLICAL BASIS FOR IMPASSIBILITY

The Bible has a good bit to say about what is really meant by impassibility. Since the term itself is not used, its necessary elements must be identified. Some of these include:

- *God does not need anything or anyone external to Himself to fill a lack or need.* God is totally self-sufficient. He does not need anything to satisfy or complete Him. We exist because of God's good pleasure alone (Job 22:2-3; 35:6-7; Ps. 50:10-12).
- *God cannot be obligated to anyone.* The concept of obligation entails a sense of duty or responsibility. When Abraham appealed to God on behalf of the people of Sodom, God agreed to spare the city if a certain number of righteous people were there. He was not obligated to do this by

Abraham's appeal; rather He was showing His mercy. God is the source of all things (Acts 17:25; Rom. 11:35–36).

- *God is not counseled or instructed by anyone.* Though some Old Testament passages indicate that God received counsel from an Abraham, or a Moses, He is all-wise and omniscient. He lacks no wisdom (Isa. 40:13–14, 28; James 1:5).
- *God cannot change.* Any outward expression of emotion does not mean that God might change what He has decided that He will do. God expresses emotion in perfect concert with His immutability (Num. 23:19; 1 Sam. 15:29; Mal. 3:6). If God cannot change, then He must be impassible. Everyone who suffers undergoes change. Hence, an immutable God is an impassible God.

THE THEOLOGICAL BASIS FOR IMPASSIBILITY

In addition to the biblical basis for impassibility, there are theological reasons why God cannot undergo passion or suffering. The most basic include:

- *Impassibility follows from Pure Actuality.* As has been shown, God is Pure Actuality. He has no potential to be anything but Who He is. But whatever has no potentiality cannot be acted upon, for to be acted upon is to have some potentiality actualized. God as Pure Actuality cannot undergo passion or suffering. If He could, He would not be Pure Actuality.
- *Impassibility flows from immutability.* All suffering involves change in the sufferer. But God cannot change, so He cannot undergo suffering. That suffering involves change is clear, since the state of nonsuffering differs from the state of suffering. Whatever suffers moves from a state of potentiality to a state of actuality. Given that God cannot change, He cannot suffer.
- *Impassibility is demanded by absolute perfection.* All passion involves a desire for what is lacking. But God lacks nothing, since He is absolutely perfect, so He cannot have passion.

He has no passion or craving for something He does not
possess. As an absolutely perfect Being, God lacks nothing
and, hence, He craves nothing.

- *Impassibility is based on God's sovereignty.* God is in sovereign
  control of the universe (see ch. 8). What is passible is
  subject to control by something. God controls all creation,
  but creation does not control Him. That which is not
  controlled by anything else, cannot be subjugated by
  anything else. Hence, God does not experience
  subjugation. He is literally impassible.
- *Impassibility is inherent in uncausality.* God is the Cause of
  all things, so He cannot be caused by anything. He is the
  uncaused Cause. An uncaused Cause acts upon other
  things but is never acted upon. What suffers is acted upon
  by another. Therefore, God cannot suffer. He is impassible.

THE HISTORICAL BASIS FOR IMPASSIBILITY

As with the other attributes of God, the doctrine of
impassibility is discussed by numerous fathers of the church,
as well as by the Reformers and Puritans. Contrary to what
neotheists are saying, the evidence of church history shows that
impassibility was held to be true.

The Patristic View of Impassibility

Ignatius of Antioch (early 2d century) wrote to Polycarp (70–
c.155), encouraging him to stand firm against those who were
spreading errors about Jesus Christ. "Weigh carefully the times.
Look for Him who is above all time, eternal and invisible, yet who
became visible for our sakes; impalpable and impassible, yet who
became passible on our account" (*Epistle to Polycarp* 3, ANF 1.99).

Clement of Alexandria wrote in his *Miscellanies*, "let the
specimen suffice to those who have ears. For it is not required
to unfold the mystery, but only to indicate what is sufficient
for those who are partakers in knowledge to bring it to mind;
who also will comprehend how it was said by the Lord, 'Be ye
perfect as your father, perfectly,' by forgiving sins, and forgetting

injuries, and living in the habit of passionlessness" (*Stromata* 7.14, *ANF* 2.549).

Origen addresses the issue of God's repentance in his *De Principiis*. He said

> And now, if, on account of those expressions which occur in the Old Testament, as when God is said to be angry or to repent, or when any other human affection or passion is described, (our opponents) think that they are furnished with grounds for refuting us, who maintain that God is altogether impassible, and is to be regarded as wholly free from all affections of that kind, we have to show them that similar statements are found even in the parables of the Gospel. . . . But when we read either in the Old Testament or in the New of the anger of God, we do not take such expressions literally, but seek in them a spiritual meaning, that we may think of God as He deserves to be thought of (*De Principiis* 2.4.4, *ANF* 4.277).

Irenaeus wrote extensively against the prevailing heretical views of his day, particularly those teachings that reduced God to nothing more than amplified humanity. He writes,

> By their manner of speaking, they ascribe those things which apply to men to the Father of all, whom they also declare to be unknown to all; and they deny that He himself made the world, to guard against attributing want of power to Him; while, at the same time, they endow Him with human affections and passions. But if they had known the Scriptures, and been taught by the truth, they would have known, beyond doubt, that God is not as men are; and that His thoughts are not like the thoughts of men. For the Father of all is at a vast distance from those affections and passions which operate among men. (*Against Heresies* 2.13.3, *ANF* 1.374)

Tertullian condemns Praxeas for affirming that God suffered. Tertullian says that there is no blasphemy in predicating of the subject that which is fairly applicable to it. . . . It is blasphemy when that is alleged concerning the subject which is unsuitable to it. On this principle, too, the Father was not associated with the suffering with the Son. *The heretics*, indeed, fearing to incur direct blasphemy against the Father, hope to diminish it by this expedient: they grant us so far that the Father and the Son are Two: adding that, since it is the Son indeed who suffers, the Father is only His fellow-sufferer. But how absurd are they in this conceit. . . . Then, again, the Father is as incapable of fellow-suffering as the Son even is of suffering under the conditions of His existence as God. (*Against Praxeas* 29, *ANF* 3.626)

Not only did Tertullian affirm that God was impassible, but he stated that the denial of impassibility is heretical. Against Tertullian's view on God's impassibility, neotheist John Sanders expresses the notion that Christ suffered to emphasize that God is conditioned by us. Moreover, Sanders states, "Perhaps more than any other early Christian theologian, Tertullian emphasized key elements of relational theism" (Sanders 1998, 143).

Athenagoras examines the true nature of God in differentiating polytheism from monotheism. He says that "God is uncreated, and, impassible, and indivisible" (*A Plea for the Christians* 8, *ANF* 2.132).

Dionysius of Alexandria (c. 190–264), speaking of the Father and the Son in a fragment preserved by Eusebius (c. 263–c. 339), "argues against certain theories of a Gnostic or Manichaean, affirming 'Let them give the reason why, if both are unoriginate, God is impassible, immutable, unmovable, active in work, but in matter on the contrary subject to passion, changeable, unstable, experiencing modification'" (Mozley 1926, 72).

Gregory Thaumaturgus, according to J. K. Mozley, provides "the most important work which comes to us from the Alexandrine School after the writings of Clement and Origen . . . dealing explicitly with the question of the divine capacity for suffering" (Mozley 1926, 63). Gregory's treatise is in the form of a dialogue between himself and a questioner, Theopompus, who asks whether God is impassible (63–72).[1] Gregory's *Twelve Topics on the Faith* states that "if anyone affirms that He who suffered is one, and that He who suffered not is another, and refuses to acknowledge that the Word, who is Himself the impassible and unchangeable God, suffered in the flesh which He had assumed really, yet without mutation, even as it is written, let him be anathema" (*Twelve Topics on the Faith* 5, *ANF* 6.51).

Novatian of Rome (c. 210–280), in chapter five of his treatise on the Trinity, argues that God is not morally corrupted by such emotions as anger, wrath, or indignation (*Treatise Concerning the Trinity* 5, *ANF* 5.615). Mozley adds that "what Novatian means is that there is a perfect concord between feeling and reason which is not to be found in man, especially not in the case of such feelings as anger and hatred" (Mozley 1926, 63).

Methodius (c. 260–312) describes the Incarnation as that state in which Christ, though enclosed in flesh, "with power He suffered, remaining impassible" (Methodius. *Three Fragments on the Passion of Christ* 3, *ANF* 6.400). Mozley notes that Lactantius, following the teachings of Arnobius the Elder (d. c. 330), asserts "the perfection of God, His incorruptibility, impassibility and freedom from all external control" (Mozley 1926, 48–49). Citing the poets regarding the one God, Lactantius writes that "there is, then, one God, perfect, eternal, incorruptible, incapable of suffering, subject to no circumstance or power" (*Epitome of the Divine Institutes* 3, *ANF* 7.225).

Arnobius, in *Seven Books of Arnobius Against the Heathen*, addresses rejection of the gospel message. Given that many reject it with disdain, he states that "God compels no one, terrifies no one with overpowering fear. For our salvation is not necessary to Him, so that He would gain anything or suffer

---

1. Unfortunately, Gregory's treatise is only available in Syriac and Latin. Mozley provides brief but incomplete English translations.

any loss, if He either made us divine, or allowed us to be annihilated and destroyed by corruption" (*Seven Books of Arnobius* 2.64, sfs 6.458).

Salvian the Presbyter (c. 400–480), commenting on Genesis 6 with regard to God's repentance that He had made man, states that "this does not mean that God is affected by emotion or is subject to any passion. Rather, the Divine Word, to impart more fully to us a true understanding of the Scriptures, speaks 'as if' in terms of human emotions" (Oden, ed., 2001, 1.127).

In his homily on Numbers, Origen writes: "Now all these sayings in which God is spoken of as sorrowing or rejoicing or hating or being glad are to be understood as uttered by the Scripture after an allegorical and human manner. The divine nature is altogether separated from every affection of passion and change, and remains unmoved and unshaken forever on that peak of blessedness" (*In Num. Hom.* 23, 2).[2]

The Medieval View of Impassibility

Augustine

Augustine affirms that Scripture's description of God's seeming emotions point to a different order of Being than humans can understand:

> That virtue of the mind which is called Patience, is so great a gift of God, that even in Him who bestoweth the same upon us, that, whereby He waiteth for evil men that they may amend, is set forth by the name of Patience, [or long-suffering]. . . . Although in God there can be no suffering, and "patience" hath its name *a patiendo*, from suffering, yet a patient God we not only faithfully believe, but also wholesomely confess. But the patience of God, of what kind and how great it is, His, Whom we say to be impassible, yet not impatient, nay even most patient, in words to unfold

---

2. Origen,; cited in *Impassibility of God*, 62.

this who can be able? Ineffable is therefore that patience, as is His jealousy, as His wrath, and whatever there is like to these.

[For] if we conceive of these as they be in us, in Him are there none. We, namely, can feel none of these without molestation: but be it far from us to surmise that the impassible nature of God is liable to any molestation. But like as He is jealous without any darkening of spirit, wroth without any perturbation, pitiful without any pain, repenteth Him without any wrongness in Him to be set right; so is He patient without aught of passion. (*On Patience* 1)

Anselm

Anselm affirmed that "the Divine nature is beyond doubt impassible, and that God cannot at all be brought down from his exaltation, nor toil in anything which he wishes to effect. But we say that the Lord Jesus Christ is very God and very man, one person in two natures, and two natures in one person." He added, "When, therefore, we speak of God as enduring any humiliation or infirmity, we do not refer to the majesty of that nature, which cannot suffer; but to the feebleness of the human constitution which he assumed. And so there remains no ground of objection against our faith." For "in this way we intend no debasement of the Divine nature, but we teach that one person is both Divine and human. In the incarnation of God there is no lowering of the Deity; but the nature of man we believe to be exalted" (*Cur Deus Homo?* 1.8).

Thomas Aquinas

According to Thomas Aquinas, "The passions in question are in sinners in one way; in the just, both the perfect and the imperfect, in another way; in Christ as man in another; and in the first man and the blessed in still another. They are not in the angels or in God at all, because in them there is no sense appetite, of which such passions are movements" (*On Truth* 26.8).

Impassibility from the Reformation

The Reformers, and theologians who followed them, embraced the doctrine of passibility.

Martin Luther

Martin Luther's statements on this subject are somewhat ambiguous. On the one hand, his so-called "theology of the cross" seems to imply that God suffered on the cross. In reacting against the Nestorian heresy that the one who died on the cross was not God, Luther seems to favor the opposite extreme of the Monophysites who confused the two natures of Christ. He wrote,

> We Christians must allow the *idiomata* [language] of the two natures of Christ, the persons, equally and totally. As a result, Christ is God and a human being in one person because whatever is said about him as a human being must also be said of him as God, namely, "Christ has died," and, as Christ is God, it follows that "God has died" — not God in isolation [*der abgesonderte Gott*], but God united with humanity. . . . For neither of the statements "Christ is God" and "God has died" are true in the case of God in isolation; both are false, for then God is not a human being. If it seems strange to Nestorius that God should die, he should find it just as strange that God becomes a human being; for by doing so, the immortal God becomes that which must die and suffer, and have all the human *idiomata*. . . .
>
> If this was not the case, what kind of human being would God have become united to, if it did not have truly human *idiomata*. It would be a phantom [*Gespenst*], as the Manicheans taught earlier. On the other hand, whatever is said of God must also be attributed to the human being. . . . "God created the world and is almighty," and the human being Christ is God; therefore, the human being Christ created the world and is almighty." The reason for this is that since God and the human being have become one person, this person bears the *idiomata* of both natures in consequence. (Luther 1959 ET, 175)

While this may seem to deny impassibility by attributing to the divine nature the suffering that occurred in Christ's human nature, Luther elsewhere declared the opposite. For example, he affirmed, "For you must immediately say that the Person [Christ] suffers and dies. Now the Person is true God; therefore it is correctly said: The Son of God suffers. For although the one part (to put it that way), namely, the divinity, does not suffer, yet the Person, who is God, suffers in the other part, namely, in His humanity."[3] Were it not for the clarification, we might understand Luther to be unorthodox on the question of impassibility. The confusion lies with his strong words against Nestorianism, and his fight with Ulrich Zwingli (1484–1531) on *alloeosis*, so that he did not state his thought as clearly as we would desire. However, Luther's subsequent words place him within the historic teaching of the church and Scriptures. Premier Lutheran theologian Franz August Pieper says of Luther's view:

> It is these definite doctrines of Scripture and not human speculation, which the Formula of Concord, Luther, and the Lutheran dogmaticians teach, when in agreement with the Scripture passages that ascribe to the Son of God suffering and death. This suffering, in the assumed human nature, however, is the suffering of the Son of God, since the human nature does not constitute a separate person, but belongs to the Person of the Son of God. (Pieper 1950–57, 2.140)

To affirm that God suffered on the cross or that Jesus suffered in His divine nature on the cross, is contrary to virtually every orthodox theologian from the earliest times through the Reformation. It is akin to a Monophysite heresy called *patripassianism*, which claimed that God the Father suffered on the Cross, since Jesus was God and Jesus suffered there as God.

---

3. By "part," Luther means "nature." See *What Luther Says: An Anthology*, 3 vols., E. M. Plass, comp. St. Louis, Concordia, 1959, 170–71.

John Calvin

John Calvin explains God's repentance as "the very same that is meant by the other forms of expression, by which God is described to us humanly. Because our weakness cannot reach his height, any description which we receive of him must be lowered to our capacity in order to be intelligible. And the mode of lowering is to represent him not as he really is, but as we conceive him." Likewise,

> though he is incapable of every feeling of perturbation, he declares that he is angry with the wicked. Wherefore, as when we hear that God is angry, we ought not to imagine that there is any emotion in him, but ought rather to consider the mode of speech accommodated to our sense, God appearing to us like one inflamed and irritated whenever he exercises Judgment, so we ought not to imagine any thing more under the term repentance than a change of action, men being wont to testify their dissatisfaction by such a change. (Calvin 1960 ET, 1.17.12–13)

Jacobus Arminius

Jacobus Arminius's position on God's impassibility is consistent with the early and medieval church fathers, as well as the teachings of major Reformers. In Disputation 4, Article 17, he writes,

> impassibility is a pre-eminent mode of the Essence of God, according to which it is devoid of all suffering or feeling; not only because nothing can act against this Essence, for it is of infinite Being and devoid of an external cause; but likewise because it cannot receive the act of anything, for it is of simple Entity. Therefore, Christ has not suffered according to the Essence of his Deity. (Arminius 1956 ET, 2.117)[4]

---

4. Cited in John Gerstner, *The Rational Biblical Theology of Jonathan Edwards* (Powhatan, Va.: Berea, 1991), 2.59.

Article XIII reads, "from the Simplicity and Infinity of the Divine sense, arise Infinity with regard to time, which is called 'Eternity;' and with regard to place, which is called 'Immensity;' 'Impassibility,' 'Immutability,' and 'Incorruptibility'" (Arminius 1956 ET, 2.116).

Francis Turretin

Reformed theologian Francis Turretin shares Calvin's basic understanding of God's repentance. He writes,

> Repentance is attributed to God after the manner of men (*anthropopathos*) but must be understood after the manner of God (*theoprepos*): not with respect to his counsel, but to the event; not in reference to his will, but to the thing willed; not to affection and internal grief, but to the effect and external work because he does what a penitent man usually does. If repentance concerning the creation of man (which he could not undo) is ascribed to God (Genesis 6:6, 7), it must be understood not pathetically, but energetically. (Turretin 1992 ET, 1.206.11)

Jonathan Edwards

Jonathan Edwards didn't leave behind a systematic presentation on the attributes of God, but frequently he commented on them. Edwards scholar John Gerstner did extensive work in the theology of Edwards, and he attempted to systematize Edwards's theology. Edwards didn't address it in the same way found in patristic, medieval, or Reformed sources. His exposition of God's happiness is the best description of how Edwards viewed God's expression of "emotion." According to Gerstner, "Edwards does not put as much emphasis on this theme as on some other attributes. Yet this is not, strictly speaking, an attribute so much as the result of the attributes, especially the harmony of natural with moral attributes."

In his discussion of the misery of men and how that affects

the will and happiness of God, Gerstner comments that, according to Edwards, "God's counsel stands fast, and so does His happiness. Edwards teaches that God's will is always done; it follows that God is infinitely happy. Therefore, the misery of men, which must fall within the will of God, cannot destroy the divine happiness but must be a part of it" (Gerstner 1991, 2.61).

OBJECTION TO GOD'S IMPASSIBILITY

The classical understanding of impassibility is rejected outright by neotheists. They insist that God not only can, but must undergo changes in feeling if He is really a personal, loving God. They offer several objections to impassibility from biblical and theological perspectives.

Objections Based on the Bible

The neotheistic objections to God's impassibility make strong appeals to Scripture. God's grief at human sin is one of the chief references used. Other expressions of emotion that suggest God is not impassible include anger, jealousy, pleasure, love, and hatred.

God Does Express Feelings

In Genesis 6:6 God is grieved over the sinful behavior of mankind and expresses sorrow that He made the human race. Second Samuel 15:35 states that God was sorry for making Saul king over Israel. God had compassion on the people of Nineveh and did not destroy them as He had warned that He would (Jon. 3:4, 10; 4:2). In Exodus 32:10–12, God's anger burns against Israel due to their idolatry. His intention is to destroy the people, but Moses intercedes and God relents.

Classical theists do not believe that God is a divine "Mr. Spock," the emotionless Vulcan in the *Star Trek* science fiction television series. God does not exude raw logic and reason devoid of emotional interaction with His creation. God does express such emotions as anger, jealousy, hatred, love, kindness, patience, grief, and sorrow. For neotheists, God's emotional reactions to His creation change Him. An example of this is the interpretation Sanders gives for Genesis 6:6, which describes God's grief over man's sin. He says that God "takes full responsibility for creating these beings who have turned toward sin, and this responsibility brings grief to God. . . . God is involved in the situation and it affects him deeply. Whatever God decides, he will never be the same again" (Sanders 1998, 49).

However, such passages as Numbers 23:19; 2 Samuel 15:29; and Malachi 3:6 support the conclusion that His immutability cannot be compromised by emotional reaction to human actions (see ch. 4). On this point classical theists and neotheists agree. However, they seriously disagree regarding how to interpret such crucial biblical texts as those cited.

Take, for example, the question, "Does God change His mind due to an emotional response on His part to the actions of an outside agent?" We know that God expresses emotions, but can He do so without compromising His immutability? Classical theists say yes; neotheists disagree. According to Sanders, "Many of us . . . read the Bible initially as saying that God responds to us and may change his mind, but once we become more 'theologically informed' we tend to reinterpret those texts in a way that does not allow for such theologically 'incorrect' views" (Pinnock et al. 1994, 59).

Sanders seems to minimize the importance of interpretation in the reading Scripture—theological interpretation in particular. His appeal to a strict prima facie approach to the text sounds good, but it doesn't always work. For example, Malachi 3:6 says, "I, the Lord, do not change." Numbers 23:19 reads, "God is not a man, that He should lie, nor a son of man, that He should repent" (NASB). According to 2 Samuel 15:29 "the Glory of Israel will not lie or change His mind; for He is not a man that He should change His mind" (NASB).

Contrary to Sanders, the only way to reconcile the apparent contradictions between these passages is to interpret them with

theological considerations. Unless Sanders is willing to admit
that the Scriptures contradict themselves and there is nothing
we can do about it, anyone concerned with handling the text
responsibly must admit that Sanders's hermeneutic is flawed.

Classical theism holds that God is not only immutable, but
His omniscience entails perfect knowledge of the future.
Therefore, God will never be surprised by any human action,
good or evil. We can conclude, then, that immutability,
omniscience, and impassibility are mutually essential, and how
they work together is crucial to a sound theological approach
to biblical interpretation. For example, God sovereignly sets in
motion a specific plan. He perfectly knows what actions people
will take in response to His plan. So when someone acts, God
responds with the perfectly appropriate emotion. However, His
emotional response is not a reaction to new knowledge, but a
response to the action based on His character. Therefore,
impassibility is consistent with God's nature and the biblical
text.

The biblical citations concerning God's feelings, which are
understood to involve change in God, can best be explained as
anthropomorphic, since God cannot change (see ch. 4).

There is a legitimate sense in which it is literally true that
God experiences feelings. God has feeling in an unchanging
way, but not in a changing way. He has feelings in an active
sense but not in a passive sense. He does not undergo feelings
(as being acted upon by another), but as actively expressing
them Himself. He expresses mercy from Himself, but He does
not experience misery from another. He has an active sensitivity
to our pain, but He does not undergo a passive sentimentality
because of it. He has active perception of our hurts but no
passive passion because of them.

God experiences emotion in accord with His nature, which
is eternal and unchangeable. Just as God knows what we know,
but not in the way we know it, so God feels what we feel but
not in the way that we feel it. Since God has no potentiality,
His nature cannot be actualized by any creature in any way. If

it were, God would be the effect, and we would be the cause. But God is the great First Cause of all things, and we creatures are merely the secondary causes and effects.

In light of what is true regarding God's attributes and how they complement each other, the biblical passages which refer to expressions of divine emotion are in harmony with classical theism's doctrine of impassibility.

THEOLOGICAL OBJECTIONS TO GOD'S IMPASSIBILITY

Most biblical and theological criticisms directed against the classical attribute of impassibility apply equally to God's attribute of immutability. Most of these have been answered in chapter 4 and will not be repeated. However, a few additional arguments have been offered:

Christ's Atonement

Several teachings are not in dispute among classical and neotheistic theologians. Both hold that Christ is God (John 1:1–17; Heb. 1:8), and both affirm that Christ suffered on the cross (Isa. 53:3–5; Col. 2:9; 1 Peter 2:24; 3:18). But given that both of these propositions find agreement, neotheists insist that a God who suffered on the cross is not impassible. It is claimed that impassibility is the most dubious doctrine of divine attribute, because it suggests that God does not experience sorrow, sadness, or pain. Classical theism appears to deny that God is touched by the feelings of our infirmities, despite what the Bible says about His love and His sorrow. How can God be loving and not pained by evil? How can God be impassible when God the Son experienced suffering and death? (Pinnock et al. 1994, 118).

In response to the neotheistic objection that God suffered on the cross, one need only point to the orthodox belief in the hypostatic union of two natures in one person. The creeds affirm that these should neither be separated, as in Nestorianism, nor confused, as in Monophysitism. It appears that this objection does the latter. Jesus had two distinct natures, one divine and the other human. He suffered in and through the latter, not the former. He who suffered was both God and man, but He did not suffer as God but as human.

Indeed, this neotheistic objection, akin to *patripassianism*, fails to recognize that the divine nature did not undergo suffering; only Christ, who shares the divine nature with the Father and the Holy Spirit, suffered on the cross—in His human nature. Only the second person of the Godhead suffered on the cross. To claim otherwise is to confuse the two natures of Christ.

The Personhood of God

A person is commonly defined as one who has intellect, emotions (feelings), and will. Yet both sides of the impassibility dispute agree that there is personhood in God. All three members of the Trinity are Persons. Therefore, reason neotheists, these persons must have feelings or emotions (including suffering). Acknowledging personhood in God implies agreement that God in all three Persons can suffer.[5]

We readily agree that God does have feelings, as numerous verses indicate. But it is equally important to point out that God does not change (see ch. 4). God cannot undergo changing emotions. That is, God is impassible. This is not the same as saying that God has no feelings. He has unchanging feelings. He always feels good about our righteousness and bad about our sin. God does not change when we repent. He always feels the same reactions to the same things, in accordance with His own nature in an active, eternal, and unchangeable way.

HISTORICAL OBJECTIONS TO GOD'S IMPASSIBILITY

Neotheists argue that Greek philosophy, not the Bible, is the basis for classical theism's view on impassibility. They also attempt to find antecedents for their view in the church fathers.

---

5. Though neotheists do not explicitly state this argument, they implicitly affirm this. See *The God Who Risks: A Theology of Providence* (Downers Grove, Ill. InterVarsity, 1998), 49, 77, 105, 118.

Greek Philosophy

The basis for divine impassibility is Greek philosophy, according to neotheists; therefore, it should be rejected. The same arguments are used against God's eternality and immutability. The same responses apply (see chs. 3, 4). The central point is that the charge simply is untrue. God's impassibility is derived from sound understanding of the biblical and theological data, apart from any thought borrowed from Greek theology. Further, the roots of biblical theism are not found anywhere in Greek thought. No pagan Greek looked to an infinite, personal God, to say nothing of a Triunity of Father, Son, and Holy Spirit—united in one essence.

Antecedents in Church Fathers

According to neotheists, the essence of the church fathers' argument is that some taught that, if a future act is foreknown, then the subject of knowledge (the knower) is conditioned by the future free act. God knows future free acts. Therefore, God is conditioned by future free acts. According to Sanders, Justin Martyr believed that God is conditioned by the creature (i.e., is passible) because Justin Martyr affirmed libertarian freedom and affirmed that God foresees what men will do (Sanders 1998, 142).

In the passage cited by Sanders, Justin states, "God foreknowing all that shall be done by all men. . . . He [God] will bestow rewards according to their merits . . . showing that He cares and provides for them" (*First Apology* 43, ANF 1.177).

Justin's statement, of course, is contrary to the neotheist position, which states that God does not know what people will do in future free acts. Further, the passage states that God does relate to His creation by His caring. And, as stated earlier, foreknowing is from our perspective. God just knows. Sanders confuses the *basis* of God's knowledge (God's essence) with the *extent* of God's knowledge (all things). Sanders presumes that if a church theologian affirmed that God foreknows, then the theologian also affirmed that God is conditioned. Therefore, he implies that Origen, Augustine, and Arminius believed that God was conditioned in some sense (Sanders 1998, 143–44, 147–51, 157).[6] But this is contrary to their own affirmations, and it does not follow that God is conditioned by His creatures as affirmed by neotheists unless one presumes that God is temporal. No good arguments have been given as to why God must be temporal (see ch. 3).

Christ's Suffering

The essence of the argument from Christ's suffering is that Jesus is God, so God suffered. According to Sanders, Tertullian is willing to speak of God's suffering in Christ on our behalf. God must be passible to substantiate his position (Sanders 1998, 143).[7]

However, Tertullian at this point is refuting the Gnostic notion that Christ did not have a material body, and he acknowledges two distinct natures of Christ. It was the person of Christ who suffered through the human nature. Tertullian states that a spirit cannot suffer.[8] Therefore, when one states "God suffered" it is true in the sense that the second person of the Godhead, Christ, suffered through His human nature. It is false if what is meant is that any other person in the Godhead suffered, for neither the Father nor the Holy Spirit have a human nature through which they can suffer.

Logically, the neotheist argument commits the formal fallacy of equivocation. The neotheist reasoning could be set out:

1. Jesus is God.
2. Jesus suffered on the cross.
3. Therefore, God suffered on the cross.

---

6. Appendix 1 contains the quotes by the same individuals, whose statements are contrary to what Sanders is affirming that they believed.
7. Sanders cites Tertullian, *On the Flesh of Christ* 5, to justify his position.
8. He reasons that God is Spirit (John 4:24). Spirits do not suffer; only bodies suffer. It follows that God does not suffer.

In the first premise, "Jesus is God," only the second person of the Godhead is meant. However, in the conclusion that God suffered, all of the whole Godhead is meant, so the term *God* does not denote the same referent. That makes the argument invalid.

Luther's Theology of the Cross

Luther refers to the suffering of Christ being inclusive of His divine nature as well as His human nature. This is a very weak historical support for God's passibility. Even if this is what Luther meant, he is the first major orthodox teacher in the history of Christianity to hold such a view. We have already seen that it is not clear at all that Luther meant to affirm God's passibility. He was confronting Nestorianism, which denied that the one and the same Jesus who died was both God and man. Luther makes statements to the contrary elsewhere. Whatever Luther believed at one time or another, orthodox Lutherans affirm God's impassibility.

CONCLUSION

The neotheistic reaction against God's impassibility is as unjustified as that against His eternality (ch. 3), His immutability (ch. 4), and His simplicity (ch. 5), for largely the same reasons. Impassibility is properly understood not to exclude emotions in God, so neotheists have launched mostly a straw man attack. The root issue and the core difference, however, is that neotheists do not ground God's feelings in His unchangeable nature. Their view makes God appear fickle.

The neotheist's view of God's passibility in the passive sense that He suffers is a serious flaw, for it gives God a potential that must be actualized by something outside Himself. This is utterly without biblical, historical, and theological support.

CHAPTER SEVEN

Relatability to the World

ONE OF THE MOST hotly disputed aspects of the classical view of God is the issue of how He relates to the material world. According to neotheists, if the traditional view of God is accurate, He is incapable of interacting with His creation. Classical theists, on the other hand, view the neotheistic concept of God as an anthropocentric attempt to recreate God in human likeness.[1]

BIBLICAL BASIS FOR GOD'S RELATION TO THE WORLD

The biblical basis for God's ability to relate to His world is found in something held in common by classical theists and neotheists, namely, the doctrine of *ex nihilo* creation ("creation out of nothing"). Numerous passages of Scripture support the fact that God created the world from nothing.

Creation is the first doctrine to be stated (Gen. 1:1) and one of the last to be restated (Rev. 4:11; 10:6; 21:5; 22:13). There are hundreds of references to creation and the Creator in the Bible, covering most biblical books.[2] The word *create* (בָּרָא, *bārā*) is used in connection with three great events in Genesis 1—the creation of matter, living things, and human beings.[3]

---

1. See Norman L. Geisler, *Creating God in the Image of Man* (Minneapolis: Bethany, 1997).
2. See Norman L. Geisler, *Knowing the Truth About Creation.* Ann Arbor, Mich.: Servant, 1989), Appendix 1.
3. The Hebrew *bārā* does not always mean to make something out of nothing directly (see Gen 2:3; Isa 41:20). However, in the context of the great origin events described in Genesis 1, it bears this meaning.

The Material Universe

Only God is eternal. Everything else had a beginning. "In the beginning God created the heavens and the earth" (Gen. 1:1). This grand statement of the initial divine act is uniquely monotheistic. That this is a reference to creation from nothing is confirmed by recent discoveries in ancient Ebla (Syria; Pettinato 1981, 259). The Ebla creation epic declares;

> Lord of heaven and earth:
> the earth was not, you created it,
> the light of day was not, you created it,
> the morning was not, you created it,
> the morning light you had not [yet] made exist."

Pure Spirit and Matter

"God is spirit" (John 4:24). As such He is the "invisible God" (1 Tim. 1:17). Indeed, "no one has ever seen God" (John 1:18). God is both invisible and immaterial (1 Tim. 6:16). As spirit He has no "flesh and bones" (Luke 24:39). He is incorporeal—pure, immaterial spiritual.

However, the universe that God created is both visible and material (Heb. 11:3). It can be seen and handled, being both physical and tangible. It has space (whereness) and time (whenness). It possesses both "here" and "now." Further, it has matter that is extended throughout space and time. It has "parts" or particles with spaces between them.

The "matter" or stuff of the universe is described by modern science in terms of atoms of physical energy with component particles and charges. As experienced by humans, matter is sensible, tangible, and visible. Bodies are real. The earth is tangible, as are the stars and planets.

The Making of Matter

God created all of this "in the beginning." "For by Him all things were created that are in heaven and that are on earth, visible and invisible" (Col. 1:16a; cf. John 1:3). His creation includes the "land," the "water" (Gen. 1:10), and all plants and animals (vv. 6–26). It includes the human body God made from the dust of the ground (Gen. 2:7). God created a real material universe.

Indeed, God brought all of matter into existence out of absolutely nothing. The Bible says that God simply spoke (cf. Gen. 1:1, 3, 6) and things came into existence by His power (Heb. 1:3; cf. 2 Cor. 4:6). "By the word of the LORD the heavens were made. . . . For He spoke and it was done" (Ps. 33:6a, 9a). "He is before all things, and in Him all things consist" (Col. 1:17). "Through him all things were made; without him nothing was made that has been made" (John 1:3). The writer of Hebrews declared, "By faith we understand that the world was framed by the word of God, so that the things which are seen were not made of things which are visible" (Heb. 11:3). It was created out of nothing. As the twenty-four elders at the throne of God proclaimed, "For You created all things, and by Your will they exist and were created" (Rev. 4:11b). In brief, the entire universe came into existence by God's will at His command. When He spoke, it appeared out of absolutely nothing.

Created by God, Not out of God

The material universe was created by God but not out of God. The cosmos is not made out of God-stuff. This is why it is a grievous sin to worship the creature, rather than the Creator (Rom. 1:25). For this reason, idolatry is condemned so strongly in the Scriptures. God commanded: "You shall not make for yourself any carved image, or any likeness of anything that is in heaven above or that is in the earth beneath, or that is in the water under the earth" (Exod. 20:4). If, on the other hand, the universe were God's "body" or part of His substance, there would be no reason that we should not worship it. God is not to be identified with the physical universe. The universe comes *from* God but it is not made *of* God. God is as different from the world as a potter from clay, or as the craftsman is from his handicraft (Job 38:4–11; Rom. 9:20).

The material universe is not made out of God, but it does reflect God. It declares His glory (Ps. 19:1). "For since the creation of the world His invisible attributes are clearly seen, being understood by the things that are made, even His eternal power and Godhead, so that they are without excuse" (Rom. 1:20). That is, God is present in creation both as its sustaining cause (Heb. 1:3; Col. 1:16) and as it reflects what He is like. Just as the mind of William Shakespeare is revealed in his works, so the Creator is seen in His workmanship.

GOD'S RELATION TO CREATION

Both classical theists and neotheists confess that God is the First Cause and the Uncaused Cause of the created universe. Both affirm that God created *ex nihilo*. However, what neotheists do not see is that God's relationship with the world is not one of interdependence and interaction. That the universe is totally dependent on God follows from the nature of God and the universe. Neotheists admit many of the following contrasts but do not draw the proper conclusions from them.

God is
1. the invisible Creator of the visible world, the immaterial Maker of all matter;
2. the noncontingent Producer of all contingent things;
3. the Uncaused Cause of all caused things;
4. the unlimited Limiter of all limited things;
5. the nontemporal Creator of all temporal things;
6. the unchanging Changer of all changing things; and
7. the noncomplex Source of all complex things.

Neotheism is inconsistent in admitting the first four of these and not the last three.

Contingent Creation

The created world, including matter, is contingent. Though the world exists, it need not exist. It is, but it might not be.

Indeed, God is holding it in existence (Heb. 1:3). "He is before all things, and in Him all things consist" (Col. 1:17). Without God's continual, sustaining causality, all of creation would cease to be—instantly.

The contingency of all creation is another way to express the biblical truth that God is not only the originating Cause of the universe, but He is also its conserving Cause. He caused it to come to be, and He also causes it to continue to be (see fig. 2).

Creation is always contingent, always dependent on its Creator. For once a creature, always a creature. Radical dependence on God for moment-by-moment existence is an essential characteristic of all created things, including the material universe as a whole. By contrast, the Creator is not contingent. If He were, then He too would need a cause. The Creator is a Necessary Being. Hence, in whatever relationship exists between the creation and the Creator, the creation must be dependent and the Creator independent.

Finite Creation

An essential property of creation is finitude. All created things are limited. Only God is infinite or unlimited. It is impossible to have two infinite beings, for *infinite* includes all, and there cannot be two *alls*. Paul declared, "In him [the Infinite God] we live and move and have our being" (Acts 17:28a). When He created finite beings there was not more being; there were simply more who had it. Just as when the teacher teaches the class there is not more knowledge; there are simply more who know.

If there were two infinite beings, they would have to differ. But they cannot differ by what they do not have. For since each is an infinite being, there is nothing essential to their beings that either does not have. And to differ in nothing is not to differ at all.

Neither can they differ by what they do have, since they both have everything proper to them. They are the same; they are

identical. Thus there can only be one infinite Being. Now if
there is only one infinite Being (God), then all other things—
the whole of creation—must be finite. God alone is unlimited;
everything else is limited. He is the Unlimited Limiter of all
limited things. He is the Uncaused Cause of all that is caused
(Geisler and Corduan 1974, ch. 9).

The very fact that all created things are caused to exist reveals
that they must be limited. For if they came to be, then they
did not always exist. Hence, their existence is not unlimited; it
had a beginning. By contrast, the Creator cannot be limited,
or He too would need a cause. He is not-finite, that is, He is
infinite. Hence, in whatever relationship that exists between
God and creatures, it must be remembered that God is
unlimited and the creature is limited. In no sense can God be
limited in the relationship.

Figure 2. God's Causality	
Originating Causality	*Conserving Causality*
Cause of beginning	Cause of sustaining
Cause of coming to be	Cause of continuing to be
Cause of becoming	Cause of being
Cause of coming together	Cause of holding together
Cause of origin	Cause of operation

Changing Creation

Furthermore, whatever is created undergoes change. Of the heavens the Scriptures declare, "They will perish, but You remain; and they will all grow old like a garment; like a cloak You will fold them up, and they will be changed. But you are the same, and your years will not fail" (Heb. 1:11–12; cf. Ps. 102:25–27). Only God is unchanging. "For I am the LORD, I do not change; therefore you are not consumed, O sons of Jacob" (Mal. 3:6).

Change is an obvious fact of all creation. It should be equally obvious that God does not change (cf. Acts 17:24–25). James declared that God "does not change like shifting shadows" (James 1:17b NIV). "Jesus Christ is the same yesterday, today, and forever" (Heb. 13:8). If God did change, then like creation He would need a Creator. Every change requires a cause for its existence, otherwise there would be no explanation as to why the change came to be. Hence, the Cause of the changing world must be unchanging. In whatever relationship exists between the unchanging God and the changing world, only the creation can change in relation to the Creator; He cannot change in relation to the creature.

Another way to see this is to note that whatever changes is limited. For if it changes, then it does not remain exactly what it was. It is limited by what it is.[4] It cannot be precisely what it once was, or it would not be changed. So all changing things are limited. God can no more change than He can become limited.

Creation Could Cease to Exist

The fact that created things change reveals that they have a potentiality for that change. Thus all created things have

---

4. In order for change in a thing to occur, there must be a part that does not change, and a part that changes, for if all parts in a thing change, this is annihilation of one thing and creation of another. The part that does not change in a thing is said to be its essence or nature. What does change is said to be its accidents. Therefore, to say that a thing is limited by "what it is" is to say that it is limited by its nature.

potentiality to change or to cease to exist. But all created things also have actuality, since they actually exist. God, on the other hand, is Pure Actuality. He has no potentiality in His Being.[5] God is the "I Am"; there is no "can be" in God's essence. He is what He is. He said, "I AM WHO I AM" (Exod. 3:14).[6] There is nothing He can be that He has not always been nor always will be. A creature, however, has the potential to be what it is not. Thus, creatures are limited by their potentials. They cannot do more than their capacities allow them to do. Just as a gallon jug has the capacity to hold a gallon of liquid, so every finite being is limited by its created capacity.

Because there is no potentiality in God to be actualized, all interaction between Creator and creatures must originate with God. Hence, in any relationship between Creator and creature, the latter will be the recipient. As Paul put it, "God, who made the world and everything in it, since He is Lord of heaven and earth, does not dwell in temples made with hands. Nor is He worshiped with men's hands, as though He needed anything, since He himself gives to all life, breath, and all things" (Acts 17:24–25).

Material Creation Is Spatial and Temporal

In addition to being contingent and limited, material creation is restricted to space and time. Time is a measurement based

---

5. God has the "potential" to *do* things other than He does, but He has no potential to *be* anything other than He is. When God is said to have no potentiality in His Being, it is not meant that He has no active power (say, to create) but that He has no passive capacities to be filled. Creation adds nothing to God's Being. He is infinite, and nothing can be added to an infinite Being.

6. When we say that God has no limiting potential, we are not saying that God can be evil if He chose to be such, for the Divine Nature which is infinite is infinitely good, and that which is infinitely good cannot be evil, for otherwise it would not be infinitely good, for it would lack some goodness. Some may say that the Divine Nature limits God so that He can only be good. However, this fails to recognize that God is unlimited in His goodness and that God is the unlimited standard, and whatever falls short of this standard is limited.

on change. It measures from the "before" to the "after" of change. Because He is an unchanging Being, God is not subject to such measurements. Since He is always the same, He cannot be the object of calculations based upon what He once was. Because He has not changed, He still is what He always was. However, in a changing being, as material things are, comparison between before and after can be made according to a measure such as time.

Time measures limited segments, whether millennia, hours, minutes, seconds, or nanoseconds.[7] Since material beings are in time (i.e., are temporal), they are limited to a "now" as opposed to a "then." We are not now living the past. We lived the past when it was the now. We cannot live both a now and a then simultaneously in the same sense. We can live the past only in memory. Time measurement is based on a real limitation that we have as material beings. We live only now; every future moment becomes a "now" when we experience it. We never live a then, only a now.

Likewise, space is a limitation. As time is a limitation to a *now*, space is a limitation to a *here*. All material things are spacio-temporal, limited to the here and now. Spatial limitations impose upon us the boundary conditions of "hereness" as opposed to "thereness." We cannot be both here and there at the same time and in the same sense. We can be there mentally, by day dreaming, but we can only be here bodily.

God, however, can be here, there, and everywhere at once, for He has no body that limits Him to being only here as opposed to there. God has no "hereness" that limits Him to one place at a time. He is not in space. God is omnipresent, that is, present everywhere in all of creation simultaneously. This is possible because He is an infinite spirit. Having no body to limit Him, nor finite capacity to fence Him in, God's presence is barred from nowhere. As the psalmist said, "Where can I go

---

7. If time were not segmentable, it would not be time; it would be like God's eternal Now, which is not divisible into past, present, and future.

from Your Spirit? Or where can I flee from your presence? If I ascend into heaven, you are there; if I make my bed in hell, behold, you are there" (Ps. 139:7–8).

Here again, given the nature of God and creation, in any relationship between them, God must remain what He is, nonspatial and nontemporal. He cannot become temporal because a temporal world is related to Him, any more than He can become spatial because a spatial world is related to Him.

Creation Is Composed

As constituted of actuality and potentiality, all creation is composed, even angels. Material things are composed of molecules, atoms, and quarks, depending on how far one wants to break down the substance. Things can change, by giving off and taking on parts or properties.

What is composed must have a Composer. And this Composer cannot be composed or He too would need a Composer (see ch. 5). Ultimately, there must be an uncomposed Composer of all composed things.

The Historical Basis for Relatability

Historically, the fathers of the church over the centuries have had no difficulty believing that an immutable, simple, nontemporal God could relate to a changeable, complex, temporal world. This is clear from the many citations given in other chapters, which will not be repeated here. It is significant that some church fathers anticipated and addressed objections of modern thought. This is particularly true of Thomas Aquinas, as we shall see.

NEOTHEISTIC OBJECTIONS

Change in Real Relationships

Keeping in mind the points discussed above, neotheist objections to God's relatability can be answered readily.

With process theology, neotheism argues that an eternal,

immutable God cannot have a real relationship with a changing world unless God relates to the universe according to its nature (Sanders 1998, 24). The implication is that all real relationships involve change.

The essential argument goes like this:

1. All real relationships involve change;
2. But an unchanging God cannot change;
3. Hence, an unchanging God cannot have a real relationship with a changing world.

They even cite Aquinas as saying that God's relationship to the world is not real but only ideal (Sanders 1998, 152).

Aquinas anticipated this objection and responded over 700 years ago. He argued that there is a real relationship between the changing world and the unchanging God (*Summa Theologica* 1a.13.7). He observed that there are three kinds of relations:

1. A relationship of ideas (e.g., the same is the same as itself).
2. A relationship between two terms that actually exist (e.g., a small thing compared to a large thing).
3. A relationship between something that exists and an idea (e.g., on the right side).

Though the following discussion was presented previously in chapter 4, we feel it is important to repeat it here.

Since creatures are really dependent on God but God is not really dependent on them, they are related as real to idea. That is, God knows about the relationship of dependence but He does not have it. Only the creature has ontological dependence. Thus, when there is a change in the creature's dependence on God there is no change in God. Just as when a person changes his position from one side of the pillar to the other, the pillar does not change; only the person changes in relation to the pillar. So, while the relationship between God and creatures is real, God is in no sense dependent in that real relationship.

It is important to note that Aquinas is only denying any *dependent relationship*, and not all *real ones*. He is denying that God changes in real relationship with the world, but not that there are no real changes in the world's relation to God. The neotheist should not have any difficulty grasping this, since they believe in *ex nihilo* creation, in which God was not related to the world before it was created, but He was after. Notwithstanding, they believe that both before and after creation God is independent of the world. For example, a concrete floor on which the chair depends does not change when the chair is removed; even so God remains independent of creation. The fact that the created universe changes from nonbeing to being does not change the Creator.

Once creatures are created, God is really related to His creatures as their Creator. And then creatures are really related to God because He is their Creator. However, the real relation of dependence is in the creature, not in the Creator. Therefore, the relation of creatures to God is real and not merely ideal. Nonetheless, it is a real relationship of dependence on the part of the creatures but not a relation of dependence on the part of God (*Summa Theologica* 1a.13.7 ad 5).

One final note on this argument: Neotheists sometimes misconstrue this as an argument to show that God is "static" like a pillar (Sanders 1998, 152). But the point of the illustration is not to define "unchanging" in a static way. It is to show that a change in a creature's relation to God does not thereby affect a change in God. In fact, as shown in chapter 4, God cannot be the object of change by any cause, since He is Pure Actuality and has no potentiality that can be actualized by a cause. Further, as Pure Actuality, God is not static but dynamic. He acted from eternity and is continually active in sustaining the universe He created. So, unlike the stereotypical view of process thought, on which neotheism depends, God is not static, completed perfection. Rather, He is dynamic Actuality, constantly causing the being of everything that exists at every moment of its existence. He is not the most unmoving Mover;

He is the most Moving Mover. He is also the supernatural God who intermittently intervenes in His creation to accomplish His eternal plan. There is, in fact, nothing static about the classical concept of a God of Pure Actuality and persistent activity.

Neotheists fail to recognize the distinction made by Aquinas that, while God, the Cause, acts from eternity, not all His acts are affected on earth at the same time. God acts as a doctor who decrees that a patient take a dose of medicine once a day for seven days. The Cause was prior to the times the patient took the pills, but the effect of taking the pills occurred successively at different times, just as the Doctor had previously willed. Even so, God acts from eternity but the results of His eternal decree happen at the appropriate points within the space-time continuum. Likewise, since God has infallible foreknowledge of how human beings will act, He pre-acts accordingly.

It is noteworthy to observe that God does not react to our acts, since He has infallible foreknowledge of what they will be and has preplanned what He will do from all eternity. Further, God has no potentiality in His nature and, hence, nothing can act on Him. Therefore, He is not really reacting to anything, since He does not have to wait to know how creatures will use their free will (see ch. 1). Like a chess master, God knows every move in advance and pre-acts accordingly. The God of the Bible and classical theism, unlike the God of neothism, is *proactive* and not *reactive*.

Unchanging Knowledge of Change?

Neotheists argue that if God is absolutely unchangeable, then how can He know a changing world? According to classical theism, God's knowledge is identical to Himself. Yet He is said to be unchangeable. Hence, His knowledge would also have to be unchangeable. But how can He have unchangeable knowledge of what is changing. For example, when time changes, God's knowledge would have to change too, otherwise He would not know what time it is. And if He did not know what time it is, then He would not be all-knowing. Hence, God cannot be omniscient and unchangeable and yet know a changing world (Pinnock et al. 1994, 128).

Their argument can be summarized in this manner:

1. God knows temporal events.
2. The truth value of temporal events changes with time (e.g., Luther is not now tacking up his Ninety-five Theses).
3. Hence, God cannot know temporal events without His knowledge changing.

While God is unchanging, and His knowledge is identical with His essence, this does not mean that God cannot know changing things. If God knows everything in one eternal "now," from the past to the future (see ch. 3), God knows the future before it happens in time (see ch. 2). Therefore, when time changes, God's knowledge does not change, since He knew it in advance.

God knows what we do but not in the way we do, in successive time frames. God knows the whole of time from eternity, but He knows what is before and what is after the temporal now of human history. God is looking down on the whole calendar of time in which He sees which days are before and after others. But God is not standing on the present day of the calendar looking back at the days just past and forward to the days yet to come.

So God knows the changing times, but He does not know them in a changing way. He has unchanging knowledge of the changing, and eternal knowledge of the temporal. Each being must know in accordance with its own being. Temporal beings know in a temporal way, and an immutable Being knows in an immutable way.

Further, as the cause of all things God knows all things as they preexist in Him.[8] So His knowledge of time is not infected by time. He knows time from beyond time, not from within it.

---

8. We are not affirming some form of Platonic or Plotinian emanation. Rather, we are affirming that God is the exemplar cause and efficient cause of all things. They exist as patterns in God's mind, and they exist in His power to bring them to being.

He knows the temporal in His eternal Self as the cause of it. Thus, He is in full mastery of the situation of the changing word, but in an unchanging way, since it is known in His unchanging nature as an effect that can and will flow from it. By knowing Himself perfectly, God knows everything He will create that will thereby participate in the likeness of Himself in some way. Hence, God does not have to "wait" for time to change before He can know it has. Rather, He knows the whole calendar of time with all its changing sequences in His unchanging Self from all eternity.

Further, since neotheists believe in *ex nihilo* creation, they must admit that, at least before creation, God was eternal and knew eternally. This is logically necessary, since time had not yet been created and, as the Kalam argument shows, God cannot live out an eternal number of moments.[9] So even the logic of the neotheistic position demands that God must know in a different way than we know.

Actions of a Temporal God

Another reason given in support of neotheism is the argument that acting in time makes God temporal. The main arguments can be summarized this way:

1. God acts in time.
2. All acts in time are tainted by time in that they have a before and an after.
3. Therefore, a God who acts in time is tainted by time, having a before and after. In short, God too is temporal in His being.

---

9. For an infinite number of moments cannot be traversed before creation or else the world would never have come into existence. But creation did occur (cf. Kalam argument). Hence, God must have been nontemporal before creation. And whatever He knew (which is everything knowable according to neotheists), He must have known nontemporally.

Clark Pinnock states, "God experiences temporal passages, learns new facts when they occur and changes plans in response to what humans do" (Pinnock et al. 1994, 118).

There is confusion here between the eternal Actor (God) and His temporal actions. The unstated assumption is that the cause of any temporal act must be temporal. But no proof is offered that this must be the case. The only argument given proves merely that the effect must be temporal, which was never a matter at issue.

Indeed, classical theists have gone to great lengths to demonstrate that this cannot be the case in both the Kalam original-cause and Thomistic current-cause arguments (*Summa Theologica* 1a.2.3).[10] Throughout this work, absolutely no reason has been raised why the cause of an effect in time must be temporal. Neotheists admit that an Independent Being (God) created a dependent universe without becoming a dependent being. And this same God who is a beginningless Being (God) made a universe with a beginning without becoming a being with a beginning Himself. Likewise, there is no reason why the Eternal Being cannot act in the temporal world without being temporal in His essence.

Neotheists also hold that God is a Necessary Being who made contingent beings without Himself becoming contingent. So, here too, the infinite God has a relationship with something finite without taking on its finitude.

What is interesting to note is that at times the proponents of neotheism come very close to recognizing this or a similar distinction when they claim that while God changes, nevertheless, His "essential nature" remains unchanged (Pinnock et al. 1994, 28). What then is changing? At times they say it is His "will," and at other times they imply that it is a nonessential part of His nature. Since the former suggestion will be discussed subsequently, the latter will be addressed here.

---

10. See William Lane Craig, *The Cosmological Argument from Plato to Leibnitz: The Kalam Cosmological Argument* (New York: Barnes & Noble, 1979).

If God has "part" of His essence that can change and another "part" that cannot, then God is not an indivisible being. He must have at least two "parts" or poles, one that is changing and another that is unchanging. But this view is the heart of bipolar panentheism—the very view that neotheism disclaims. To put the objection another way, if God is necessary in the unchanging part (pole) and not necessary (i.e., contingent) in the changing part (pole), this raises a whole nest of metaphysical problems. Which attributes of God are necessary and which are not? How do we know which are which? How do we know God's moral attributes (love, purity, truthfulness, etc.) are part of His unchanging nature?

Further, if God is contingent in one part of His being, then this means that this part of God has the possibility not to be. For only a Necessary Being has no possibility not to be. But as Aristotle affirmed, and good reasoning supports, no mere potentiality for existence can actualize itself. For it cannot be in a state of actuality and potentiality at the same time. The potentiality to be cannot actualize anything. Only what actually exists can actualize anything. Hence, we would have a self-actualizing God. But to actualize means to cause. Thus, God would be a self-caused being—a notoriously incoherent concept in which God lifts Himself by His own ontological bootstraps.

Of course, as in process theology, neotheists may wish to claim that God is only causing His own becoming, not His own being, thus avoiding the contradiction of a self-caused being. But in this case what He causes to come to be is not uncreated but created. It is not part of His Creatorhood but has its own creaturehood. In short, it is part of creation, not of the Creator. In this case, the Cause that actualized this creation is Pure Actuality, just as classical theists argue. And what is actualized is not part of God but is nothing but a creature whose existence He actualizes. So here again, neotheism finds itself in a no-man's-land with no firm ground of its own on which to stand. It can return to classical theism or slide into panentheism.

The Creation of a Temporal World

Unlike panentheism, the new theism maintains that "the triune God is the Creator of the world out of nothing. This means that God does not simply influence preexisting matter but that everything depends on God for its existence." And "it also implies that God has the power to intervene in the world, interrupting (if need be) the normal causal sequences" (Pinnock et al. 1994, 109). But if God can act in time then, argue neotheists, God must be temporal. For whatever acts in the temporal world is part of the temporal process. Thus God is tainted with time by the very fact that He created in time.

There is a difference between saying God created *in time* and that He is the Creator *of time*. According to classical theism, there was no time before God made the temporal world. Time began with the world. God "framed the ages" (Heb. 1:2 cf. John 17:5). So God was ontologically prior to time but not chronologically prior to it. Hence, it is not impossible for God to create a temporal world without being temporal. Before God created, no temporal continuum existed that would have made it necessary for Him to choose a moment in time to create. Rather, from all eternity God chose to create the temporal continuum itself.

It appears to be incoherent to speak of God being eternal before creation and temporal after creation. William Craig concludes that the Creator of the universe "exists changelessly and independently prior to creation and in time subsequent to creation" (Craig 1979, 152). If this means God is temporal in His being after creation, then it is difficult to make any sense of it. If it simply means that God is nontemporal in His unchanging essence both before and after creation but can relate to a temporal world after it is created, then it is what Aquinas meant.

For a classical theist the nature of God does not change in the process of creating the world. The world is not created *ex Deo* (out of God); that is pantheism. For theism the world is created *ex nihilo* (out of nothing). Hence, God does not change "internally" that is, in His essence by creating something else. The only thing that changes is "external," namely, His relationship with the world. Prior to creation, God had no relationship to a created world, because there was none to which He could relate. At creation and after, God became "Creator" for the first time. It is not possible for God to be a Creator until He creates something. Prior to creation He was God but not Creator. That is, God gained a new relationship but not any new attributes. He did not change in His essence but in His external activity. At creation there was no change in what God is but only in what He does. Failure to make this disinction leads to the confusion of speaking of God changing in His nonessential nature.

The neotheist seems to make the same errors that were noted in the previous objection. The objection assumes that to act in time is to be temporal. But there is no evidence that the Actor is temporal, only that His acts are. Classical theists do not deny that God's actions are temporal. They only insist that God's attributes are not temporal. God cannot have a nonessential nature. "Nonessential" means something God has but does not need to have. But a nature is what is essential to a thing. For example, without a human nature we would not be human. So a nonessential nature is a contradiction in terms. Since nature means essence, it would be a nonessential essence, which is nonsense.

Even neotheists recognize that there is a real difference between an uncreated Creator and a created world. One has no beginning, and the other does. One has no temporal starting point, and the other does. Thus, it would be meaningless to speak of a created Creator or a beginningless beginning. In this way, classical theists insist that God is beyond time, even though He made time. This should not be difficult to understand. After all, the Creator is beyond His creation the way an artist is beyond his painting or a composer is beyond his composition.

Creating and Relating

Neotheists may attempt to avoid this logic by claiming that there is a significant difference between God acting to bring the world into existence and His acting in the world (or knowing it) after it came into existence. They may affirm the former act is meaningful but the latter is incoherent. After all, there were no moments of time before God made time. Hence, there was no problem of how a nontemporal Being could know (or act in) time, since there was no time to know. This is not so after time was made.

However, this move is doomed to failure for at least two reasons. First, admitting that God can be related to a finite, temporal, changing world at any point destroys the heart of their argument from the alleged impossibility of the classical God relating to such a world.

Second, neotheists, not being Deists, believe that God not only originated the world, but that He sustains it in existence. This means that God is actively related to the world as its sustaining Cause at every moment of its existence. So, He remains an Independent Being related to the world as its Cause at every moment of its dependent existence, but He does not become a dependent being. The same is true of God remaining the infinite, necessary, and uncreated Cause of the finite, contingent, and caused beings at every moment of their existence. But if neotheists admit this, as indeed they must, then there is no reason for them to deny that God can remain a nontemporal, unchangeable Being who is the Cause of all temporal and changing beings at every moment of their existence.

Thus, unless neotheists revert to a Deistic denial of the sustaining relationship of God to a finite, contingent, caused world, they must admit that there is no incoherence in the belief that the nontemporal and changeless God of classical theism can continue His relationship with a temporal and changing world.

Referring to a Non-temporal God

According to neotheistic reasoning, no references from our temporal perspective can be made to a nontemporal being. For:

1. All statements made by a temporal being are temporal.
2. God is nontemporal.
3. Therefore, none of our statements about God can really apply to Him.

What neotheists apparently fail to see is that temporal language is not necessarily an argument against God's nontemporality, but rather an argument for the analogous use of religious language. It is true that temporal statements cannot be correctly applied to God temporally. If they could, then God would have to be temporal. But who is to say there are not other ways to make statements about God?

Unless we are willing to accept the absolute, self-defeating agnostic view that "no statements can be applied to an eternal God," including that statement, then we must accept that statements may be applied to God in a nontemporal way. This is precisely what classical theists like Aquinas did, arguing that all finite and limited temporal conditions must be negated of a term before it applies to God.[11] If we say God is good, He cannot be good in any temporal or changing sense of the term. He can only be eternally and unchangeably good.

So statements can be made about a nontemporal God, as long as they are not made univocally, that is, in the same way they are made of temporal changing things. One may use the same meaning (definition) of a term (say, "being" for that which is), but it cannot be applied to God in the same way. For God is infinite Being, and all other beings have being only finitely. Hence, *what* is signified is the same (that which is), but the *mode* of signification is different. This is what Thomas Aquinas meant by analogous predication about God (Geisler and Corduan 1974, ch. 12).

---

11. See Battista Mondin, *The Principle of Analogy in Protestant and Catholic Theology* (The Hague: M. Nijhoff, 1963).

THE BASIC INCONSISTENCY OF NEOTHEISM

Based on the biblical data, certain theological conclusions can be drawn about God's relatability to the world. Since biblical arguments were addressed in previous chapters, only theological objections based on them will be discussed here. Classical theists and neotheists agree that God is related to the world; He brought it into existence, and He sustains its existence. There is both an original and a continual relationship between the infinite, uncreated Creator and the finite, created world. Observe the contrast in Figure 3. Of course, neotheists disagree with classical theists on a number of crucial attributes of the classical view of God, insisting that a Being with these attributes cannot relate to the world. Figure 4 presents the contrasting attributes of Creator and creation.

Figure 3. Uncreated Creator and Created World	
God	*World*
Uncreated	Created
Always was	Came to be
Beginningless	Had a beginning
Not finite	Finite
Necessary	Contingent
Independent	Dependent
Not material	Material
Not running down[12]	Running down

---

12. Though the neotheist would deny that God is actually running down, logically, they say something very much like that when they tell us that God gave away power when He created. See Gregory A. Boyd, *God of the Possible: A Biblical Introduction to the Open View of God* (Grand Rapids: Baker, 2000), 97.

What is important to observe, however, is that there is no more difficulty in explaining the contrasts between God and the world in those attributes that both sides agree upon than there is in those that neotheists reject.

Relating to an Uncaused Being

All neotheists agree that God is an Uncaused Being. Likewise, they concur that all creatures are caused. And all neotheists who accept the Bible must recognize that this relationship continues after creation, since God is the sustaining Cause of all creation. So an Uncaused Cause can and does continually relate to what is caused. Why, then, cannot a nontemporal Cause relate to a temporal world? For example, the continued relationship between a God who is not finite (i.e., is infinite) and a world that is finite is no more problematic than the relationship of a God who is not in time and a world that is in time. Likewise, if God, an independent Being, can be continually sustaining a dependent being, why cannot a nontemporal God relate to a temporal world? One is no more difficult to understand than the other.

Further, if a Necessary Being can be continually related to a contingent being, as its sustaining Cause, then why cannot an unchanging God be continually related to a changing world as

Figure 4. **Contrasting Relational Attributes of God and World**	
God	*World*
Not temporal	Temporal
Not complex	Complex
Not Changeable	Changing
No Potentiality	Potentiality

its Cause? If one is consistent, then so is the other. Finally, if an infinite Being can be continually related to a finite being as its conserving Cause, then why cannot a simple Being be related to a complex being as its conserving Cause? There is no more problem in holding one than the other.

On the basis of what neotheism admits regarding God's relation to the world, there is no basis for denying the relatability of the characteristics of classical theism's God to a temporal, changing world.

Relating Opposites

The law of noncontradiction dictates that opposites cannot be the same. However, there is no logical law mandating that opposites, while remaining distinct things, cannot relate to each other.

For all but those who hold a self-defeating monistic view of the nature of human beings, there should be no difficulty in believing that logical opposites can relate. Intellect is not material and matter is not intellect. Yet mind and body relate, be it interactionally (as dualists believe), hylomorphically (as Thomists believe), or however else. Certainly, anyone who believes that the mind survives the dissolution of the body (as do orthodox Christians) cannot deny that the immaterial and the material can and do continually interact in human beings in some way. To deny these two dimensions in human beings is to accept some form of monism, whether it be a pure idealist's denial of matter or a materialist's denial of mind.

Less controversially, virtually all neotheists believe that God is immaterial intellect, yet He made matter with which He has been interacting. He has sustained it and miraculously intervened in its operation. Why then should neotheists find it problematic that a nonchanging God should interact with a changing world and a nontemporal God with a temporal world?

Simply because a pendulum moves at the bottom does not mean its axis must move at the top. Likewise, God can be the unmoved Mover of all that moves without being moved Himself.

He can be the unchanged Changer of all that changes without changing Himself. He can be the nontemporal Cause of all that is temporal. The radii of a circle are many and yet the center is one. If the many can relate to the one without the one becoming many, then why cannot God be the simple Center to which all complex beings are related as their Cause. Further, the spokes of a wagon wheel move faster near the circumference, slower near the center, and not at all at the absolute center of the hub. Why, then, cannot God be like an absolute and unmoved Center around which all moving things relate.

The neotheistic view has failed to demonstrate any incoherence in the classical view of how a nontemporal, simple, and changeless Being can relate to a temporal, complex, and changing world. Every kind of argument that they can adduce to demonstrate the alleged incoherence of classical theism would destroy their own belief in an independent, infinite, and Uncaused Being that continually relates to a dependent, finite, and caused world as its efficient cause.

The Painful Alternatives

Painful as the dilemma is for neotheists, they have several alternatives. One alternative is to admit that their view collapses into panentheism or process theology.[13] That is, they could admit that they view a God with two or more poles in His Being, one pole that is unchanging, eternal, and simple and another pole that is changing, temporal, and complex. This they deny at present, but this option is open to them, and some appear to be moving closer to it (see Appendix 3).

The second alternative is to settle back on the position that their unchanging dimension of God is the equivalent of what

---

13. This is the standard position of process theology following Alfred North Whitehead's *Process and Reality: An Essay in Cosmology*, ed. D. R. Griffin and D. W. Sherburne (1929 corr. ed.; repr. ed., New York: Free Press, 1979).

classical theists call God's nature or essence. But the changing aspect is not really part of God's nature but of His activity. By distinguishing between what God is and what He does, both the unchanging and the changing can be accounted for and yet be related. But, of course, this is exactly what classical theist's claim. So, on this alternative, neotheism reverts back to a form of classical theism, along with whatever innovations they may have about God's changing activity.

Finally, neotheists may acknowledge that their view entails some form of polytheism. For however many parts, aspects, poles, dimensions, or the like they many find in God (having unanimously denied His absolute simplicity), they seem to be reduced logically to the conclusion that there are many different beings in God, however they may be relationally associated. On the other hand, if these so-called dimensions in God turn out to be no more than many attributes affirmed of His one indivisible essence, then their view reduces to the classical view of the simplicity of God's Being (see ch. 5) and the multiplicity of many attributes affirmed (analogously) of His one absolute essence.[14] We shall see that this is precisely what Aquinas held.

Logically speaking, the alternatives to classical theism are painful for the neotheist: panentheism or a return to theism. Neothesim embraces an incompatible set of divine attributes. Some are consistent with process theology and others with classical theism.

CONCLUSION

The neotheistic objections that an immutable, eternal God cannot relate to a changing temporal world fail. They confuse God's attributes with His actions, and they fail to recognize that God knows what we know but not in the same way we know. In fact, as a basis for their criticism they presuppose that God is changing and temporal. Hence, their arguments are circular.

---

14. See Norman L. Geisler, *Baker Encyclopedia of Christian Apologetics* (Grand Rapids: Baker, 1999): "Analogy, Principle of."

There is no more difficulty in affirming what neotheists do not believe about God (namely, His eternality and immutability) than there is in what they do affirm about God, namely, His infinity and necessity. If it is not incoherent to affirm that God can be Independent and Necessary and yet continually related to a dependent, contingent world, then neither is there any contradiction in asserting that an unchanging and nontemporal God can continually relate to a changing and temporal world.

CHAPTER EIGHT

Sovereignty

THE MEANING OF GOD'S SOVEREIGNTY

While both sides of the battle for God believe He is sovereign in some sense, the meaning of the term differs significantly between them. Classical Christian theology believes that God is in complete control of the entire universe, including every event caused by free agents. Neotheists, however, believe that such control would mean the future is not open to truly free acts.

According to classical theism, God is in complete control of all things. As the *Westminster Confession of Faith* (3.1) puts it, "God, from all eternity, did, by the most wise and holy counsel of His own will, freely, and unchangeably ordain whatsoever comes to pass." Nothing catches God by surprise. All things come to pass exactly as He ordained them from all eternity. From His vantage point of eternal foreknowledge, everything is known as a certainty in advance. Hence, God takes no risks. For even though He has made free creatures, He knows exactly how each will freely act and, hence, has determined the end from the beginning.

Neotheists' denial that God has infallible knowledge of future free acts (see ch. 2) significantly curtails His ability to direct the outcome of events. His limited omniscience leads to a limited sovereignty.

Further, neotheists hold a libertarian view of free choice, whereas not all classical theists do. And the neotheists who believe in libertarian free choice hold a stronger view on the degree of influence God exercises on that free choice. What is more, neotheists believe God has libertarian free will. From this they infer that "if libertarian freedom is not predicated of God, then God is 'captive' to his own nature in that God is not free to do otherwise than what he does" (Sanders 1998, 185). So "God is the sovereign determiner of the sort of sovereignty he will exercise. God is free to sovereignly decide not to determine everything that happens in history. He does not have to because God is supremely wise, endlessly resourceful, amazingly creative and omnicompetent in seeking to fulfill his project" (Sanders 1998, 169).

The kind of sovereignty God chooses to have is limited because He gives away some of it to His free creatures. In John Sanders's words, "If God wants a world in which he tightly controls every event that happens, then God is free to do so. If God wants a world in which he sovereignly elects to establish genuine give-and-take relations such that God's will, for some things, be conditioned by the decisions of the creatures, then God is free to do so." Thus, "It is God's free decision whether or not to set up reciprocal relations between himself and his creatures" (Sanders 1998, 184).

According to Clark Pinnock, "God willingly surrenders power and makes possible a partnership with the creature" (Pinnock et al. 1994, 113). He is open to take risks. Indeed, "God is so confident in his sovereignty, we hold, he does not need to micromanage everything. He could if he wanted to, but this would demean his sovereignty." So "he chooses to leave some of the future open to possibilities, allowing them to be resolved by the decisions of free agents. It takes a greater God to steer a world populated with free agents than it does to steer a world of preprogrammed automatons" (Boyd 2000, 31).

THE BIBLICAL PRINCIPLES OF SOVEREIGNTY

Now that the two views have been set in contrast, an examination of the biblical basis is necessary. Does God, as classical theists claim, have complete control over the universe, including all free actions? An affirmative answer is found in the following biblical texts. God is not only before all things, but He also created all things, upholds all things, is above all things, knows all things, can do all things, rules over all things, and, therefore, is in control of all things.

God Before All Things

As the first verse of the Bible puts it, "In the beginning God. . . ." Before there was anything else, God was present (Col. 1:17). Moses wrote: "From everlasting to everlasting, Thou art God" (Ps. 90:1 KJV). He is called "the First," "the Beginning," and "the Alpha" (Rev. 1:8; 21:6). Repeatedly, the Bible speaks of God as being there "before the foundation of the earth" (Matt. 13:35; 25:34; John 17:24; Rev. 13:8; 17:8).

God was not only prior to all things, He was there "before the beginning of time" (2 Tim. 1:9). In fact God brought time into existence when He "framed the world" (lit: "the ages"; Heb. 1:2). God "alone has immortality" (1 Tim. 6:16). We get it only as a gift (Rom. 2:7; 1 Cor. 15:53; 2 Tim. 1:10).

God Producing All Things

Not only is God prior to all things, but He produced all things. "In the beginning God created the heavens and the earth" (Gen. 1:1 KJV). "Through him [Christ] all things were made; without him nothing was made that has been made" (John 1:3). "For by him all things were created: things in heaven and on earth, visible and invisible, whether thrones or powers or rulers or authorities; all things were created by him and for him" (Col. 1:16).

God Sustaining All Things

Further, God upholds all things. Hebrews declares that God is "sustaining all things by his powerful word" (Heb. 1:3). Paul adds, "He is before all things, and in him all things hold together" (Col. 1:17). John informs us that God not only brought all things into existence but that he keeps them in existence. Both are true, for "they were created and have their being" from God (Rev. 4:11). Paul added, there is "one Lord, Jesus Christ, through whom all things came and through whom we live" (1 Cor. 8:6 cf. Rom. 11:36). Hebrews asserts "it was fitting that God, for whom and through whom everything exists, should make the author of their salvation perfect through suffering" (Heb. 2:10).

God Transcending All Things

The God who is prior to all things, who created and upholds all things, is above them. He is transcendent. The apostle affirmed that there is "one God and Father of all, who is over all and through all and in all" (Eph. 4:6). The psalmist declared: "O Lord, our Lord, how majestic is your name in all the earth! You have set your glory above the heavens" (Ps. 8:1). "Be exalted, O God, above the heavens; let your glory be over all the earth (Ps. 57:5). "For you, O Lord, are the Most High over all the earth; you are exalted far above all gods" (Ps. 97:9 cf. 108:5).

God Knowing All Things

What is more, the God of the Bible knows all things (see ch. 2). He is omniscient (Lat. *omni* = all; *scientia* = knowledge). That God is all-knowing is declared numerous times in Scripture. The psalmist declared: "Great is our Lord, and mighty in power: His understanding is infinite" (Ps. 147:5, NKJV). God knows "the end from the beginning" (Isa. 46:10). He knows the very secrets of our heart. The psalmist confessed to God: "Before a word is on my tongue you know it completely, O Lord. . . . Such knowledge is too wonderful for me, too lofty for me to attain" (Ps. 139:4, 6). Indeed, "Nothing in all creation is hidden from God's sight. Everything is uncovered and laid bare before the eyes of him to whom we must give account" (Heb. 4:13). The apostle exclaimed: "Oh, the depth of the riches of the wisdom and knowledge of God! How unsearchable his judgments, and his paths beyond tracing out! (Rom. 11:33). Even the elect were known by God (1 Peter 1:2) before the foundation of the world (Eph. 1:4). By His limitless knowledge God is able to predict the exact course of human history (Daniel 2, 7), and He is able to predict infallibly the names of individuals long before they are born (cf. Isa. 45:1). Nearly two hundred predictions were made by God about the Messiah, not one of which failed. God knows all things past, present, and future (see ch. 2).

God Able to Do All His Will

Furthermore, God is all-powerful. He not only knows all things eternally and unchangeably, but God can do all things.

Before performing a great miracle, God said to Abraham, "Is anything too hard for the LORD? (Gen. 18:14). In fact, "Nothing is impossible for God" (Matt. 19:26). God is literally omnipotent (Lat. *omnis* = all; *potentia* = power). He is not only infinite (not-limited) in His knowledge, He is also infinite in His power. God declared: "I am the LORD, the God of all mankind. Is anything too hard for me?" (Jer. 32:27). That God's power is supernatural is evident by the miracles He performs that overpower the forces of nature. Jesus, as the Son of God, walked on water and stilled the storm (John 6), and even raised the dead (John 11).

What is more, God's omnipotent power is manifest in the creation of the world from nothing. He simply spoke and things came into being (Gen. 1:3, 6, 9, 11). Paul described Him as the "God, who said, 'Let light shine out of darkness' (2 Cor. 4:6).

Of course, God cannot do what is actually impossible to do. Since it is impossible for God to do things contrary to His unchanging nature, it is understandable that He cannot do any contradictory thing. The Bible says that God cannot lie (Titus 1:2) for "it is impossible for God to lie" (Heb. 6:18). "And also the Strength of Israel will not lie nor relent. For He is not a man, that He should relent" (1 Sam. 15:29). For example, God cannot make a square circle. Nor can he make a triangle with only two sides. Likewise, God cannot create another God equal to Himself. It is literally impossible to create another being that is not created. There is only one uncreated Creator (Deut. 6:4; Isa. 45:18). Everything else is a creature.

So, God can do whatever is possible to do. There are no limits on His power, except that it be consistent with His own unlimited nature. That is, He can do anything that does not involve a contradiction. The Bible describes Him as "the Almighty" (all-mighty) in numerous places (e.g., Gen. 17:1; Exod. 6:3; Num. 24:4; Job 5:17). He has all the might or power there is to have.

God Governing All Things

It is because God knows all and can do all that He can rule all. The Bible affirms God's sovereignty in many ways. Just as every sovereign controls his domain, even so the heavenly King governs His creation. Isaiah's vision of God was of a heavenly King whose train fills the temple (Isaiah 6). Yahweh is called "the great King" (Ps. 48:2). His reign is eternal, for "the LORD sits as King forever" (Ps. 29:10b). And He is king over all the earth, for "the LORD is King forever and ever; the nations have perished out of His land" (Ps. 10:16). He is also the almighty king: "Who is this King of glory? The LORD strong and mighty, the LORD mighty in battle" (Ps. 24:8). As such, God rules over all things: "Yours, O LORD, is the greatness, the power, and the glory, the victory and the majesty, for all that is in heaven and in earth is Yours. Yours is the kingdom, O LORD, and you are exalted as head over all. Both riches and honor come from You, and You reign over all. In Your hand is power and might; in Your hand it is to make great and to give strength to all" (1 Chron. 29:11–12).

God Controlling All Things

Not only is God in charge of all things, He controls them. Nothing happens apart from God's will. Job confessed to God: "I know that You can do everything, and that no purpose of Yours can be withheld from You" (Job 42:2). The psalmist added, "Our God is in heaven; He does whatever He pleases" (Ps. 115:3). Again, "Whatever the LORD pleases He does, in heavens and in earth, in the seas and in all deep places" (Ps. 135:6). This has important implications.

First, earthly kings are under God's control. The great king Solomon acknowledged that "the king's heart is in the hand of the LORD, like the rivers of water; He turns it wherever he wishes" (Prov. 21:1). God is the Sovereign over all sovereigns. He is "King of Kings and Lord of Lords" (Rev. 19:16). No human power is not under God's power.

Second, human events are under God's control. As God controls the hearts of kings, He ordains the course of history. He predicted through Daniel that the great world kingdoms of Babylon, Medo-Persia, Greece and Rome would rise (Daniel 2, 7). The great king Nebuchadnezzar learned the hard way that "the Most High rules in the kingdom of men, [and] gives it to whomever He will, and sets over it the lowest of men" (Dan. 4:17). "The LORD of hosts has sworn, saying, 'surely, as I have thought, so it shall come to pass, and as I have purposed, so it shall stand. . . . For the LORD of hosts has purposed, and who will annul it?'" (Isa. 14:24, 27a). His word "shall accomplish what I please, and it shall prosper in the thing for which I sent it" (Isa. 55:11).

Third, the angels are under God's control. God not only rules in the visible realm but also in the invisible domain. "He is the image of the invisible God, the firstborn over all creation" including "visible and invisible, whether thrones or dominions or principalities or powers" (Col. 1:15–16). The angels come before His throne to get their orders to obey (1 Kings 22; Job 1:6; 2:1). They constantly worship God (Neh. 9:6). Indeed, they are positioned before the throne of God, and "day and night they never stop saying: 'Holy, holy, holy, Lord God Almighty, Who was, and is, and is to come'" (Rev. 4:8).

This sovereignty extends to the free choices of evil angels (Eph. 1:21). They too will bow before God's throne in total subjection to Him, for "at the name of Jesus every knee should

bow, in heaven and on earth and under the earth" (Phil. 2:10).
Indeed, the evil spirits who deceived king Ahab were dispatched
from the very throne of God. The Prophet Micaiah told Ahab:

> Therefore hear the word of the LORD: I saw the LORD sitting
> on His throne, and all the host of heaven standing by, on
> His right hand and on His left. And the LORD said, "Who
> will persuade Ahab to go up, that he may fall at Ramoth
> Gilead?" So one spoke in this manner, and another spoke in
> that manner. Then a spirit came forward and stood before
> the LORD, and said, "I will persuade him." The Lord said to
> him, "In what way?" So he said, "I will go out and be a lying
> spirit in the mouth of all his prophets." And He said, "You
> shall persuade him, and also prevail. Go out and do so."
> (1 Kings 22:19–22)

Even Satan is under God's control. Satan came among the
good angels before God's throne in the book of Job (1:6; 2:1).
Although he wished to destroy Job, God would not permit him.
Satan complained, saying to God, "Have you not made a hedge
around him, around his household, and around all that he has
on every side? You have blessed the work of his hands, and his
possessions have increased in the land" (Job 1:10). God has
power to bind Satan any time He desires, and He does it for a
thousand years in the book of Revelation (Rev. 20:2). The
demons who fell with him knew they are doomed, crying out
to Jesus "What have we to do with You, Jesus, You Son of God?
Have you come to torment us before the time?" (Matt. 8:29;
cf. Rev. 12:9; Jude 6). Satan was defeated by Christ on the cross.
"Having disarmed principalities and powers, He made a public
spectacle of them, triumphing over them in it [the cross]" (Col.
2:15). Therefore, Satan "knows that he has a short time" (Rev.
12:12). He roams the earth (1 Peter 5:8) but on a leash held
firmly by God's sovereign hand.
    Christ came, "that through death He might destroy him who
had the power of death, that is, the devil" (Heb. 2:14b). John said

that "for this purpose the Son of God was manifested, that He might destroy the works of the devil" (1 John 3:8). John foretells how "the devil, who deceived them, was cast into the lake of fire and brimstone where the beast and the false prophet are. And they will be tormented day and night forever and ever" (Rev. 20:10). Fourth, human decisions are under God's control. The Bible affirms that God is in sovereign control of everything we choose, even our own salvation. For "in him we were also chosen, having been predestined according to the plan of him who works out everything in conformity with the purpose of his will" (Eph. 1:11 NIV). "For whom He foreknew, He also predestined to be conformed to the image of His Son, that He might be the firstborn among many brethren. Moreover, whom He predestined, these He also called; whom He called, these He also justified; whom He justified, these He also glorified" (Rom. 8:29–30). According to Paul, "He chose us in Him before the foundation of the world" (Eph. 1:4a). Peter said that Jesus had been handed over to the Jews "by the determined counsel and foreknowledge of God" (Acts 2:23). Indeed, only those who are elect will believe, for Luke wrote that "as many as had been appointed to eternal life believed" (Acts 13:48b).

John declared that we are children of God "who were born, not of blood, nor of the will of the flesh, nor of the will of man, but of God" (John 1:13). Likewise, Paul affirmed that "it is not of him who wills, nor of him who runs, but of God who shows mercy" (Rom. 9:16). He adds in even stronger terms, "He has mercy on whom He wills, and whom He wills He hardens" (Rom. 9:18).

God's sovereignty over human decisions includes both those for Him and those against Him. Peter wrote of Christ: He is "'A stone of stumbling and a rock of offense.' They stumble, being disobedient to the word, to which they also were appointed" (1 Peter 2:8). Likewise, God has destined the "vessels of wrath" who were "prepared for destruction" (Rom. 9:22) as well as the "vessels of mercy" (Rom. 9:23). Indeed, no one comes to the Father except he is drawn by God (John 6:44).

Even actions that the Bible declares as freely chosen by human beings are said to be determined by God in advance. For example, Jesus said, "I lay down my life that I may take it again. No one takes it from Me, but I lay it down of myself" (John 10:17b–18a). He said that He did this freely, yet in Acts 2:23 the Cross is said to be a result of God's set counsel and foreknowledge. This can also be rendered "determined counsel" (NKJV) or "God's definite plan" (TCNT). God determined it from all eternity, yet Jesus did it freely.

Jesus proclaimed: "And truly the Son of man goeth, as it was determined: but woe unto that man by whom he is betrayed!" (Luke 22:22 KJV). In other words, God determined that it must happen, but when it occurred it did so as a result of a free and responsible act of Judas.

In other texts, both God's determination and human free choice are affirmed. Peter said that Jesus, "being delivered by the determined counsel and foreknowledge of God, you have taken by lawless hands, have crucified, and put to death" (Acts 2:23). While God determined their actions from all eternity, nevertheless those responsible for crucifying Jesus were free to perform these actions—and were morally culpable.

The Bible declares that God is in complete control of everything that happens across history. This includes even free choices, both good and evil, which He ordained from all eternity.

THE THEOLOGICAL BASES FOR GOD'S SOVEREIGNTY

The point has been made that the doctrine of God's sovereignty is particularly grounded in certain key attributes, especially His omniscience and omnipotence. The exercise of His sovereignty is determined by one's view of what kind of free choice He gave to His rational creatures. Since both classical theists and neotheists agree on omnipotence, and since we have already argued against neotheism for unlimited omniscience, it remains to discuss the nature of human free choice.

The Nature of Foreknowledge

First, let's recall what has been established. If God knows everything, including every future free act, then nothing catches Him by surprise. He knows everything that can occur, and He knows what will happen and, hence, can, at a minimum, plan in advance for it. Further, God has all power, so that He can do anything that is not impossible to do. He cannot do what is contradictory or intrinsically impossible. For example, God cannot make square circles. This would mean that God could not force a free creature to do something against his or her will. But God has the power to achieve anything other than a contradiction.

Given these two attributes, God can control every future event, including free ones, in at least the sense of knowing for certain how everything would turn out prior to creating the world. Thus, not only are there no surprises for Him, but the way the world will turn out is exactly the way He chose it and knew it would turn out from all eternity. But this complete control of every future action and event is what is meant by the classical concept of sovereignty. So, given these attributes (see ch. 2), the classical theist's concept of sovereignty follows, and the neotheist's view fails.

The Nature of Free Choice

The nature of human free choice, particularly since the Fall, is an intramural debate among those who hold the classical view of God. Most classical theists hold to a libertarian view of the power of contrary choice. Some, following Jonathan Edwards, claim that free choice is simply doing what one desires. They add quickly, that it is God who gives the desire to do good.

The Power of Contrary Choice

With the exception of the later Augustine, most orthodox theologians through the Reformation held a libertarian view of free will, similar to the view held by neotheists: Free choice involves noncoerced actions springing from a will that has the power of contrary choice (Geisler 1999, appendix 1). A few examples will illustrate the point.

Augustine

The early Augustine[1] wrote:

> Free will, naturally assigned by the Creator to our rational soul, is such a neutral power, as can either incline toward faith, or turn toward unbelief (*On the Spirit and the Letter* 58). In fact, sin is so much a voluntary evil that it is not sin at all unless it is voluntary. (*Of True Religion* 14)
>
> For every one also who does a thing unwillingly is compelled, and every one who is compelled, if he does a thing, does it only unwillingly. It follows that he that is willing is free from compulsion, even if any one thinks himself compelled. (*Two Souls, Against the Manichaeans* 10.14)

Augustine's point is that all evil is resistible, "because whoever has done anything evil by means of one unconscious or unable to resist, the latter can by no means be justly condemned" (*Two Souls, Against the Manichaeans* 10.12).

Anselm

Anselm affirmed:

> A man cannot will against his will because he cannot will unwillingly to will. For everyone who wills, wills willingly. . . . Although they [Adam and Eve] yielded themselves to sin, they could not abolish in themselves their natural freedom of choice. However, they could so affect their state that they were not able to use that freedom except by a different grace from that which they had before their fall. . . . [For] if

---

1. By "early" Augustine we mean before 417. By "later" Augustine we mean 417 and after, beginning with *On the Correction of the Donatists*. See Norman L. Geisler *Chosen but Free* (Minneapolis: Bethany, 1999), appendix 3.

temptation can conquer the will, it has the power to conquer it, and conquers the will by its own power. But temptation cannot do this because the will can be overcome only by its own power. . . . I wonder whether even God could remove uprightness from a man's will. Could he? I'll show you that He cannot. (Anselm 1967, 125, 130, 132, 136)

Aquinas

Thomas Aquinas also held a libertarian view of free choice: "Necessity comes from the agent when the latter so coerces something that he cannot do the contrary. . . . Such necessity by coercion is contrary to the will."[2] Thus, "something cannot be absolutely coerced or violent and simultaneously voluntary. . . . Consequently man does not choose necessarily but freely" (*An Aquinas Reader* 1972 ET, 291–92).

According to Thomas, "Man has free choice, otherwise counsels, exhortations, precepts, prohibitions, rewards, and punishment would all be pointless . . ." (Aquinas 1951 ET, 261–62). "To be free is not to be obliged to one determinate object. . . . [Thus, a free judgment] leaves intact the power of being able to decide otherwise" (Aquinas 1951 ET, 259).

The Late Augustinian and Reformed View

Following the late Augustine, and some Reformers, there was a move away from the traditional libertarian view in favor of the position that free will was lost in the Fall.[3] In contradiction to his own early view, Augustine wrote: "For it was by the evil use of his free-will that man destroyed both it and himself. For, as a man who kills himself must, of course, be alive when he kills himself, but after he has killed himself ceases to live, and cannot restore himself to life; so, when man by his own free-

---

2. Cited in Mary T. Clark, ed., *An Aquinas Reader* (New York: Doubleday, 1972), 291–92.
3. See *Chosen but Free*, appendixes 1 and 3.

will sinned, then sin being victorious over him, the freedom of his will was lost" (*Enchiridion* 30).

Thus, when we act, it is God empowering us to act. For "'it is God who worketh in you, even to will!' It is certain that it is we that act when we act; but it is He who makes us act, by applying efficacious powers to our will, who has said, 'I will make you to walk in my statutes, and to observe my judgments, and to do them'" (*On Grace and Free Will* 32).

Luther

Martin Luther conceded only that we may

> allow man a "free-will," not in respect of those which are above him, but in respect only of those things which are below him . . . although, at the same time, the same "Free-will" is overruled by the Free-will of God alone, just as He pleases; but . . . God-ward, or in things which pertain unto salvation or damnation, he has no "Free-will," but is captive, slave, and servant, either to the will of God, or to the will of Satan. (*Bondage of the Will*, 79)

Luther insisted that only God has a truly free will (*Bondage of the Will*, 122). However, "God cannot do evil, although He thus works the evils by evil men, . . . but He uses evil instruments, which cannot escape the sway and motion of His omnipotence." The fault, therefore, "is in the instrument, which God allows not to remain actionless; seeing that, the evils are done as God Himself moves. [Hence,] it is, that the wicked man cannot but always err and sin; because, being carried along by the motion of the Divine Omnipotence, he is not permitted to remain motionless, but must will, desire, and act according to his nature" (*Bondage of the Will*, 224).

Calvin

John Calvin also believed that free choice was lost in the Fall, contending that only "in this upright state [before the Fall], man possessed freedom of will, by which, if he chose, he was able to obtain eternal life. . . . Adam, therefore, might have stood if he chose, since it was only by his own will that he fell. . . . Still he had a free choice of good and evil . . . until man corrupted its good properties, and destroyed himself" (Calvin 1960 ET, 1.169).

Calvin insisted that "the will, so far as regards divine things, chooses only what is evil. So far as regards lower and human affairs, it is uncertain, wandering, and not wholly at its own disposal" (Calvin 1960 ET, 2.679). Therefore, "man is so enslaved by the yoke of sin, that he cannot of his own nature aim at good either in wish or actual pursuit" (Calvin 1960 ET, 1.265).

Hence, "those who, while they profess to be the disciples of Christ, still seek for free-will in man, notwithstanding of his being lost and drowned in spiritual destruction, labour under manifold delusion, making a heterogeneous mixture of inspired doctrine and philosophical opinions, and so erring as to both" (Calvin 1960 ET, 1.169).

Arminius

Arminius's view of free will is more Calvinistic than neotheists would care to admit. Arminius states,

> In his primitive condition as he came out of the hands of his creator, man was endowed with such a portion of knowledge, holiness and power, as enabled him to understand, esteem, consider, will, and to perform THE TRUE GOOD, according to the commandment delivered to him. Yet none of these acts could he do, except through the assistance of Divine Grace. But in his lapsed and sinful state, man is not capable, of and by himself, either to think, to will, or to do that which is really good; but it is necessary for him to be regenerated and renewed in his intellect, affections or will and in all his powers by God in Christ through the Holy Spirit, that he may be qualified rightly to understand, esteem, consider, will, and perform whatever is truly good. When he is made a partaker

of this regeneration or renovation, I consider that, since he is delivered from sin, he is capable of thinking, willing and doing that which is good, but yet not without the continued aids of Divine Grace." (Arminius 1853 ET, 2.252)

Edwards

According to Jonathan Edwards, free choice is simply the choice to follow our strongest desire in a given situation. Naturally the strongest desires flowing from our evil natures are always evil. And the desire to do good is always given by God. Edwards's point in writing his treatise *On Religious Affections* is that the will follows the desire that is strongest to the individual at a given moment.

As for the libertarian view of the power of contrary choice, Edwards wrote that a self-determining power in the will is "plainly absurd." He found it "a manifest inconsistence to suppose that the will itself determines all the free acts of the Will" (Edwards 1865 ed., 283).

Wesley

John Wesley believed that God is sovereign and that God even allows suffering according to His purposes. Wesley declared, "O what do we want here, either for life or godliness! If suffering, God will send it in his time" (Wesley 1984 ed., 48).

Virtually all theists up to modern times have held a strong view of God's complete sovereignty over all events, including free ones. Almost all theists up to the Reformation held a libertarian view of free choice, insisting that it was compatible with the God-given ability to do otherwise. Despite intramural differences, there is no reason, even under the libertarian view of free will, to deny God's complete sovereignty over all events.

THE HISTORICAL BASIS FOR GOD'S SOVEREIGNTY

In addition to the strong biblical and theological arguments for God's complete sovereignty, there is a strong and unbroken tradition from the earliest times in favor of this doctrine.

The Patristic View of Sovereignty

The Didache

The Didache (c. 80–140) states, "Accept as a blessing all of the things that befall you. For nothing comes to pass apart from God" (*Didache*, 7.378).[4] This early Christian manual states that all things are sovereignly ordained by God.

Polycarp

Polycarp wrote that "all the martyrdoms were blessed and noble, and they took place according to the will of God. For it befits those of us who profess greater piety than others to ascribe to God authority over all things" (*Martyrdom of Polycarp* 1.39).

Irenaeus

According to Irenaeus,

> Not a single thing that has been made or that will be made, escapes the knowledge of God. Hither, through his Providence, every single thing has obtained its nature, rank, number, and special quantity. Nothing whatever has been produced (or is produced) in vain or by accident. Instead, everything has been made with precise suitability and through the exercises of transcendent knowledge. (*Against Heresies* 2.26.3)

Irenaeus adds of God, He is "the Maker of the universe the Father, for He exercises a providence over all things and arranges the affairs of our world" (*Against Heresies* 3.25.1). Further, "God rules over men and Satan too. In fact, without the will of our Father in heaven not a sparrow falls to the ground" (*Against Heresies* 5.22.2).

---

4. David Bercot, *A Dictionary of Early Christian Beliefs* (Peabody, Mass.: Hendrickson, 1998), 629.

Clement

Clement of Alexandria stated, "Nothing happens without the will of the Lord of the universe. It remains to say that such [evil] things happen without the prevention of God. For this alone saves both the providence and the goodness of God. . . . Rather, we must be persuaded that He does not prevent those beings who cause them. Yet, He overrules for good the crimes of His enemies" (*Stromata* 4.12).

Moreover, Clement affirmed that human free will and sovereignty are compatible, for "many things in life take rise in some exercise of human reason, having received the kindling spark from God. . . . Now, all these things truly have their origin and existence because of divine providence—yet not without human cooperation as well" (*Stromata* 6.27).

Tertullian

Tertullian wrote that "God hardened the heart of Pharaoh. However, he served to be influenced to his destruction, for he had already denied God" (*Against Marcion* 2.14). He also states, "Some things seem to indicate the will of God, seeing that they are allowed by Him. However, it does not necessarily follow that everything that is permitted proceeds out of the unqualified and absolute will of Him who permits it (*On Exhortation to Chastity* 4.3).

Origen of Alexandria

Origen contended that "after the resurrection a person will also learn the judgment of the Divine Providence on each individual thing. He will learn that among those events that happen to men, none occur by accident or chance, but in accordance with a plan so carefully considered and so stupendous that it does not overlook even the number of hairs on the heads." He added, "I speak not only of the saints, but perhaps of all human beings. A son will learn that the plan of this Providential government extends even to caring for the sale of two sparrows for a denarius" (*De Principiis* 2.11.5).

Yet, Origen also believed that man is free: "Some say that we are moved externally, and they put the blame away from ourselves by declaring that we are like stones and pieces of wood. They say we are dragged about by those forces that act upon us externally. However, this is neither true nor in conformity with reason. Rather, it is the statement of someone who desires to destroy the conception of free will" (*De Principiis* 3.1.5).

No matter what happens to a believer, "in respect of all these occurrences, every believer should say, 'You would have no power at all against me, unless it were given you from above.' For notice that the house of Job did not fall upon his sons until the devil has first received power against them" (*De Principiis* 3.2.6).

Novatian of Rome

Novatian stated, "We should not think that such an inexhaustible providence of God does not reach to even the very least of things. For the Lord says, 'One of two sparrows will not fall without the will of the Father. For even the very hairs of your head are all numbered.'" Thus, "His care and providence did not permit even the clothes of the Israelites to [become] 'Worn out. . . .' Since He embraces all things and contains all things . . . His care consequently extends to all things" (*Treatise Concerning the Trinity* 8).

Cyprian

Cyprian writes, "For, in our temptations, nothing is permitted to do evil unless power is given from Him" (*Treatises of Cyprian* 4.25). This includes "pestilence and plague which seems horrible and deadly." (*Treatises of Cyprian* 7.16).

Lactantius

Lactantius stated that "Apart from divine providence and power, nature is absolutely nothing!" (*Divine Institutes* 1.91). Further, "The Most High Father arranged from the beginning, and ordained all things that were accomplished. . . . All the events that where necessary to carry out the plan of salvation had been orchestrated by God from the beginning—from the first Adam to the last Adam all things were ordained by God" (*Divine Institutes* 4.26).

The Medieval View of Sovereignty

Augustine

Augustine affirmed that "He left no part of this creation without its appropriate peace, for in that last and least of all His living things the entrails are wonderfully ordered—not to mention the beauty of birds' wings, and the flowers of the fields and the leaves of trees." How "can anyone believe that it was the will of God to exempt from the laws of His providence the rise and fall of political societies" (*City of God* 1983 ET, 5.10).

"God allows nothing to remain unordered and . . . he knows all things before they come to pass" (*City of God* 1983 ET, 5.8).

"Nor are we dismayed by the difficulty that what we choose to do freely is done of necessity, because He whose foreknowledge cannot be deceived foreknew that we would choose to do it" (*City of God* 1983 ET, 5.9).

Certainly, "God knows all things before they happen; yet we act by choice in all things where we feel we know that we cannot act otherwise than willingly." But Augustine hastens to add,

> We do not deny, of course, an order of causes in which the will of God is all-powerful. On the other hand, we do not give this order the name fate. . . . [However,] our main point is that, from the fact that to God the order of all causes is certain, there is not logical deduction that there is no power in the choice of our will. . . . Our choices fall within the order of the causes which is known for certain to God and is contained in His foreknowledge—for human choices are the causes of human acts. . . . As He is the Creator of all natures, so is He the giver of all powers—though He is not the maker of all choices. Evil choices are not from Him, for they are contrary to the nature which is from Him. (*City of God* 1983 ET, 5.9)

Augustine stresses that, ultimately, everything in creation is subject to the will of God—including all wills, since their Maker knows exactly what they will do with freedom. "Our conclusion is that our wills have the power to do all that God wanted them to do and foreknew that they could do. Their power, such as it is, is a real power" (*City of God* 1983 ET, 5.9).

In view of our freedom, how can God be all-powerful? "We call Him omnipotent because He does whatever He wills to do and suffers [permits] nothing that He does not will to suffer. He would not, of course, be omnipotent, if he had to suffer anything against His will" (*City of God* 1983 ET, 5.10).

As to evil choices, "He whose foreknowledge cannot be deceived foresaw, not the man's fate or fortune or what not, but that the man himself would be responsible for his own sin. No man sins unless it is his choice to sin; and his choice not to sin, that, too, God foresaw" (*City of God* 1983 ET, 5.10). For "He is the Cause of all causes, although not of all choices" (*City of God* 1983 ET, 5.8).

Anselm

Anselm affirmed that God can control the entire universe, including free actions, because of His infallible foreknowledge. For "God, who knows all truth and only truth, sees all things just as they are—whether they be free or necessary; and, conversely, as He sees them so they are" (*Trinity, Incarnation, and Redemption, Theological Treatises* 1970 ET, 159). Hence, the future is certain for "what is foreknown must happen in the future, and that what is able not to happen in the future can't be foreknown" (*Truth, Freedom, and Evil, Theological Treatises* 1970 ET, 185).

This, of course, does not mean humans are not free. "For God, who foresees what you are willingly going to do, foreknows that your will is not compelled or prevented by anything else; hence this activity of the will is free" (*Trinity, Incarnation, and Redemption, Theological Treatises* 1970 ET, 154).

"Therefore, it is true that what God foreknows will necessarily occur, but also true that God foreknows what event will occur without any necessity" (*Trinity, Incarnation, and Redemption, Theological Treatises* 1970 ET, 153).

God's control of all events is secure because, for example, "when Satan turned his will to what he should not, both that willing and that turning were something; and yet he had this something only from God and by the will of God, since he could neither move his will nor will anything except through the permission of the One who makes all substantial and accidental and universal and individual natures." Thus, "insofar as Satan's will and its turning, or movement, are something, they are good and they are from God. But insofar as his will lacks the justice that it shouldn't lack, it is something evil—though not purely evil; and whatever is evil is not from God but from willing, or from the moving of the will" (*Truth, Freedom, and Evil, Theological Treatises* 1970 ET, 183).

However, "God does not cause injustice, neither does He cause anything to be unjust. But He does cause all actions and movements, in that He causes the things from which, out of which, by which, and in which they come to be. Every creature possesses only such power to will or to do anything as God has given" (*Trinity, Incarnation, and Redemption, Theological Treatises* 1970 ET, 167).

Thomas Aquinas

For Thomas Aquinas, a sovereign is one who governs. God as the Supreme Sovereign governs the whole universe. In his "Treatise on Divine Government" in the *Summa Theologica*, Aquinas argued against "certain philosophers [who] denied the government of the world, saying that all things happened by chance" (*Summa Theologica* 1.103.1).

Further, "God possesses, in its very essence, the government of all things, even the very least." With the exception of His sustaining causality of all things, God does not govern all things directly. For "God so governs things that He makes some of them to be causes of other things in government; as in the case of a teacher, who not only imparts knowledge to his pupils, but also makes some of them to be the teachers of others" (*Summa Theologica* 1.103.6).

Thomas declared that nothing can happen outside "the order of the divine government." For while it is possible for an effect to happen outside the order of some particular cause, it is not possible that it happens outside the order of the Cause of all things (*Summa Theologica* 1.103.7).[6] Since God is the universal Cause of all being, even evil does not escape God's sovereign control. Sometimes it may appear that something has slipped past God, when seen from the perspective of one cause and effect. But we do not see all the causes that extend back to God's ordered plan (*Summa Theologica* 1.103.7).

As to how God controls the future of humans who are free, Aquinas's answer is twofold. First, "things known by God are contingent because of their proximate causes, while the knowledge of God, which is the first cause, is necessary" (*Summa Theologica* 1a.4.14). Second, "when a thing is properly disposed to receive the movement of the first mover, a perfect action in accord with the intention of the first mover follows, but if a thing is not properly disposed and suited to receive the motion of the first mover, an imperfect action follows. . . . For this reason we maintain that the action pertaining to sin is from God, but the sin is not from God" (*On Evil* 110).

"Similarly when something moves itself [in an act of free will], it is not precluded that it is moved by another from whom it has this very ability to which it moves itself" (*On Evil* 11). That is, God gives us the power of free choice, but we are responsible for exercising it. He gave the fact of freedom, but we are responsible for the acts of freedom.

---

6. In other words, a particular final cause may fail to occur, but God's ultimate purpose will not be frustrated. This can be seen in the book of Jonah, where a particular cause (Jonah's going to Nineveh) initially fails to occur. Nonetheless, the Ultimate Final Cause (Jonah preaching at Nineveh) does not fail.

Finally, according to Aquinas, nothing can resist the order of the divine government in general. For "every inclination of anything, whether natural or voluntary, is nothing but a kind of impression from the first mover: just as the inclination of the arrow toward a fixed point is nothing but an impulse received from the archer. Hence, every agent, whether natural or voluntary, attains to its divinely appointed end, as though through its own accord. For this reason God is said to order all things sweetly" (*Summa Theologica* 1.103.8).

The Reformation View of Sovereignty

Martin Luther

God has in His hand the hearts of all human beings, in Martin Luther's understanding. Thus, God testifies that He set the limits for the sea in Job 38:10–11: "I fixed limits for it and set its doors and bars in place, when I said, 'This far you may come and no farther; here is where your proud waves halt.'" Luther wrote, "Just so hearts of men, inflamed by anger, rage terrible. But God has set limits for their fury and angers—limits which they are not allowed to pass" (Luther 1959 ET, 879).

Further, "God so governs the physical world in matters external that if you consult and follow the judgment of human reason, you are either compelled to say that there is no God or that God is unjust" (Luther 1959 ET, 1529).

Luther approved of Augustine's position "that God controls the things He has created in such a way that He allows them to take their own natural course" (Luther 1959 ET, 1453).

John Calvin

"Since the arrangement of all things is in the hand of God, since to him belongs the disposal of life and death, he arranges all things by his sovereign council, in such a way that individuals are born who are doomed from the womb to certain death and to glorify him by their destruction" (Calvin 1960 ET, 3.23.6). In making such a comprehensive statement, John Calvin declared, "we must consider, that what each individual possesses has not fallen to him by chance, but by the distribution of the sovereign Lord of all" (Calvin 1960 ET, 2.8).

Divine risk was not an option for Calvin, because "the conditions of men do not come about by chance. God directs in hidden ways all that takes place" (Calvin 1847–51 ET, 23.6). Even suffering is ordained. In his exposition of 1 Peter 1:11, Calvin commented, "He puts suffering first and the glories which are to follow second. It is clear that this order can neither be changed nor reversed. . . . Since God himself has ordained this conjunction, it is not for us to tear one part away from the other. . . . Hence we also know that we suffer not by chance but by the solid providence of God" (Calvin 1847–51 ET, 23.4).

Although God sovereignly ordains all things, evil is not attributable to God. Calvin said that "we must also hold that God's action is distinct from Man's, so that Providence is free from all iniquity and his decrees have not affinity with the wrong doing of man" (Calvin 1847–51 ET, 23.6).

The Post-Reformation View

Jacobus Arminius

"I consider Divine Providence to be the solicitous, continued, and universally present inspection and oversight of God, according to which he exercises a general care over the whole world," declared Jacobus Arminius, adding that he means that God "preserves, regulates, governs and directs all things, and that nothing in the world happens fortuitously or by chance." Besides this, "I place in subjection to Divine Providence both the free-will and even the actions of a rational creature so that nothing can be done without the will of God, not even any of those thing which are done in opposition to it" (Arminius 1853 ET, 1.251).

Arminius ascribed dominion over all things to God by right of creation. His rule is primary, "being dependent on no other dominion." It is supreme "because there is none greater. . . .

It is absolute, because it is over the entire creature, according to the whole, and according to all and each of its parts, and to all the relations which subsist between the Creator and the creature. It is, consequently perpetual, that is, so long as the creature itself exists" (Arminius 1853 ET, 2.66).

God's dominion also is abundant in goodness and sufficiency. God presides over those He deems worthy in His kingly and paternal authority. "Hence, it is that, when God is about to command some thing to his rational creature, he does not exact every thing which he justly might do, and he employs persuasions through arguments which have regard to the utility and necessity of those persuasions."[8]

Francis Turretin

Francis Turretin (1623–87) stated that God's sovereignty is founded on his preeminence and beneficence.

"First, eminence of power above others, for it is in accordance with the nature of things that the superior and more excellent should have dominion over the inferior and more ignoble. Second is beneficence by which one man acquires a right over another. He is therefore lord because he is kind. Since, then, God is established in the highest preeminence and has bestowed upon His creatures as His work innumerable blessings, He is most justly called the Lord of all" (Turretin 1992 ET, 250).

Turretin wrote, "The former [natural dominion] is founded upon the decree of Providence by which He [God] predetermined all things and events." God's dominion is universal, absolute, and unlimited. As the only fully independent Being, God is liable to no censure for any action (Job 9:12; Dan. 4:25). He can do with His own whatever He wishes (Matt. 20:15). No one has a right to complain, "although the reason of his works and judgments may be hidden from us (Job 33:13)" (Turretin 1992 ET, 251).[9]

---

8. See Jacobus Arminius, *The Writings of James Arminius*, 3 vols., trans. J. Nichols and W. R. Bagnall (1853 ed.; repr. Grand Rapids: Baker, 1956), 2.66.

9. Turretin means that God is not held liable or accountable when he says irresponsible (not responsible).

Stephen Charnock

Stephen Charnock testified that God

> hath an absolute right over all things within the circuit of
> heaven and earth; though his throne be in heaven, as the
> place where his glory is most eminent and visible, his
> authority most exactly obeyed, yet his kingdom extends itself
> to the lower parts of the earth. . . . [For] He doth not muffle
> and cloud up himself in heaven, or confine his sovereignty
> to that place, his royal power extends to all visible, as well as
> invisible things: he is proprietor and possessor of all (Deut
> 10:14). . . . He hath right to dispose of all as he pleases"
> (Charnock 1971 ET, 362).

Contrary to the neotheist position, Charnock said that God
"is not determined by his creatures in any of his motions, but
determines the creatures in all; his actions are not regulated
by any law without him, but by a law within him, the law of his
own nature." So there can be no rule outside of Him, because
none is His superior. "Nor doth he depend upon any in the
exercise of his government; he needs no servants in it, when
he uses creatures: it is not out of want of their help, but for
the manifestation of his wisdom and power. What he doth by
his subjects, he can do by himself" (Charnock 1971 ET, 373).

Jonathan Edwards

Jonathan Edwards strongly defended the absolute sovereignty
of the Father and the Son. In Christ, as God, are joined absolute
sovereignty and perfect *resignation*. Edwards differentiates
between God's sovereign decrees and His sovereign acts in
creation and providence. By both He "worketh all things
according to the counsel of his own will. Col. i. 16, 17. 'By him,
and through him, and to him, are all things.' John x. 17. 'The
Father worketh hitherto, and I work.' Matt. viii. 3. 'I will, be
thou clean'" (Edwards 1842 ed., 1.682).

Edwards defined God's sovereignty as His "ability and

authority to do whatever pleases him: whereby 'he doth according to his will in the armies of heaven and amongst the inhabitants of the earth, and none can stay his hand, or say unto him what doest thou?'" Within sovereignty the theologian found

1. Supreme, universal, and infinite power to do whatever He wills.
2. Supreme, absolute authority, the perfect right to do what He wills, as well as complete independence from all other beings.
3. Supreme, underived, and independent will, which is determined by His own counsel.
4. Supreme, underived, and perfect wisdom, which determines His will.

"It is the glory and greatness of the Divine Sovereign that His Will is determined by his own infinite, all-sufficient wisdom in everything; and is in nothing at all directed either by inferior wisdom, or by no wisdom; whereby it would become senseless arbitrariness, determining and acting without reason, design, or end" (Edwards 1842 ed., 1.71).

OBJECTIONS TO SOVEREIGNTY BASED ON SCRIPTURE

Neotheists have challenged the biblical, historical, and theological bases of God's sovereignty. We will first examine their challenge to the biblical basis. Neotheists attempt to offer biblical support for their denial of complete sovereignty.

Prayer that God's Will Be Done

One such passage is taken from the Lord's Prayer. Sanders writes that in the Lord's Prayer, Jesus instructs His disciples to pray that the Father's will would be done on earth as it is in heaven (Matt. 6:10). Sanders says Jesus' prayer proves that "God's sovereignty has not been realized yet. There is an eschatological element to the divine project, for not everything happens on earth as the Father desires. We are to work and pray for God's will to be done in our lives now and in the age to come. But it is not yet a complete reality in our world—this Jesus well knew" (Sanders 1998, 114–15).

A careful look at Sander's qualified language answers his own objection. The key phrase is "not yet." Of course, God's sovereign will is not yet completely accomplished on earth. No traditional theist argues that it is. God did not sovereignly will that everything be accomplished on earth all at once. He willed that it would be accomplished by the end. Nothing in this or any other text even hints that the complete sovereign will of God might fail in the end. To the contrary, passages affirm that "our God is in heaven; he does whatever pleases him" (Ps. 115:3). "The LORD does whatever pleases him, in the heavens and on the earth, in the seas and all their depths" (Ps. 135:6).

Human Dominion

Using Genesis 1:28, Pinnock argues,

> In a world reflecting a triune community, God does not monopolize the power. Were he to do so, there could be no created order, certainly not a dynamic one with free agents, and not one producing love and communion. To achieve that kind of creation, God needs to deploy his power in more subtle ways. Though no power can stand against him, God wills the existence of creatures with the power of self-determination. This means that God is a superior power who does not cling to his right to dominate and control but who voluntarily gives creatures room to flourish. By inviting them to have dominion over the world (for example), God willingly surrenders power and makes possible a partnership with the creature. (Pinnock et al. 1994, 113)

One problem here is the failure to see that a God with infallible foreknowledge can sovereignly will to accomplish things through the free will He gives to His creatures. Infallible knowledge of what each creature will do with freedom is sufficient to assure that He has complete sovereign control over every event and the final outcome (see ch. 1). Otherwise, He would not have willed to create such a world. And this does not include the power that God has to persuade and even overrule free choices. Even neotheists admit that God does overrule choices on occasion (Pinnock et al. 1994, 38).[10]

The neotheistic objection seems to be based on the idea that God cannot give power without giving away power. But this is a denial of infinite power. When an infinitely powerful Being exercises power, He does not have finite power left; He still has infinite power. God does not cease being infinite by creating. He is not transformed from an infinite God to a finite God by the act of creating a world.

God gives power to creatures without giving it away. For He is the Primary Cause, and free choice is a secondary cause. All effects pre-exist in their Primary Cause.[11] Hence, God is in ultimate and complete control of the universe through the causes He has produced, including free causes.

As Aquinas puts it, "When something moves itself [in an act of free will], it is not precluded that it is moved by another from whom it has this very ability by which it moves itself. And therefore it is not contrary to liberty that God is the cause of the act of free will" (*On Evil* 111).

OBJECTIONS TO SOVEREIGNTY FROM THEOLOGY

Neotheists disagree with the strong view held by classical theists regarding God's sovereignty on two main grounds. First, they claim God does not have infallible foreknowledge of the future and, hence, cannot have absolute control over every

---

10. That is to say that God's mind is the exemplar cause after which all created things are patterned, and He is the efficient cause of their coming to be, so they pre-existed in His power insofar as He had the power to bring them into existence.
11. See Irenaeus, *Against Heresies* 4.37.1–2.

event. Second, they aver that absolute control and a libertarian view of free choice are incompatible.

Limits to Foreknowledge

First of all, neotheists claim that God does not have infallible foreknowledge of future free acts. Since this has been discussed in chapter two, it will be briefly summarized here.

At the heart of the neotheistic view of limited omniscience is this reasoning:

1. God knows infallibly whatever is possible to know.
2. It is not possible to know infallibly future free acts.
3. Therefore, God does not know future free acts infallibly.

Classical theists have no difficulty with the logical form of this basic argument about God's omniscience. Of course, God cannot know the impossible. The disagreement is with the content of the second premise: It is not possible to know infallibly any future free acts. Classical theists contend that this premise is unproven. An examination of each argument for the nature of free choice reveals why God can know future free acts.

Free Choice

The basis of the neotheist's objection to God's complete sovereignty (control) is that each human being is free in a libertarian sense of having the ability to choose otherwise. However, strong Calvinists do not grant this definition of free will. Even if one accepts it, neotheists have not demonstrated that this is incompatible with God's complete control.

According to this reasoning:

1. Free acts (in the libertarian sense) are those that could have been otherwise.
2. God's infallible knowledge of events means they cannot be otherwise (for if they could then God would have been mistaken and not infallible in His knowledge).

3. Hence, infallible knowledge of free acts is impossible.

This conclusion can be challenged in either of two ways. First, it assumes a particular view of free choice called libertarianism, which not all theists accept. Those who are strong Calvinists in particular argue that free acts simply are acts that one desires to do. God is capable of giving free agents the desires He decrees. Hence, future free acts in this sense can be free and yet determined and, therefore, infallibly known in advance.

Second, other classical theists, in the tradition of the early fathers, the early Augustine, Anselm, and Aquinas, moderate Calvinists, and Arminians, point out that there is no contradiction involved in claiming both that a future free act is determined from the perspective of God's infallible foreknowledge and yet also free when viewed from the relationship of our free choice (in the sense of the power to do otherwise). Thus, infallible foreknowledge and free choice are not contradictory. The law of noncontradiction demands that, to be contradictory, two propositions must affirm and deny the same thing in the same sense in the same relationship. But in this case one and the same event is determined in one relationship but not determined in a different relationship—one in relation to God's knowledge and the other in relation to our free choice.

As to the relation between God's absolute and unchangeable foreknowledge and man's free will, the early Augustine held that God's "foreknowledge cannot be deceived." God infallibly foreknows exactly how we are going to use our free choice. "The conclusion is that we are by no means under compulsion to abandon free choice in favor of divine foreknowledge, nor need we deny—God forbid!—that God knows the future, as a condition for holding free choice" (*City of God* 1983 ET, 5.10).

Hence, said Augustine, "a man does not sin because God foreknew that he would sin. Nay, it cannot be doubted but that it is the man himself who sins when he does sin, because He, whose foreknowledge is infallible, foreknew . . . that the man

himself would sin, who if he wills not, sins not. But if he shall
not will to sin, even this did God foreknow" (*City of God* 1983
ET, 5.10).

Anselm argued that God's omniscience included infallible
foreknowledge of everything, including free acts. "For He
foreknows every future event. But what God foreknows will
necessarily occur in the same manner as He foreknows it to
occur. . . . God, who foresees what you are willingly going
to do, foreknows that your will is not compelled or prevented
by anything else; hence this activity of the will is free"
(*Trinity, Incarnation, and Redemption, Theological Treatises* 1970
ET, 153–54).

Anselm points out that God's necessary foreknowledge does
not make the event necessary. "For, although He foreknows all
future events, nevertheless He does not foreknow every future
event as occurring by necessity. . . . He foreknows that some
things are going to occur through the free will of rational
creatures" (*Trinity, Incarnation, and Redemption, Theological
Treatises* 1970 ET, 158).

God sees only what will truly occur, "whether this results from
necessity or from freedom" (*Trinity, Incarnation, and Redemption,
Theological Treatises* 1970 ET, 161). Anselm stresses that a
necessary attribute of God is that He exhaustively knows truth
and sees all things just as they really are" (*Trinity, Incarnation,
and Redemption, Theological Treatises* 1970 ET, 159). Thus, God's
knowledge of everything, including future free acts, is necessary,
unchangeable, eternal and immutable" (*Trinity, Incarnation, and
Redemption, Theological Treatises* 1970 ET, 162–63).

God is the efficient Cause of all things, writes Aquinas. But
all effects pre-exist in their efficient cause. Hence, whatever
exists must pre-exist in God, who is its efficient cause. And God
knows Himself perfectly. But to know Himself perfectly entails
knowing all of the various kinds of perfection in Himself as
well as those which can participate in His likeness. Therefore,
it follows that God knows whatever exists or will exist perfectly
insofar as they all pre-exist in Him" (*Summa Theologica* 1a.14.5).

God knows everything in one eternal *now*, including the past, present, and future. And God knows the future before it happens in time. Therefore, when time changes, God's knowledge does not change, since He knew in advance it would change. God knows what we know but not in the way we know it, that is, in successive time frames. God knows the whole of time from within eternity, but He knows what is before and what is after the temporal *now* of human history (*Summa Theologica* 1a.14.15).

God does not know things sequentially, since He is timeless and knows all things eternally at once. Nor can God know things inferentially, for He is simple and knows all things through the oneness of Himself (*Summa Theologica* 1a.14.7). So God does not have to wait for things to happen before He can know them. He knows them eternally in Himself as the Primary Cause of all things including the power of free choice. In brief, God knows the created effects in Himself but not through Himself in a discursive way (*Summa Theologica* 1a.14.7ad2).

God not only knows all things in and through Himself, but He also causes all things by His knowledge. For God causes all things by His being. His Being is the cause of all other beings. But God's Being and His knowledge are identical. Hence, God causes all things by His knowledge including future free choices (*Summa Theologica* 1a.14.8).

Further, God's knowledge is not simply of the actual; He also knows the potential. He knows both what is and what could be. For God can know whatever is real in any way it can be known. Now both the actual and the potential are real. Only the impossible has no reality (*Summa Theologica* 1a.14.9). Hence, God cannot know what is impossible to know, since contradictions do not fall under the omniscience of God. However, God can know future contingents, that is, things that are dependent on free choice. For the future is a potential that pre-exists in God. And God knows whatever exists in Himself as the cause of those things (*Summa Theologica* 1a.14.13).

Therefore, as an omniscient Being, God knows future

contingents as necessarily true. He knows necessarily that what will be must be. That is, if it will be and God knows it, then what God knows about what will be must be true. An omniscient mind cannot be wrong about what it knows. Therefore, the statement "Everything known by God must necessarily be" is true if it refers to the statement of the truth of God's knowledge, but it is false if it refers to the necessity of the contingent events (*Summa Theologica* 1a.14.4).

In brief, God has infallible knowledge from all eternity of everything that would ever occur, including all free actions. This infallible knowledge does not diminish the freedom of the creature, since God knew for sure (= determined) what they would freely do (= free act). No contradiction is involved with God's complete control of the world in advance, because He has absolute certainty of how everything will turn out, including all free acts.

OBJECTION TO SOVEREIGNTY FROM HISTORY

As in the case of other dimensions of the historical argument concerning God's characteristics, the neotheist's argument is very weak (see the response in chs. 3 and 4). Since no Greek philosophers had a view of an infinitely personal triune God whose sovereign will determined all events, including free ones, in advance, neotheists cannot make appeal to their usual historical argument against the traditional orthodox view of complete sovereignty. Indeed, great Christian Fathers who held this view argued for it over against Greek fatalistic views (*City of God* 1983 ET, 5.8).

Sanders states that Irenaeus "affirms libertarian human freedom and rejects any predetermination on God's part concerning human decision" (Sanders 1998, 143).

Sanders is correct insofar as Irenaeus in the text cited does affirm that God gave man free will. The text also states that God does not coerce anyone. However, the text does not state that God has not predetermined all things. However, Sanders asserts that this is what Irenaeus teaches (Sanders 1998, 143).

It is interesting that Sanders fails to mention that in Book Two of *Against Heresies*, the same work, Irenaeus states:

> But, as each one receives his body through the skillful working of God. . . . For God is not so poor or destitute of resources that He cannot confer its own proper soul on each individual body, so does he also possess his soul. And therefore, when the number [fixed upon] is completed, [that number] which He [God] had predetermined in His own counsel, all those who have been enrolled for life [eternal] shall rise again, having their own bodies, and having their own souls, and their own spirits, in which they had pleased God. (*Against Heresies* 2.33.5)

Irenaeus believed that God predetermined each individual that would be saved, and Irenaeus believed that each individual is truly free. In terms of the elect, we are chosen but free. This is contrary to the neotheistic position, which denies that God sovereignly predetermined each elect individual. Moreover, several things are of significance in responding to the neotheist's arguments. First, virtually all major figures in the history of Christian thought have held to God's complete control of the future. This is true of Thomists and Molinists, of Calvinists and Arminians.

Second, the only notable figures who held deviant views were both minor and unorthodox. Not until contemporary times and the development of process theology were there significant deviations within professing evangelicalism of the neotheistic variety.

CONCLUSION

The biblical, historical, and theological foundation of God's complete and sovereign control over all human events, past, present, and future, stands firm. Neotheistic challenges are easily answered. The only significant debate is intramural within classical theism, and it is between Thomists and Molinists and between Calvinists and Arminians. It concerns the nature of free choice and how much influence God exercises on human free will in bringing about His sovereign will and whether God is in any way dependent on free choices in His sovereign decrees. Be that as it may, all classical theists agree that God is in complete control of the universe and its future, with infallible foreknowledge of all that will happen and infinite power to accomplish His will.

CHAPTER NINE

Theological Dangers of Neotheism

ALL ERRORS IN theology are dangerous. Some errors are more dangerous because they hold profound implications for other doctrines and practices for believers. By any standard, errors about the Person and attributes of God are serious errors. Every other teaching is connected to the doctrine of God. Errors in this foundational area affect our entire worldview. For example, to affirm that "the Bible is the Word of God" is totally dependent for its strength on what is meant by the word *God*. If by *God* is meant a finite, limited being, the whole of traditional theology comes crashing down. Likewise, the declaration that "Christ is the Son of God" is no stronger than what is meant by *God* in the sentence. Clearly, if it means the Son of Zeus, the statement about Him is not orthodox Christianity.

Likewise, every area of theology is skewed by deviant views of the nature of God. And views that are seriously deviant or heretical command our utmost attention. Such is the case with neotheism, which by its own confession deviates significantly from the historically orthodox view of God (Pinnock et al. 1994, 8–9).

THEOLOGICAL DANGERS OF NEOTHEISM

If one adopts the teachings of neotheism, many disastrous consequences follow. This includes consequences for predictive prophecy, the infallibility of the Bible, assurance of ultimate salvation, and the final defeat of evil.

Uncertain Prophecy

If all predictive prophecy involving free choices is conditional, the Bible could not have predicted where Jesus would be born. But Micah did predict that He would be born in Bethlehem, as He was (Micah 5:2). Indeed, the Bible predicted when He would die (Dan. 9:25–27), how He would die (Isaiah 53), and that He would rise from the dead (Ps. 16:10 cf. Acts 2:30–31). But either these are infallible predictions or else they were just guesses on God's part. If they are infallible, then neotheism is wrong, since their view espouses that God cannot make infallible predictions involving future free acts (see ch. 2). On the other hand, if they are not infallible, then God was merely guessing.

The same is true of most, if not all, prophecies about the Messiah, which involved free choices somewhere along the line, which, according to neotheists, God did not know for sure (cf. Dan. 9:25f; Isaiah 53). For example, if God does not know future free acts for certain, then He could not know that Satan will deceive the nations and gather them for war and surround the camp of the saints and the beloved city (Rev. 20:8–9). Hence, either this prophecy could be false or else neotheism is not correct.

Before leaving prophecy, another point must be addressed. Neotheists claim that "the problem with the traditional view on this point is that there is no *if* from God's perspective. If God knows the future exhaustively, then conditional prophecies lose their integrity" (Pinnock et al. 1994, 52). But this is a confusion of two perspectives. Of course, from God's perspective (since He knows the future infallibly) every thing is certain. But as noted earlier (in chs. 2, 8), this does not mean that from the human standpoint these actions are not chosen freely. It is simply that God knew for certain how they would freely exercise their choice.

Discerning False Prophecy

If all prophecy involving free choice is conditional, then there could not be any test for a false prophecy. But the Old Testament lays down tests for false prophets, one of which is whether the prediction comes to pass. For "If what a prophet proclaims in the name of the LORD does not take place or come true, that is a message the LORD has not spoken. That prophet has spoken presumptuously. Do not be afraid of him" (Deut. 18:22). But if neotheists are correct, this test is not valid.

As a matter of fact, according to neotheism, God Himself could be a false prophet, since some of His predictions may not come to pass. Of course, it is absurd to claim that God can be a false prophet. Neotheism leads to absurdity. God is not even smart enough to know that He may get caught in His own test for a false prophet? Indeed, Pinnock claims Jesus made a false prophecy (see appendix 3)!

Confidence in Infallibility

Not only does the neotheist's denial that God knows future free acts deny God omniscience and omnipotence, but it entails a denial of the infallibility and inerrancy of the Bible which some neotheists (e.g., Clark Pinnock) claim to believe. If all prophecies are conditional, we can never be sure that they will come to pass. Yet the Bible speaks with certainty that these events would come to pass. If such pronouncements are not infallible, they may be in error.

Indeed, on the premise that God is only guessing the results of many free choices, it is reasonable to assume that some prophecies *are* in error. It is begging the question to assume that it just so happened that all of God's guesses turn out to be right. If any prophecy possibly might be wrong, the doctrine of inerrancy fails in theory. If any in fact do miss the mark, then the Bible not only can err, but it is in error. Logically speaking, neotheism's denial of biblical inerrancy is inescapable. Pinnock confirms this in his recent statement listing many alleged false prophecies in the Bible (see appendix 3).

The Door to Universalism

Neotheists believe in libertarian free will, that a free agent is one who could have done otherwise. They also believe that God generally does not constrain anyone against human will, unless it is necessary for God to so intervene to guarantee His ultimate desire to provide salvation for all humankind.

This exception may seem a convenient way to avoid some problems with neotheism, but it is at the end of the day a fatal flaw if neotheists genuinely want to be evangelical. This exception backs one into universalism. If God willingly violates freedom sometimes for the benefit of our salvation, and His desire is that none should perish (2 Peter 3:9; 1 Tim. 2:4), then ultimately He is forced to deny His will or to move in such a way that all are saved (Boyd 2000, 34). If God really wants everyone to be saved, and He can violate their will to assure their salvation, then certainly He would do so. Hence, the logic consistently applied leads to universalism.

Realizing the trap, some neotheists try to avoid universalism by positing the annihilation of all who do not choose God's way of salvation.[1] But this does not solve the neotheist's problem that God violates free will to accomplish His plan of salvation. Annihilation is the ultimate violation of free choice—the total destruction of it. This is to say nothing of the fact that both Scripture (e.g., Luke 16; Rev. 19:20; 20:10) and centuries of orthodox Christian teaching stand against this aberrant teaching.

Ultimate Victory of God

Since neotheists insist that God does not know the future for sure (see ch. 2), and that He rarely intervenes against freedom, it seems to follow that there is no guarantee of ultimate victory over evil. How can God be sure that *anyone*

---

1. Clark Pinnock takes this approach. See his reasoning in *A Wideness in God's Mercy: The Finality of Jesus Christ in a World of Religions* (Grand Rapids: Zondervan, 1992).

will be saved without tampering with their freedom, which contradicts the neotheists libertarian view of free will. So the neotheist God cannot guarantee that a single person will be in heaven. Since God determined before the foundations of the world that Christ would die for the sins of the world, then He risked the supreme sacrifice of His only Son, not knowing for sure that a single person would be saved.[2]

What is more, the Bible predicts that Satan will be defeated, evil will be vanquished, and many will be saved. However, if according to the neotheist, this is a moral question that involves (libertarian) free will, then God could not know this infallibly. The Bible is unjustified in stating as a certainty that evil will be defeated (Revelation 21–22). Again the consistent neotheist must conclude that neither God nor the Bible can be completely infallible and inerrant. Yet some, notably Pinnock, say Scripture is infallible, yet, inconsistently, admit errors in it (see appendix 3).[3]

THE PHILOSOPHICAL DANGERS OF NEOTHEISM

Not only does neotheism have serious theological problems, it has grave philosophical dangers. The chief dangers are that although it is confessionally a form of theism, it leads logically to some clearly heretical views of God. For in spite of some basic beliefs such as God is infinite, creation is *ex nihilo*, and miracles occur, nonetheless, it holds to attributes of God, such as mutability, temporality, and complexity, that logically lead to non-Christian views of God.

Finite Godism

As was shown in chapter 2, the God of neotheism does not have infallible knowledge of future free actions. But human

---

2. Neotheists interpret Rev. 13:8 as "the incarnation" being determined before the foundation of the world. According to the neotheist, it should not be interpreted as Christ's vicarious death on the cross (John Sanders, *The God Who Risks: A Theology of Providence* [Downers Grove, Ill. InterVarsity, 1998], 102).

3. See *A Wideness in God's Mercy.*

history is composed of billions of free actions. All of these are beyond God's ability to know with certainty. At best, God can only make good guesses about them. At worst, He has no real idea what will happen. This drastically limits the exercise of His power. He cannot act freely to accomplish His will if He does not know for sure what people will do in relation to His actions.

Further, if neotheists consistently interpret anthropomorphisms as literal, God did not even know where Adam and Eve were hiding in the Garden. This means that God cannot be omnipresent.

Add to this the temporal nature of God, as neotheists do, and He cannot be eternal. A temporal God lives in an endless series of moments that never begin and never end. But an endless series of actual moments before the present moment are impossible. For the present moment is the end of the series of all moments before it, and an infinite series has no end. Hence, there could not have been an infinite number of moments before today. They must have been finite. Thus, if God is temporal, He must be finite in duration, having a beginning. But whatever has a beginning has a cause. Hence, this alleged "God" of neotheism is not God at all but a creature with a beginning in time.

Some have attempted to avoid this painful logic by claiming that God is omnitemporal, or above time in some way, so as to avoid the ravages of time just mentioned. This move will not work, since God must be either temporal or not temporal. There are no in-between alternatives, since these are logically exhaustive. If He is temporal, then He has moment after moment of existence of life like everything else in time. But such an existence, as we have seen, cannot be beginningless.

On the other hand, if God is not temporal, but is somehow above time, then God is the Being defined by classical theists. In making this move, neotheists back into the very traditional theism they are trying to avoid. So, in attempting to avoid time, neotheists place God in eternity above time. They bring in the

back door the very timeless God of classical theism that they
have pushed out the front door.[4]

If God is in time, as they claim He is (see ch. 3), He must also
be spatial and material, according to Einstein's conception of
the universe, which never allows one without the other. It is the
space-time-material universe. A temporal God Who is material
would be subject to the Second Law of Thermodynamics. He
would be running out of useable energy. Such a God would not
only be finite (since one cannot run out of an infinite amount
of energy) but would also be in the process of self-destructing.
Such a god is not only sub-Christian; it is subpagan. At least pagan
gods have tended to be immortal.

Further, neotheists deny the simplicity of God (see ch. 3).
But a God who is not simple has parts. What has parts cannot
be infinite, since there cannot be an infinite number of parts.
No matter how many parts there are, one more can always be
added. And there cannot be more than an infinite number.
Hence, if God is simple, then He must be infinite.

Neotheists define a God that is finite in power. Gregory Boyd
states,

> Though this is simplistic, it might help if we think of God's power
> and our say-so in terms of percentages. Prior to creation, God
> possessed 100 percent of all power. He *possessed* all the say-so there
> was. When the Trinity decided to express their love by bringing
> forth a creation, they *invested* each creature (angelic and human)
> with a certain *percentage of their say-so*. The say-so of the triune
> God was at this point no longer the only one that determined
> how things would go. (Boyd 2000, 97, emphasis added)[5]

---

4. The attempt to create a third category between temporal and not temporal is not only logically impossible (because they are contradictories),
   but it is semantically fruitless. For "omnitemporality" turns out to be
   only another term for timelessness. Of course, there are different views
   of timelessness, but all of them—to be timeless—could not be subject to
   changing moments, one after the other, which is at the core of what it
   means to be temporal.
5. Emphasis added.

Process Theology

Neotheists claim that God can change in His nature (see ch. 5). But in all change there must be a potentiality for the change. So along with His actuality, God must have potentiality. Hence, God must have an actual dimension or pole and a potential pole. But this is the core of the bipolar process view of God.

It is no longer a monopolar God of theism but a dipolar God of panentheism. Such a God has serious problems, not the least of which is that it is self-actualized. Indeed, one of its major proponents, Charles Hartshorne, said that we are co-creators of God with God (Hartshorne 1967, 113). In short, God is creating Himself, and creatures He created are helping to create Him too. It seems best to leave this tangled web of metaphysical nonsense without further comment.

Further, in all real change in a thing, something remains and something is added or taken away. Otherwise there would be no real change, so something does not change and something else does.[6] But if God has a dimension of His Being that changes and one that does not, then God must have two aspects or poles. A dipolar God belongs to process theology. Thus neotheism inevitably approaches panentheism, which is a clearly heretical view of God.

Likewise, the denial of simplicity in God (see ch. 5) leaves neotheism with a multiplicity within their Deity. Assuming these are multiple aspects of one God and not multiple beings or entities within a Godhead, then neotheism again reduces to panentheism or process theology. Either the manyness is within the oneness of God, or it is many gods. If the former, then this duality in God is the heart of process theology.

---

6. Of course, it is possible that all change is a substantial change, namely, creation—annihilation—and recreation. But this view of change has two serious problems: First, this is not a change in a thing, being, nature, substance, entity, or whatever one wishes to call it. Rather, it is a change from one thing to another. It is a replacement of one thing for another, not a transformation in one thing. Second, who is doing the annihilation and recreation out of nothing? This is something that only a theistic God can do.

Polytheism

Actually, some neotheists believe that God has no essence but is a bundle of properties. Each of God's many properties has existence like a Platonic Form. But there is no one essence that unites all other properties. In fact, this would not be possible, since each property is predicated of something univocally (the same way). And something cannot be both one and many in the same univocal sense. But if each property in God, who has no one unifying essence, is a distinct existence of its own, then there are really many little entities (beings) in the Godhead. That is, each property would be an entity or being in itself. In this case, God would be as many beings (entities) as He has properties. But this form of neotheism reduces to polytheism, which is a heretical view by any Christian standard for God. To posit a conjunctive property of all properties is not possible on univocal predication. And if all properties are applied to one essense analogically then we are back to classical theism.

Of course, a neotheist might respond by arguing that there is one property or essence that unites all other properties, which are predicated of it in an analogous way. This would avoid the contradiction of being one and many in the same way. However, it would no longer be neotheism but classical theism, which affirms that there is one simple essence in God and that all properties (attributes) are attributed to this one essence in an analogous way (*Summa Theologica* 1.13.3.5). So, either neotheism must return to classical theism or collapse into process theology or polytheism.

A neotheist might take refuge in the mystery of the Trinity, claiming that there are many in One and One in many here. But there is a significant difference between the triunity of three *Persons* in one Essence (trinitarianism), and having three *essences* in one Essence, when *essence* means the same thing in both cases. *Person* does not mean the same thing as *essence*. A person is a "who" and an essence is a "what." *Person* refers to an "I" and essence to an "it." A person is a Subject and essence an

Object. Having three "whats" in one "what" is a contradiction. Having three "whos" in one "what" is a mystery, but not a contradiction.

THE ROAD TO RECOVERING CLASSICAL THEISM

Granting the attributes of God that neotheists share with classical theism, they could find the road home at lot easier than they think. For these attributes lead logically to classical theism.

Timelessness and creation *ex nihilo*

Neotheism affirms many of the traditional attributes and activities of God. Among these is that God created the universe *ex nihilo*. God is ontologically independent of His creation. That is, if there were no world, there would still be God. Yet at the same time, they claim to reject God's traditional attributes of aseity and eternality (nontemporality). But it would seem that logically these attributes follow from creation *ex nihilo*.

If God created the spatio-temporal universe out of nothing, and time is part of it, then time is part of the nature of the cosmos He created. That is, time began with creation. In short, God created time. But if time began and God did not begin, then time is not of the essence of God. That is, God is not in time or subject to time by nature. Rather, He is beyond time and above time as the Creator of time. Thus, the neotheistic belief in creation *ex nihilo* appears to contradict its belief in creation within time. The logic of their understanding, were they consistent in its application, would lead to the classical view of God as beyond time.

If on reconsideration neotheists opt to hold that time existed before creation, then further logical problems emerge. If time was "inside" God as part of His nature, how can God be without a beginning, since an infinite number of temporal moments appears to be incoherent (as proponents of the Kalam argument for God's existence have affirmed).

If, on the other hand, time is "outside" of God, then some

sort of dualism emerges. We must ask whether the time that is outside of God had a beginning. If it did not, then it could be argued that there is sometime outside God that He did not create, since it is as eternal as He is. This belief is no longer theism in either the classical or the neotheistic sense. But if time is outside of God and had a beginning, then it must have been created by God (since everything with a beginning had a cause). And in this event we are right back to the classical theistic position that time is created by God, and that God as the Creator of time is not temporal. What is made is not part of God, for it was not created out of God but out of nothing. And what is part of the world (as time is) is not part of God.

Transcendence and Timelessness

According to neotheism, God is beyond creation. He is other than the entire spatio-temporal world. Yet they believe that He lives in time. This is a problem, since time is part of the space-time world. And time had a beginning, although God did not. If God is beyond time, He cannot be temporal.

The neotheist might reply that God is also immanent in the temporal world, and whatever is immanent in the temporal is temporal. But this conception of God's immanence makes God part of the world, as in pantheism. In the theistic sense of immanence, God is *present* in the world but not part of it. God is in the world in accordance with who He is, and who He is must be nontemporal.

This should not be difficult for neotheists to accept, since they believe God to be a Necessary Being. He is immanent in a contingent world, but neotheists do not believe that this makes God a contingent being. God is immanent in creation as the Creator, which certainly does not mean He is part of creation. It means that He is present to those things He has made. In no sense does immanence of a nontemporal God in a temporal world demand that He is temporal. In every sense, His transcendence over the spacio-temporal demands that He is nontemporal.

An Uncaused Being

Neotheists believe that God is an Uncaused Being. He is the Cause of all other beings but is Himself not caused. If God is uncaused in His being, He must be Pure Being or Pure Actuality. For whatever is not caused never came to be.[7] And whatever never came to be has no potentiality to be anything but what it is. But if it has no potential, then it must be Pure Actuality. If God is uncaused then He has no potential. For to be caused means to have one's potential actualized. But what has no potential must be Pure Actuality. Thus, the neotheists' belief that God is an Uncaused Being leads logically to the attribute of Pure Actuality, which they reject.

Necessity

The classical theistic view of God also follows from the neotheists' belief that God is a Necessary Being. If God is a Necessary Being, then He cannot not be. That is, God has no potential in His Being not to be.

But if God has no potentiality in His Being, then He is Pure Actuality. So the classical theistic view of God follows from what neotheists admit about God. Neotheism is inconsistent and incoherent. To make their view coherent with the attributes that neotheists accept, they need only return to classical theism.

Because neotheists do believe that God is an infinite, omniscient, and ontologically independent Creator *ex nihilo* of this world, then the belief that He is mutable, temporal, and does not know future free acts sets their view at war within itself. Indeed, the only consistent way to believe in these finite attributes is to forsake theism and adopt panentheism. The neotheistic half-way house has no consistent structure. Its proponents live in a theological no-mans land. They cannot have

---

7. Only that which has never come to be (God) is pure actuality. God never has potential for ceasing to be or coming to be. All creatures had the potential of existing, and they have the potential of not existing. Only things that are contradictory like square circles have no potential for existence.

it both ways. There is no logical stopping point between classical theism and contemporary panentheism. The traditional attributes of God stand or fall together. Hence, the exhortation becomes: "Choose you this day whom you will serve."

On one side, the choice of theism is the self-existent I AM who says, "I am the Lord, I do not change" (Mal. 3:6a). This God knows the end from the beginning (Isa. 46:10). The only other consistent option is the finite god of process thought, who is waiting with bated breath to see how things will turn out.[8] As for us and our houses, we will choose "AAA theism" as the only safe way to travel the theological road. This is the theism of Augustine, Anselm, and Aquinas.

Simplicity

Neotheism holds that God is infinite in His Being, as does classical theism. But we have seen that an infinite Being cannot be divided, for He cannot have an infinite number of parts. One more can always be added, and more cannot be added to an infinity. Hence, an infinite Being must be absolutely simple (see ch. 3).

Simplicity follows logically from the neotheist's view of God's infinity. Again, what neotheists believe leads logically to what they reject. To be consistent, they should return to classical theism.

CLASSICAL THEISM AND FREE CHOICE

Neotheists do have motivations for rejecting classical theism. Two of their reasons are among the strongest. First, they are guided by their view of libertarian freedom. Second, they believe in an "interactive" God. As we have seen, neither of these is logically inconsistent with classical theism. God can have infallible foreknowledge, while human beings still are free (see ch. 8).

---

8. See Alfred North Whitehead, *Process and Reality: An Essay in Cosmology*, ed. D. R. Griffin and D. W. Sherburne (1929 corr. ed.; repr. ed., New York: Free Press, 1979).

Free choices are simply determined in relation to God's infallible foreknowledge and yet not determined in relation to our free choices. So they are determined and not determined in different relationships. But the law of noncontradiction finds two propositions contradictory only if they both affirm and deny the same thing at the same time in the same relationship. Thus, the neotheist's desire for libertarian freedom is consistent with the classical view of God who has infallible foreknowledge of future free acts.

Classical Theism and Interaction with God

Likewise, the neotheist can return to classical theism and still have an interactive God. Their failure to see how God is relationally interactive with a changing temporal world is based on the misunderstanding that only a temporal God can relate to a temporal world and only a changing God to a changing world. As we saw in chapter 7, a changing world can be constantly related to a changeless God, as a dependent world can be constantly related to an Independent God and a contingent world can be related to a Necessary God. Just because the pendulum is moving does not mean its axis changes. Simply because a person moves in relation to the pillar does not mean the pillar moved in relation to the person.

The fact is that free agents (in the libertarian sense) can be just as free and interactive with the God of classical theism as with the highly problematic God of neotheism. The difference is that God is not *reactive* but *proactive*. He can act as many times and in response to as many prayers as is needed. The difference is that with the classical view of God, He pre-knows and pre-acts from all eternity. He does not have to "wait" to see what will happen and then react to it. Neither does anything catch God by surprise, since He has infallible foreknowledge from the fulcrum of eternity of all that has happened, is happening, and will happen.

Not only is the God of classical theism as interactive with free agents as is the Zeus-like God of neotheism, but He is in a much better position to be interactive, since He has infallible knowledge in advance. He is never guessing. He is in complete and sovereign control over everything without destroying the freedom of anyone (see ch. 8).

SOME ROOT PROBLEMS WITH NEOTHEISM

To understand what is at work behind the scenes in this controversy, it is helpful to see the basic premises that lead neotheists astray. These will be briefly described here, but a detailed response to each can be found elsewhere in this book.

Creating God in Man's Image

Although not intentionally, neotheists constantly argue from a time-bound, anthropocentric point of view. They insist that God must know in the way we do in order to know what we do. He must know in a temporal way if He is to know the temporal world. He must act in a temporal way if He is to act in a temporal world. But as we have shown (chs. 3, 7), this does not follow. God must know in accordance with His nature, not ours. And if He is infinite, eternal, and/or nontemporal, then He must know in these ways.

Misunderstanding Classical Theism

After nearly a half-century in the study of classical theism, the authors cannot help but be amazed at how contemporary thinkers misunderstand it. As pointed out in the above chapters, the objections raised by current neotheists were answered centuries ago. Past errors are being repeated.

Improper Metaphysics

Much of contemporary neotheism, particularly on the philosophical level, comes out of contemporary analytic philosophy. While a critique of this movement is beyond the scope of this discussion, we commended Etienne Gilson, *The*

Unity of Philosophical Experience,[9] and Henry Veatch, *Two Logics: The Conflict Between Classical and Neo-analytical Philosophy.*[10]

We are reminded in this connection of the quip of contemporary philosopher Jerry Gill, who spoke of his colleagues as physicians who have the cleanest hands and the sharpest tools with which to operate. They lack only a body on which to operate. By and large analytic philosophy is a logic in search of a metaphysics. Nowhere is this failure of the logical method of analytic philosophy more apparent than in the brilliant, but largely metaphysics-less works of Alvin Plantinga.[11] With incisive logic applied to God, he comes up with a metaphysically empty hand—a God who has no real nature in the traditional sense. Rather, God's nature is a bundle of properties (Plantinga 1974, 7). He, like neotheists, cannot understand a God who is a simple, indivisible substance and essence because no metaphysical rationale exists to allow for a substance with many different characteristics or attributes.

A Misunderstanding of Analogy

When one's whole system is reducible to univocally predicated "properties," undefined "objects," and "states of affairs," it is little wonder that traditional metaphysical theism is thrown out with the bath water of ancient physics. For if properties are all distinct and each one exists, then it is difficult to see how anyone could believe in a simple, indivisible Being with many properties (attributes).

However, in traditional Aristotelian-Thomistic terms, there can be one simple substance (essence) that has many properties. These characteristics are attributable to it in an analogous way.

---

9. Etienne Gilson, *The Unity of Philosophical Experience* (New York: Scribner's Sons, 1937).

10. Henry Veatch, *Two Logics: The Conflict Between Classical and Neo-analytical Philosophy* (Evanston, Ill.: Northwestern University Press, 1969).

11. Alvin Plantinga, *Does God have a Nature?* (Milwaukee: Marquette University Press, 1980); *The Nature of Necessity* (Oxford: Clarendon, 1974).

Again, the failure to understand traditional metaphysics leads to an untraditional and unorthodox view of God. As an antidote, one would recommend the excellent book by Battista Mondin on *The Use of Analogy in Protestant and Catholic Theology*.[12]

Alfred North Whitehead was right when he described modern philosophy in broad terms as a series of footnotes on Plato. Plato had the same problem as does modern philosophy. His entire metaphysical system reduced to a plurality of simple forms that could not be predicated univocally (in the same way) of the one Super Form (the *Agathos*). This led, on the one hand, to Plotinian mysticism, in which the ultimate Form (called the One) was beyond all positive predication. Or, on the other hand, it led to the logical atomism of Betrand Russell behind analytic philosophy's vain attempt to apply symbolic logic to understand the real world. The result is the presupposition that all truth can be understood univocally in terms of properties. This in turn leads to a denial of God's simplicity, since ultimate reality consists of tiny forms or properties that have no essence to hold them together.

Ironically, the very neotheists who disclaim "Greek Philosophy" because of its alleged influence on classical theism (see ch. 5) have themselves fallen into the pit of Greek Platonic philosophy.

Misused Metaphor and Anthropomorphism

Not all neotheists come at the subject from a strictly philosophical perspective. Some, with Gregory Boyd, claim a biblical basis. However, one finds that their changing, temporal God is based largely on anthropomorphisms. Boyd takes the metaphor of God "repenting" literally instead of metaphorically. He argues that it is not "ridiculous" to say that God truly repented. So one must take the expression as literal (Boyd 2000, 118).

---

12. Battista Mondin, *The Principle of Analogy in Protestant and Catholic Theology* (The Hague: M. Nijhoff, 1963).

Boyd admits that anthropomorphisms are used of God in the Bible (Boyd 2000, 118–19). So, it is possible that God's repenting is one. Neotheists are inconsistent in choosing what to take literally, since the Bible also speaks of God as having eyes (Heb. 4:13), arms (Deut. 33:27), and even wings (Exod. 19:4). They do not take these literally, though it may be argued that the "repentance" of God is just as ridiculous as to speak of God's eyes. Yet Boyd takes such expressions as God "forgetting" our sins to be metaphorical (e.g. Isa. 43:25). If so, then why should we not also take God's "learning" to be the same? At best, the criterion of "ridiculousness" is subjective and inconsistently applied. Even Boyd admits that speaking of God as repenting, which he believes to be literally true, strikes some as ridiculous (Boyd 2000, 118).

Boyd acknowledges that even anthropomorphisms can tell us something literally true of God, but he rejects that this can be true of God's alleged "mind change." Classical theists have long observed that human repentance tells us something about God's alleged "repentance," namely, that God has more than one attribute upon which He must act consistently. Hence, before a person repents, he is under God's attribute of wrath, and after he repents he is under God's attribute of mercy (Charnock 1971 ET, 341–42). God is really both wrathful and merciful, and when one repents there is a real change in his relationship with the unchanging God. For when a person repents of his sin, he moves from under the unchanging attribute of God's wrath to under the unchanging attribute of God's mercy.

Classical theists believe that God knew from eternity who would repent. And God's will includes intermediate causes, such as human free choice. So God knows what the intermediate causes will choose to do. And God's will is in accord with His unchangeable knowledge. Therefore, God's will never changes,

---

13. Further, what God wills to happen, He knows will happen. For both willing and knowing are coordinate and eternal acts in God.

since He wills what He knows will happen.[13] That is to say, what is willed by conditional necessity does not violate human freedom, since what is willed is conditioned on their freely choosing it. God wills the salvation of men only conditionally (2 Peter 3:9). Therefore, God's will to save them does not violate human free choice; it utilizes it.[14]

Of course, while God's will does not change, the effects in time of His will do change. God wills unchangeably from all eternity that many different and changing things will happen at different times, so that eventually His sovereign purpose will be accomplished. Just as a doctor knows and wills in advance to change the patient's medicine as physical status changes, so God wills unchangeably from all eternity to meet the changing conditions of His creatures in order to accomplish His ultimate purposes. An omniscient Mind cannot be wrong about what it knows (*Summa Theologica* 1.14.2–7).

There is a more objective criteria for deciding what in Scripture is to be taken literally (albeit analogously) when applied to God and what is not to be taken literally. Since it is known from both special (John 4:24) and general revelation (Acts 17:29; Rom. 1:19) that God is immaterial (cf. John 4:24), then any term applied to God whose meaning cannot be abstracted from materialness cannot be applied to God literally. This applies to terms like rock, arms, eyes, legs, and wings—all of which are material. Hence, they must be applied to God metaphorically. Further, classical theists and neotheists agree that God is infinite. Hence, any term whose meaning cannot be separated from what is finite must be applied to God in a nonliteral or metaphorical way. Since an infinite rock, arm, leg, eye, or wing is impossible, then these must be taken metaphorically of God.

In like manner, if it is known that God is infinite in His understanding, then forgetting or changing His mind must be understood metaphorically. This is an objective criterion and

---

14. See Thomas Aquinas, *Summa Theologica* 1.19.7.

would rule out the kinds of things many neotheists take literally that are really metaphorical. Absent taking these metaphors literally, neotheists lose much of the alleged biblical support for their view.

CONCLUSION

Neotheism is a serious theological danger with regard to belief in the triune God who really is, and also with respect to every other significant Christian doctrine. By buying into the God of process theology, neotheism sacrifices the God of orthodox theology, whose attributes of timelessness, unchangeability, and simplicity are firmly based in the Bible, theology, and history.

The God of neotheism is admitted to be finite in knowledge, and logic demands that He is finite in being and activity. He is more like the Greek Zeus than the Plotinian One. He is a God made more in human image than the God who made humankind in His image (Gen. 1:27).

If neotheism would carry through consistently with the attributes of God they hold in common with classical theism, like infinity, necessity, and uncausality, they could retain their view of libertarian freedom and fulfill their desire for an interactive God, yet return to classical theism.

CHAPTER 10

Practical Dangers of Neotheism

FOR A LOT OF THE people in today's church, who have not been well taught and who are not accustomed to theological disputes, and for some who are, the discussion of neotheistic ideas may raise the question "So what? What practical difference does it make who is right in this discussion?"

The answer recalls the title of Richard M. Weaver's excellent book, *Ideas Have Consequences*.[1] In the twentieth century, Adolf Hitler's application of social Darwinism cost 12 million lives in a holocaust. Josef Stalin's use of Karl Marx's thought resulted in the liquidation of more than 18 million people. And Mao Tse-tung's adherence to the ideas of Marx and Leon Trotsky caused more than 30 million deaths.

While no one suggests that the battle for God will feed a mad man's passion to rival these statistics, even more important consequences lies in the balance—the eternal souls of spiritual seekers. Theological ideas have longer-lasting consequences than do mere political ones.

While neotheism may seem a lightweight controversy compared to those that rage even now over the deity of Christ and the Trinity, the dangers are more grave than the average person in the pew might appreciate. Traditional theism's view

---

1. Richard M. Weaver, *Ideas Have Consequences* (Chicago: University of Chicago Press, 1948).

of God is the gateway to virtually every other Christian doctrine. A serious deviation on this topic can erode every other pillar supporting the orthodox church.

The doctrine of God underlies or profoundly affects virtually every major doctrine of Christianity. For example, the claim that the Bible is the Word of *God* or that Christ is the Son of *God* is entirely dependent on what is meant by *God* in His nature and attributes.

The concept of *God* also makes a difference in a believer's personal life. As A. W. Tozer put it, "What comes into our minds when we think about God is the most important thing about us" (Tozer 1961, 1). In fact, we can rise no higher in our spiritual lives than the God we worship. So our concept of God will have a marked effect on our practical lives. Since the neotheist's view of God is a significant deviation from the historic orthodox view, the practical results of this teaching on the church are likely to be enormous. The following are but a sampling of some practical dangers relating to the neotheist's view of God.

CONFIDENCE IN THE CHARACTER OF GOD

As was shown, neotheists deny the immutability (ch. 4) and true sovereignty of God (ch. 8), along with the infallibility of His foreknowledge (ch. 2). In many ways the new God of the new theism is both finite and imperfect. Indeed, by logical reduction, such a God has been found to be limited in perfection, in presence, and in power as well. Such a view of God undermines confidence in the One we need to trust the most.

Any God worthy of the term must be worthy of our ultimate admiration and commitment. As Paul Tillich correctly observed, religion involves an ultimate commitment. And any commitment to a God who is less than ultimate is ultimately unworthy (Tillich 1965, 7–8). But such is the finite and imperfect God of neotheism. By their own admission, God is not absolutely perfect in nature. He lacks the unchanging character of the God of Scripture who said, "I am the LORD, I do not change" (Mal. 3:6a).[2] Indeed, "if we are faithless, He remains faithful; He cannot deny Himself" (2 Tim. 2:13). It is this God of the Bible in which one can place absolute confidence, not the changeable, fallible God of neotheism.

Our spiritual confidence in God can be no greater than the nature of the God in whom we place our confidence. For "it is impossible for God to lie." Hence, "we might have strong consolation, who have fled for refuge to lay hold of the hope set before us" (Heb. 6:18). But a God who is limited in perfection, power, and performance—such as the God of neotheism—cannot engender the confidence that Scripture calls upon us to have. For we are asked to love Him with all our heart (Matt. 22:37), to commit our very souls to Him eternally (2 Tim. 1:12), and even to sacrifice our lives for Him (Rev. 2:10).

What is more, the rejection of God's complete sovereignty (see ch. 8) has a grave and disconcerting practical effect on one's spiritual life. One has no real basis to endure the type of things Job did unless he has the type of sovereign God Job had. After all his trials, Job confessed "I know that You can do everything, and that no purpose of Yours can be withheld from You" (Job 42:2). This is something hardly possible with a God who is less sovereign than one that knows "the end from the beginning" (Isa. 46:10), whose plan has been secure from before the foundation of the earth (Rev. 13:8) and "who works all things according to the counsel of His will" (Eph. 1:11b). Such is not the God of neotheism, as we have seen.

Our godliness can be no greater than our view of God. Our confidence in God can be no higher than our concept of God. And by any realistic biblical assessment, the God of neotheism falls seriously short of being worthy of our utmost for His highest.

---

2. The neotheist would respond that God's character does not change, but His actions and experiences change. However, this involves complexity in God, and it begs the question as to what actually changes.

CONFIDENCE IN THE WORD OF GOD

The psalmist said, "When the foundations are being destroyed, what can the righteous do?" (Ps. 11:3). And surely the Bible is the foundation of all Christian doctrine and practice (2 Tim. 3:16–17). What undermines confidence in the Bible will likewise seriously diminish the practice of the Christian life.

We are called upon in Scripture to trust God's Word completely, for it is "perfect" (Ps. 19:7). Jesus said, "the Scripture cannot be broken" (John 10:35). It is imperishable, for Jesus also declared that, "till heaven and earth pass away, one jot or one tittle will by no means pass from the law till all is fulfilled" (Matt. 5:18). It is effective, as God affirmed through Isaiah: "So shall My word be that goes forth from My mouth; it shall not return to Me void, but it shall accomplish what I please, and it shall prosper in the thing for which I sent it" (Isa. 55:11).

That the Bible speaks with divine authority is evidence that it is infallible. Jesus asked the religious leaders of His day: "Why do you also transgress the commandment of God because of your tradition? . . . Thus you have made the commandment of God of no effect by your tradition" (Matt. 15:3, 6b). Our Lord also cited Scripture with divine authority to rebuke the Devil, saying repeatedly, "It is written" (Matt. 4:4, 7, 10). Indeed, Paul speaks of God's Word as "the oracles of God" (Rom. 3:2 NASB). Jesus declared that the Bible is indestructible (Matt. 5:17–18). Isaiah confirmed the same when he wrote, "The grass withers, the flower fades, but the word of our God stands forever" (Isa. 40:8). The psalmist added, "Your word, O LORD, is eternal; it stands firm in the heavens" (Ps. 119:89 NIV). Now it is simply impossible to rest the heavy weight of these truths of Scripture on the weak frame of the neotheistic God. Only a sovereign, omniscient God can support infallible Scriptures.

The neotheistic God is simply too weak to support the superstructure of an infallible and inerrant Scripture.[3] We saw

---

3. Some neotheists admit this. Others seem afraid to draw the logical conclusion that a God with fallible foreknowledge cannot inspire an infallible Book.

in chapter 2 that this has obvious implications for the trustworthiness of the Bible. On the premises of neotheism, God is only guessing about future free acts. Thus, it is reasonable to assume that God is wrong at least part of the time. But an errant Word from God will lead to errant lives for God. What Jesus told the Sadducees seems to apply here: "You are mistaken, not knowing the Scriptures nor the power of God" (Matt. 22:29).

CONFIDENCE IN THE PROMISES OF GOD

Likewise, if, as a result of God's fallible foreknowledge, all predictions are conditional, then this undermines confidence in God's promises. If we cannot be sure that even God can keep His word, then it undermines belief in His faithfulness. But the Bible says we can accept God's word unconditionally. Sometimes it says this explicitly in the context of affirming that He knows "the end from the beginning" (Isa. 46:10). In this context Paul wrote, "if we are faithless, he remains faithful; He cannot deny Himself" (2 Tim. 2:13). Again, he reminds us that "the gifts and the calling of God are irrevocable" (Rom. 11:29). Hence, with regard to these unconditional promises, "it is not of him who wills, nor of him who runs, but of God who shows mercy" (Rom. 9:16).

The Christian life depends on being able to take God at His word, knowing that what He promises He will do. But virtually all events that affect human lives depend at some point on free actions. According to neotheism, God does not know these things infallibly, so how do we know He can keep any particular promise unless He violates the free will of His creatures? Any such violation in the neotheist schema of reality is a serious breach of God's intention. That the neotheist finds this *Deus ex machina* intervention necessary is a serious weakness in their system.[4] Further, if God sometimes violates free will to

---

4. Literally: "The God out of the machine," a phrase used to criticize a view that invokes special intervention (such as from God) to keep it from collapsing. The term developed in the ancient Greek theatre, where

accomplish His plan of salvation, then why can and does He not do it to overcome the stubborn will of unbelievers to save them?

The Bible is filled with promises from God—some of them vastly important promises about our salvation. These promises are said to be irrevocable and immutable (Rom. 11:29; Heb. 6:18), even though free will is involved. There is no contradiction here, because a God with infallible foreknowledge knows exactly how every free creature will exercise his freedom (see ch. 2). So, without destroying our ability to do otherwise, God knows in advance for certain how things will turn out. On this basis He is able to make absolute promises about the future, including those about our salvation. Otherwise, Paul could not say, "I am persuaded that neither death nor life, nor angels nor principalities nor powers, nor things present nor things to come, nor height nor depth, nor any other created thing, shall be able to separate us from the love of God which is in Christ Jesus our Lord" (Rom. 8:38–39). Likewise, if neotheism were true, Jesus could not say, "I give them eternal life, and they shall never perish; neither shall anyone snatch them out of my hand. My Father, who has given them to Me, is greater than all; and no one is able to snatch them out of My Father's hand" (John 10:28–29).

Acts 27 contains a beautiful illustration of how God can make unconditional promises that involve free choice. Paul said to his fellow passengers on the boat, "I urge you to take heart, for there will be no loss of life among you, but only of the ship. For there stood by me this night an angel of the God to whom I belong and whom I serve, saying, 'Do not be afraid, Paul; you must be brought before Caesar; and indeed God has granted you all those who sail with you'" (Acts 27:22–24). Yet later he warned those who wanted to jump ship, "Unless these men stay in the ship, you cannot be saved" (Acts 7:31).

---

playwrights tended to back their characters into an impossible corner and then call in the miraculous intervention of a god to save the day—and the story line.

An even better illustration comes from the fact that God guaranteed that Christ would die for our sins before the foundation of the earth (cf. Eph. 1:4; Rev. 13:8). Peter declared that Jesus "was handed over to you by God's set purpose and foreknowledge; and you, with the help of wicked men, put him to death by nailing him to the cross" (Acts 2:23). Yet we hear from Jesus' own lips that the Cross happened because of His own free choice: "I lay down my life— only to take it up again. No one takes it from me, but I lay it down of my own accord. I have authority to lay it down and authority to take it up again. This command I received from my Father" (John 10:17–18). Thus, God can make unconditional promises to us—promises that involve truly free choices—that are absolutely trustworthy. Such is not possible with a neotheistic God who cannot predict with certainty anything about the future involving free actions without violating human free choice.

It is clear that not all God's promises in the Bible are given to everyone. Some are only to some people (Gen. 4:15). Others are only to a certain group of people (Gen. 13:14–17). Some are conditioned on human behavior. They have a stated or implied "if" in them. The Mosaic covenant is of this type. God said to Israel, "'Now *if* you obey me fully and keep my covenant, then out of all nations you will be my treasured possession. Although the whole earth is mine, you will be for me a kingdom of priests and a holy nation.' These are the words you are to speak to the Israelites" (Exod. 19:5–6).

Other promises of God are unconditional. Such was the land promise to Abraham and his offspring. This is clear because

1. no conditions were attached to it;
2. Abraham's agreement was not solicited; it was initiated while Abraham was in a deep sleep (Gen. 15:12);
3. the covenant was enacted unilaterally as God passed through the split sacrifice (Gen. 15:17–19);
4. God reaffirmed this promise even when Israel was unfaithful (2 Chron. 21:7).

Such unconditional promises that involve free choices of creatures would not be possible unless God knew all future free choices.

Neotheists offer 1 Kings 2:1–4 as an example of how a seemingly unconditional promise is really conditional. God promised David of his son Solomon: "My love will never be taken from him, as I took it from Saul, whom I removed from before you" (2 Sam. 7:15–16). Yet later God seemed to take this back, making it conditional on whether he would "walk faithfully before me" (1 Kings 2:1–4). Thus, they argue that all seemingly unconditional promises are really conditional.

This argument fails. First, it is a *non sequitur,* since the conclusion is much broader than the premises. Even if this were an example of an implied conditional, it would not show that all promises are conditional. Second, it overlooks promises that are irrefutably unconditional, such as the Abrahamic covenant in Genesis 15. These counter-examples refute the contention that all God's promises are conditional.

Third, the argument as stated is inconsistent with the neotheistic view of God. For neotheists insist that God is an ontologically independent Being. But God's knowledge is part of His essence or being. How then can God's knowledge be dependent on anything else?[5]

Finally, the argument is based on a failure to see that the texts refer to different things. In 2 Samuel, God was speaking to David about never taking the kingdom away from his son Solomon. This promise was fulfilled for, in spite of his sins, the kingdom was not taken from Solomon during his entire lifetime. In fact the fulfillment is explicitly stated when God said to Solomon: "Since this is your attitude and you have not kept my covenant and my decrees, which I commanded you, I will most certainly tear the kingdom away from you and give it

---

5. See John Sanders, *The God Who Risks: A Theology of Providence* (Downers Grove, Ill. InterVarsity, 1998); R. Garrigou-LaGrange, *God: His Existence and Nature* (St. Louis: Herder, 1946), appendix 4.

to one of your subordinates. Nevertheless, for the sake of David your father, I will not do it during your lifetime. I will tear it out of the hand of your son" (1 Kings 11:11–12). God did keep His promise to David about Solomon.

The other text (1 Kings 2:1–4) is not speaking about God's promise to David about his son Solomon. Rather, it refers to God taking the kingdom from any of Solomon's sons. There was no unconditional promise made here. From his death bed David exhorted Solomon

> Keep the charge of the LORD your God: to walk in His ways, to keep His statutes, His commandments, His judgments, and His testimonies. . . that the LORD may fulfill His word which He spoke concerning me, saying: "If your sons take heed to their way, to walk before me in truth with all their heart and with all their soul," He said, "you shall not lack a man on the throne of Israel." (1 Kings 2:3–4).

This promise was both conditional ("if") and limited to Solomon's sons. It said nothing about Solomon, concerning whom God apparently made an unconditional promise not to take his throne during his lifetime.

From this it seems clear that God does make unconditional promises. But this is not possible if neotheism is true. For, according to neotheists, God does not have infallible foreknowledge of free acts. Hence, neotheism must be false.

GOD'S ABILITY TO ANSWER PRAYER

Most of our prayers involve human free choices at some point. Yet God does hear and answer our prayers. James said, "The effective, fervent prayer of a righteous man avails much" (James 5:16b). He added, "You do not have, because you do not ask" (James 4:2c). Jesus said, "Ask and it will be given to you" (Matt. 7:7a). He added, "If you abide in me and my words abide in you, you will ask whatever you desire, and it shall be done for you" (John 15:7).

This does not mean, of course, that everyone will get anything they asked of God (see 2 Cor. 12:8–9; James 4:3; 1 John 5:16). But when we pray in His will and according to His Word (John 15:7; 1 John 5:14), and when God answers, we can be sure that free acts in the chain of events leading to the answer will not be an obstacle. This is not the case with the God of neotheism. We have no assurance that He is able to answer prayer.

Neotheists make much of God's dynamic ability to answer prayer, but it would appear that their concept of God undermines God's use of special providence. Neotheists admit that most answers to prayer do not require direct supernatural intervention in the world. God works through special providence in unusual ways to accomplish unusual things, but a God who does not know for sure what any future free act will be is severely limited in His logistic ability to do usual or unusual things. Only a truly omniscient God has the information necessary to exercise perfect wisdom. Ironically, the neotheistic God is a liability to the answered prayer that they consider so important in a personal God.

OUR ABILITY TO TEST FOR FALSE PROPHECY

God's people through the ages have depended on the discernment to know a false prophecy from a true one. The Bible exhorts us to test the spirits (1 John 4:1). It warns against lying spirits (1 Tim 4:1) and "false prophets" (Matt. 7:15). Indeed, it provides tests for a false prophet, one of which is whether the prophecy comes to pass. Moses wrote, "When a prophet speaks in the name of the LORD, if the thing does happen or come to pass, that is the thing which the LORD has not spoken; the prophet has spoken it presumptuously; you shall not be afraid of him" (Deut. 18:22).

According to neotheists, God cannot make infallible predictions that involve free choice. Therefore, all prophecies could be false, whatever their divine inspiration. Even a true prophet can only pass on God's projections and prognostications. Again, there is no certain knowledge of what will come to pass. If neotheists are correct, then this test from God is not valid. It is not a way to distinguish a true prophet, since either can utter prophecies that remain unfulfilled. Indeed, God Himself could be judged a false prophet by this test. A neotheist God's predictions involving free agents are just guesses, no matter how good God may be at guessing. In fact, given the openness of the future and the fickleness of free will, it is reasonable to assume that some of God's predictions will be inaccurate. Hence, this test, which is laid down by God in His Word, would prove that God is a false prophet. This is clearly absurd.

GOD'S KNOWLEDGE OF THE ELECT

If neotheists are correct, then even God does not know for sure who will accept His salvation, persevere, and be in heaven. Neotheists opt for a *corporate election*, in which God knows that Christ is elect and, hence, all who are in Him will be elect— whoever they are. Sanders states, "According to corporate election, it is the group—the body of Christ—that is foreordained from the foundation of the world, not specific individuals selected by God for salvation" (Sanders 1998, 102). God predestines the "bus" [Christ] will get to heaven. Whoever gets on it and does not get off before it gets to heaven will make it. The rest will not.

There are serious objections to this view. First, on the basis of neotheism, God cannot even be sure that the "bus" [Christ] will be in heaven. For, along with being God, Christ was a human being with unpredictable libertarian freewill. Jesus Himself said of His free choice, "No one takes it from me, but I lay it down of my own accord (John 10:18a). Since that is the case, the neotheist God could not be sure that Christ would assume His mission of salvation or that anyone would accept it. However, such a notion is clearly contrary to the Bible. Scripture informs us that Christ was the lamb slain from the foundation of the world (Rev. 13:8) and that some elect were chosen in Him before the world began (Rom. 8:29; Eph. 1:4).

Further, the cross was determined from all eternity (Acts 2:23). But this would not have been possible for the Bible to affirm unless God infallibly knew their future free acts. Neotheists claim that He did not. So God would not even have been able to predict with certainty that Christ would carry through with His mission of the Cross. But the Bible does say that God knew for sure that Christ would freely chose to fulfill His divinely appointed mission. Therefore, the neotheist's view must be false. God did know from all eternity that the "bus" [Christ] would be in heaven.

Second, according to neotheism, even if somehow God could have predestined the bus to be in heaven, He cannot be sure who will be on board. God does not know who the elect are. At best, He is making a good guess about some, but he Has no certainty about any. The bus destined for heaven could arrive empty. So, for all God knows for sure, there may be no elect in heaven. For a neotheist, the only thing God knows for sure is that He does not know for sure who, if anyone, is going to be on the bus. Finally, Paul includes himself among those whom God knew and chose before the foundation of the world (Eph. 1:4). But if God cannot know future free acts, then this would not have been possible. But this neotheistic view is contrary to both traditional Calvinistic and Arminian views. Indeed, it has no basis in the whole history of orthodox Christianity.

GOD'S ABILITY TO DEFEAT EVIL

As neotheists insist that God does not know the future for sure and that He does not intervene against freedom except on rare occasions, no victory over evil can be guaranteed. How can He be sure that anyone will be saved without tampering with freedom, which contradicts the neotheist libertarian view of free will.

What is more, it is contrary to the Bible, which predicts that Satan will be defeated, evil will be vanquished, and many will be saved. But since, according to the neotheist, this is a moral question that involves (libertarian) free will, then it follows that

God could not know this infallibly. However, the Bible does inform us that evil will be defeated (Revelation 21–22).

Further, in spite of Satan's libertarian free will, God predicts that he is doomed (Matt. 25:40–41; Rev. 20:10), even though he is now loose. But if neotheism is correct, God cannot know this for sure, unless God violates Satan's free choice. This would give up the whole theodicy, which is based on the fact that Satan and all who are doomed have the power of contrary choice. Again the neotheistic view breaks down. The Bible proclaims that God knows for sure that Satan will end in the lake of fire. He can know that for sure only if He has infallible foreknowledge.

CONCLUSION

What one believes does affect how one behaves. It is a fact that people tend to act on their beliefs. And a change in one's ultimate beliefs can make an ultimate difference in behavior. Such is the case with neotheism. It not only undermines the orthodox view of God, but orthodox doctrine in general.

The practical consequences of neotheism are enormous. To adopt this truncated theism is to undermine confidence in the character of God, the Word of God, and the actions of God.

These actions on which we depend include God's promises to us, His salvation of us, the ability to trust His Word, and His ability to keep His Word. Political and theological ideas do have consequences, whether the ideas are philosophical, political, or theological. Bad theological ideas have bad consequences. And seriously bad ideas have seriously bad consequences. Neotheism is a seriously bad idea.

CHAPTER ELEVEN

Is Neotheism Orthodox?

SOME NEOTHEISTS SEEM sensitive to the charge of heresy. Gregory A. Boyd, for example, denies it repeatedly (Boyd 2000, 8, 9, 12).[1] To use a less emotive word, let us ask whether neotheism is "unorthodox." Several points are significant in helping us make a determination.

GROUNDS FOR NEOTHEISM'S ORTHODOXY

From the start, one must reject the claim that Christians should not divide over such "peripheral" issues (Boyd 2000, 8, 9, 19, 20). The nature of God is no peripheral matter. It is fundamental to every essential Christian teaching. Further, it is possible to have unorthodox views of God, as even Boyd acknowledges when discussing his former beliefs as a Oneness Pentecostal.[2] Boyd's stated criterion for orthodoxy is faulty. He contends that "no ecumenical creed of the orthodox church has ever included an article of faith on divine foreknowledge" (Boyd 2000, 116).

This misses the point, since more is involved in neotheism than divine foreknowledge. Boyd also denies God's eternality, immutability, and simplicity—which are addressed directly in creeds. And not all credal teachings are found in individual

---

1. See also in Boyd, pp. 19, 20, 84, 115, 116, 172 regarding the orthodoxy of neotheism.
2. See Boyd's excellent refutation of this heretical view in his book, *Oneness Pentecostals and the Trinity* (Grand Rapids: Baker, 1992).

"articles." Some doctrines are subsumed within articles on other things. The simplicity (indivisibility) of God is a case in point (see ch. 5). Several creeds include it under the one nature of God in a section on the Trinity. Nor do the creeds contain an article on the inspiration and infallibility of Scripture, but it is clear that this teaching was entailed in all their pronouncements.[3] This does not make it any less true or orthodox. This neotheist test for orthodoxy is too narrow.

Likewise, the implication that unity should be achieved at any price falls short of being a viable Christian principle (Boyd 2000, 8, 9, 19). The same logic could be used to include Latter-Day Saints, Jehovah's Witness, or someone who denies the infallibility and inerrancy of the Bible.

Separating the Questions

Two distinctions will help us consider whether neotheism is orthodox. First, a person can be orthodox on most essential Christian doctrines and be unorthodox on one. Many Christians, for example, accept the central teachings of Christian Faith, yet have a low view of the inspiration and authority of the Bible. They are orthodox in general but unorthodox in a particular doctrine.

Second, someone can be unorthodox on a doctrine such as inerrancy and still be saved. Salvation depends upon believing certain soteriological doctrines, centrally the death of the second Person of the Trinity for our sins and His resurrection (1 Cor. 15:1–4). Salvation does not hinge on explicit acceptance of all evangelical doctrines, such as the inspiration of Scripture and the bodily return of Christ. A neotheist may be orthodox on crucial soteriological doctrines, while remaining unorthodox on others.

That is not to downplay the crucial nature of one's concept

---

3. See Philip Schaff, *The Creeds of Christendom: With a History and Critical Notes* (repr. ed., Grand Rapids: Baker, 1983). Also, Norman L. Geisler, *Decide for Yourself: How History Views the Bible* (Grand Rapids: Baker, 1982), chs. 2–3.

of God. Every evangelical doctrine is connected, directly or indirectly, to who God is. Since these traditional doctrines are based on the classical view of God, an errant view will infect other areas of faith. This is demonstrated in the truncated version of omniscience held by neotheists. As we saw in chapter 2, the extent of God's knowledge effects both soteriology and eschatology. A God limited in foreknowledge is limited in what He can do to save a people and secure their future.

Defining Orthodoxy on God's Nature

Typically, an unorthodox teaching denies a fundamental doctrine that church fathers, creeds, and confessions have regarded as important. In evaluating neotheism, two points must be kept in mind.

First, there is a difference between explicit unorthodoxy and implicit unorthodoxy. Explicit unorthodoxy formally denies a central tenet of faith. Implicit unorthodoxy denies by implication. Its position logically entails the denial of a central teaching.

Second, neotheism, as held by some evangelicals, is implicitly unorthodox on the infallibility and inerrancy of Scripture. If they are right, then the Bible contains unconditional predictions about the future that could be wrong. For example, the Bible predicts that the Devil is free, but his ultimate fate in the lake of fire is predetermined (Rev. 20:10). According to neotheism, this prediction cannot be infallible, so at least this part of the Bible is not infallible. The same logic would apply to unconditional predictive prophecy about Christ (cf. Ps. 16:10; Dan. 9:24f cf. Mic. 5:2; Acts 2:30–32). Boyd admits that God made an infallible prediction of the cross, but He has no right to do that under His own system, for Jesus said He freely chose to go to the cross (John 10:18; Boyd 2000, 46).[4]

Neotheist evasions of this conclusion are inadequate. Clearly

---

4. For an elaboration on these prophecies, see J. Barton Payne's *The Encyclopedia of Biblical Prophecy* (Grand Rapids: Baker, 1980).

not all biblical predictions are conditional, and God's knowledge of the character of individuals is no guarantee that they will not change (Boyd 2000, 160, 171). If God can know for sure in advance that they will change, then He has infallible foreknowledge of free will, which is exactly what neotheists deny. The least that can be said of neotheism is that it logically undermines at least this crucial tenet of orthodoxy.

Some object to denying the orthodoxy of those caught in implicit error. A bad theological method can cause just as much error, yet many evangelicals are unwilling to label these methods as unorthodox, at least not in the sense they would label other beliefs. However, excusing a bad theological method seems myopic. Truly, a bad method *often is* just as devastating to faith as outright denial of major doctrines.

For example, evangelicals within the academic community tend to be members of the Evangelical Theological Society (ETS). ETS would not tolerate in its membership someone who claims to believe in biblical inerrancy but uses a method of interpretation that allegorizes away all literal, historical truth. This can be said with certainty, because 75 percent of ETS members voted to exclude from the society a New Testament scholar who used a midrash method to interpret Matthew. His method denied the historicity of parts of that Gospel, although he accepts the historical death and resurrection of Christ.[5]

With most ETS members, we conclude that orthodoxy must be implicit as well as explicit, methodological as well as confessional. Indeed, the former can be as harmful to orthodoxy as the latter.

Does neotheism engage in more than implicit or methodological unorthodoxy? That is, does it explicitly deny a

---

5. In defending his view in *JETS* (March 1983): 114, Gundry agreed that no one who confesses belief in inerrancy should be eliminated from ETS because of an unorthodox method, even if it were the method of total allegorization of Scripture, such as held by the founder of Christian Science, Mary Baker Eddy.

fundamental tenet of the Christian Faith? The answer to this seems to depend on the answer to two other questions:

- Is the nature of God a fundamental tenet of the Christian Faith?
- Are early creeds, councils, and confessions a test for orthodoxy?

COMPARING NEOTHEISTS AND FATHERS

The Neotheists

Inasmuch as early pronouncements of the church expressed the beliefs of the fathers, their views on these matters provide a test of orthodoxy. We have looked at their statements on various attributes of God in chapters 2–8, but here are a small selection of statements by neotheists and answers from early theologians:

Neotheism: God Is Not Eternal.

Brian Hebblethweite: If God creates a temporally structured universe, then, whatever his own eternal being may be he must relate himself to his creation in a manner appropriate to its given nature, i.e. temporally. (quoted in Sanders 1998, 24)

William Hasker: It is clear that the doctrine of divine timelessness is not taught in the Bible and does not reflect the way the biblical writers understood God. (Pinnock et al. 1994, 128)

Neotheism: God Is Not Omniscient.

Clark Pinnock: God experiences temporal passage, learns new facts when they occur and changes plans in response to what humans do. (Pinnock et al. 1994, 118)

Pinnock: God is the best learner of all because he is completely open to all the input of an unfolding world. (Pinnock et al. 1994, 124)

Gregory Boyd: Our omniscient Creator knows us perfectly, far better than we even know ourselves. Hence, we can assume that he is able to predict our behavior far more extensively and accurately than we could predict it ourselves. This does not mean that everything we will ever do is predictable, for our present character doesn't determine all of our future. But it does mean that our behavior is predictable to the extent that our character is solidified and future circumstances that will affect us are in place. (Boyd 2000, 35).

Neotheism: God Is passible.

Pinnock: God does not just imagine what it would be like to suffer, he actually suffers because of his decision to love. (Pinnock et al. 1994, 119)

Sanders: God forbears with the sin of humanity, but it takes its toll on the divine life. The cost to God is great in terms of personal suffering. (Sanders 1998, 49)

John Sanders: As Creator, God is impassible in the sense that God is not forced to be open or vulnerable. However, if God freely decides to be passible and vulnerable in relation to us, who is to say that God *cannot* sovereignly do this? (Sanders 1998, 178)

Neotheism: God Is Mutable.

Boyd: While classical theologians have always considered the notion that God changes his mind as denoting a weakness on God's part, this passage and several others (Jonah 4:2; Joel 2:12–13) consider God's willingness to change to be one of God's attributes of greatness. When a person is in a genuine relationship with another, willingness to adjust to them is always considered a virtue. Why should this apply to people but not to God? (Boyd 2000, 78)

Pinnock: The difference between them [classical and neo-theism] is not that one views God as changeless while the other doesn't. The difference is that everything about God must be changeless for the traditional view, whereas the open view sees God as both changeless and changeable. . . . We can attribute both change and changelessness to God if we apply them to different aspects of his Being. They [neotheists] apply the "changeless" statements to God's existence and character, to his love and reliability. They apply the "changing" statements to God's actions and experience. (Pinnock et al. 1994, 48)

Hasker: When God began to create the universe he changed, beginning to do something that previously he had not done. (Pinnock et al. 1994, 133)

Neotheism: God Is Not Simple in Being.

Hasker: This [divine timelessness] might be something we would have to accept, if there were compelling reasons forcing us to affirm divine timelessness. But do such reasons exist? I think not; my own conclusion on the matter is that divine timelessness is strongly dependent for its justification on neo-Platonic metaphysics, and in particular on the doctrine of divine simplicity (whose intelligibility has also been strongly challenged). Once this metaphysical taproot has been severed, the prospects for divine timelessness are not bright—nor, I think, should they be. (Pinnock et al. 1994, 129)

Neotheism: God Is Not Completely Sovereign.

Boyd: Indeed, God is so confident in his sovereignty, we hold, he does not need to micromanage everything. He could if he wanted to, but this would demean his sovereignty. So he chooses to leave some of the future open to possibilities, allowing them to be resolved by the decisions of free agents. It takes a greater God to steer a world populated with free agents than it does to steer a world of preprogrammed automatons. (Boyd 2000, 31)

Boyd: Though this is simplistic, it might help if we think of God's power and our say-so in terms of percentages. Prior to creation, God *possessed* 100 percent of all power. He *possessed* all the say-so there was. When the Trinity decided to express their love by bringing forth a creation, they *invested* each creature (angelic and human) with a certain *percentage* of *their say-so*. The say-so of the triune God was at this point no longer the only one that determined how things would go. (Boyd 2000, 97; emphasis added)

The Fathers

Ignatius of Antioch

The earliest known precredal statement of a church father (c. 107) reveals crucial elements of a classical view of God. Written to encourage Polycarp, it reflects a predictive prophecy from Scripture that implies God's infallible foreknowledge that Christ is awaiting in heaven the consummation of history (*Creeds* 2.12). Ignatius advised Polycarp, "Look for Him who is above all time, eternal and invisible" (*Ignatius to Polycarp*, ANF 1.94). He spoke "of the nature of God, which fills His works with beauty, and teaching both where God must be, and that He must be One" (*Ignatius to Polycarp*, ANF 2.131).

Justin Martyr

Justin Martyr described God's simplicity as "an uncompounded intellectual nature, admitting within Himself no addition of any kind; so that He cannot be believed to have within him a great and a less" (*ANF*, 4.243). Justin added, "For Moses said, 'He who is' and Plato, 'That which is." But neither of the expressions seems to apply to the ever-existent God. For He is the only one who eternally exists, and has no generation" (*ANF*, 1.282).

Clement of Alexandria

Clement of Alexandria declared that "All things, therefore, are dispensed from heaven for good . . . according to the eternal foreknowledge, which He purposed in Christ" (*ANF*, 2.319–20). Clement said that God shows "both His divinity in His foreknowledge of what would take place, and His love in affording an opportunity for repentance to the self-determination of the soul" (*ANF*, 2.228).

Tatian

Tatian declared: "I was led to put faith in . . . the foreknowledge displayed of future events, the excellent quality of the precepts, and the declaration of the government of the universe as centered in one Being" (*ANF*, 2.77).

Irenaeus

Philip Schaff calls Irenaeus "the most important witness of the doctrinal status of the catholic church at the close of the second century." Irenaeus affirmed there was "one God" (a reference to God's unity and possibly His simplicity) who "made the heaven and the earth" "out of nothing" and who made predictions of Christ's "birth from the Virgin," of His "passion," "the resurrection from the dead," His "bodily assumption into heaven" and His "appearing from heaven" at the Second Coming. That God's foreknowledge is infallible is seen in the fact that His Son "was always heard in the prophets" (*Creeds*, 12–19).

In his seminal work, *Against Heresies,* Irenaeus declared that only God remains "truly and forever the same" (*Against Heresies*, *ANF* 1.411). In comparing God to humanity, Irenaeus remarks that "He who makes always remains the same" (*ANF* 1.474). God is referred to as "the Father invisible" (denoting immateriality). He implies God's infallible foreknowledge that the angels would never change their will and thus will be sent into "eternal fire." Likewise, the "Rule of Faith" is said to be "immovable and irreformable," thus reflecting the character of God whose Word it is.

Irenaeus also wrote: "He also ascended to the heavens, and was glorified by the Father, and is the 'Eternal King'" (*ANF* 1.577).

"Now what has been made is a different thing from him who makes it. The breath, then, is temporal, but the Spirit eternal" (*ANF* 1.538).

He said of God that "He is a simple, uncompounded Being without diverse members, and altogether like, and equal to Himself" (*ANF* 1.374).

Athenagoras

The early Athenian Christian thinker Athenagoras affirmed that "It is evident that we are not atheists, therefore, seeing that we acknowledge one God, uncreated, eternal" (*ANF* 2.133).

Tertullian

Tertullian replies to Marcion by noting, "We must . . . vindicate those attributes in the Creator which are called in question–namely, His goodness and foreknowledge, and power" (*Five Books Against Marcion* 2.5). Moreover, he affirms the eternality of God when he states, "This rule is required by the nature of the One-only God, who is One-only in no other way than as the sole God; and in no other way sole, than as having nothing else (co-existent) with Him. So also will He be first, because all things are after Him; and all things are after Him, because all things are by Him; and all things are by Him, because they are of nothing" (*Against Hermongenes* 17, ANF 3.162f).

Theophilus

Theophilus declared that, "As God, because He is uncreated, is also unalterable." Citing Scripture, he also said, "'Thou art the same, and Thy years shall not fail . . .' pointing out plainly . . . who it is that doth endure for ever–God" (*Theophilus to Autolycus* 2.4, ANF 2.172).

Origen of Alexandria

Although Origen embraced some unorthodox teachings, He did not appear to deny the classical attributes of God. He declared: "For God, comprehending all things by means of His foreknowledge, and foreseeing what consequences would result from both of these, wished to make these known to mankind by His prophets" (*ANF* 4.594). He also wrote of "One God" who "created and framed everything" as well as God's omnipotence in Christ's birth of the "Virgin" and "resurrection" from the dead (*Creeds of Christendom*, 23).

Novatian of Rome

Novatian speaks also of God as "Almighty" and "Maker of all things," including this temporal world (which places Him beyond time; *Creeds of Christendom*, 21).

Gregory Thaumaturgus

Gregory's belief embraces "one God" with "eternal power" whose power "produces all creation." This God is both "Invisible," "Immortal," "Incorruptible," "Everlasting," "a perfect Trinity," and "not divided," having both "eternity" and "sovereignty." God is "ever the same, unvarying and unchangeable." Here in the mid-third century are almost all the attributes of classical theism, including immutability, eternality, and simplicity (indivisibility) that are denied by neotheists (*Creeds of Christendom*, 24–25).

Alexander of Lycopolis

Alexander of Lycopolis (3d century) wrote, "In truth I think it to be more accurate doctrine to say that God is of a simple nature" (*Of the Manicheans* 6.10).

Lucian of Antioch

Lucian of Antioch (240–312). He confessed belief in "one God the Father Almighty, the maker and Provider of all things." God is "unchangeable," "unalterable," and "immutable." He then "anathematizes all heretical and false doctrine" (*Creeds of Christendom*, 26–27).

Arius

Even though his view of Christ was unorthodox, in the "Private Creed of Arius" Arius (d. 336) confessed that God was almighty and that by him all things were made. Noteworthy is the phrase "before all ages," which reveals His belief that God is before time, namely, nontemporal. This attribute is rejected by neotheism (*Creeds of Christendom*, 28–29).

Eusebius

Eusebius affirmed the central attributes of classical theism, declaring at one point, "We believe in one God the Father Almighty, Maker of all things visible and invisible." He describes God as "Light" and "Life." The resurrection and ascension of Christ are acknowledged to be manifestations of God's omnipotent power (*Creeds of Christendom*, 29–30).

Cyril of Jerusalem

Eusebius's fourth-century contemporary, Cyril of Jerusalem, confessed most of the same points. Cyril said, "We believe in one God the Father Almighty, Maker of heaven and earth; and in one Lord Jesus Christ, . . . begotten of the Father before all ages, very God, by whom all things were made." This affirms both God's unity and eternality (*Creeds of Christendom*, 31).

The Creeds of Epiphanius

In his first formula Epiphanius (c. 315–403) confessed in 374, "We believe in one God the Father Almighty, Maker of heaven and earth, and all things visible and invisible. . . ." God and His Son are eternal, existing "before all worlds [ages]." He speaks of God's one "substance" or "essence," which Christ shared. He adds the attribute of "perfection" as well as the ability to make predictions through the "Prophets." He denies that Christ is "changeable" or "variable" in "substance or essence" from God the Father (*Creeds of Christendom*, 33–34; 37–38).

Reformers

Since it is well known that Augustine, Anselm, and Thomas Aquinas made clear statements of classical theism, they need not be added here.[6] Likewise, it is well known that the Reformers were classical theists.[7] Indeed, no major father up to and through the Reformation deviated from the central attributes of the God of classical theism—even a few who deviated seriously on other elements of Christian teaching.

The Statements of the Creeds

In addition to teachings of the early fathers behind creeds, many of the attributes of God denied by neotheism are embedded in the creeds themselves. Consider the following selection:

Nicene Creed (325)

Nicaea refers to "one God the Father All—sovereign, maker of all things . . . one substance." There is a statement of anathema on those who say God is "created, or changeable, or alterable, these the Catholic and Apostolic Church anathematizes" (Bettenson 1971, 36).

Dedication (Antiochan) Creed (341)

The Council of Antioch, called to deal with the Arian controversy, refers to "one God, Father all, sovereign, framer, maker and providential ruler of the universe, from all things came into being." "before all ages," "unchangeable and immutable" (Bettenson 1971, 57–58).

---

6. For a discussion of Augustine's view and citations, see Norman L. Geisler, *What Augustine Says* (Grand Rapids: Baker, 1982), ch. 3. For Anselm's views see Anselm, *Anselm of Canterbury: Trinity, Incarnation, and Redemption*, trans. by Jasper Hopkins and Herbert Richardson (New York: Harper Torchbook, 1970), esp. 152–99. For Thomas Aquinas's thought, see *Summa Theologica* 1.1–19.

7. See, for example, John Calvin's treatment in Book 1, *Institutes of the Christian Religion*.

Nicaeno-Constantinopolitan Creed (381).

Like its precursors, this creed confessed "one God the Father Almighty; Maker of heaven and earth, and of all things visible and invisible." Likewise, God was "before all worlds." He has one substance (essence). God's omnipotence is manifest, not only in His ability to create the world, but in the virgin birth, bodily resurrection, and ascension of Christ (*Creeds of Christendom*, 58–59).

Definition of Chalcedon (451).

Although stressing the deity of Christ, this creed refers to God as perfect, existing "before all ages," having a nature, producing the supernatural virgin birth, and making predictions through "the prophets from the beginning" (*Creeds of Christendom*, 62–63).

Athanasian Creed (373).

This creed, of unknown origin but influential in church history, begins by declaring: "Whosoever will be saved: before all things it is necessary that he hold the Catholic Faith. Which Faith except every one do keep the whole and undefiled: without doubt he shall perish everlastingly." This includes believing that there is "Unity" in God's "Substance [essence]" without "dividing"; that each member of the Trinity is eternal, uncreated and "incomprehensible" or "unlimited." God is almighty. He is not three gods but one. He is also "perfect God." God has power to raise the dead (*Creeds of Christendom*, 66–69).

CONCLUSION

It is evident that the early Creeds and Confessions of the Faith embraced classical theism on the crucial attributes denied by neotheism: simplicity, eternality, immutability, and infallible foreknowledge of all events, including future freely chosen ones. What is more, the teachings of the fathers is unequivocally on the side of classical theism and opposed to the new kind of theism that has been proposed.

The doctrine of God is crucial to Christian faith by any standard. Who God is in His being figures into the essentials of anything related to faith and life. Given these facts it would seem undeniable by either side, that neotheism is a fundamentally different view of God from that of historical orthodox Christianity. To consider it to be within the realm of Christian orthodoxy would mean a new test of, and definition for, orthodoxy.

Whatever one chooses to call neotheism's view of God, it must be conceded that this view is:

- contrary to the great orthodox creeds, confessions, and councils of the Christian Church;
- contrary to the virtually unanimous teachings of the fathers from the early church to modern times;
- internally inconsistent;
- a system that reduces logically to process theology; and
- destructive to the integrity of Scripture as infallible.

If such problems are not sufficient to merit the charge of unorthodoxy, then one must ask what level of deviation on the fundamental doctrines of God would qualify as unorthodox? What possible standard of authority could be used to make the determination?

APPENDIX ONE: WHAT THE CONFESSIONS TEACH

Document	Reference	Simplicity	Impassibility	Relatability	Sovereignty
Ante-Nicene Creed by Gregory Thaumaturgus Date: 270	P. Schaff *Creeds of Christendom* Vol. 2, 24–25	There is one God, the Father of the living Word, who is substantive wisdom and eternal power and image of God . . . a perfect Trinity not divided. . . .	The true Son of the true Father . . .Incorruptible of Incorruptible The Trinity is ever the same unvarying and unchangeable.	. . . the power which produces all creation. . .	. . . a perfect Trinity not divided in glory eternity and sovereignty. . . .
Apostles' Creed (Italian) Date: 350	*Creeds of Christendom* Vol. 2, 50			We believe in God the Father Almighty, Ruler and Creator of all ages and creatures.	
Athanasian Creed Date: 373	*Creeds of Christendom* Vol. 2, 66	We worship one God in Trinity and Trinity in Unity; neither confounding the Persons nor dividing the substance [essence].			
Augsburg Confession Date: 1530	*Creeds of Christendom* Vol. 3, 7	. . . there is one divine essence, which is called and is God . . . indivisible [without parts]			
French Confession Date: 1559	*Creeds of Christendom* Vol. 3, 359	We believe and confess that there is one God, who is one sole and simple essence, spiritual, eternal, invisible, immutable, infinite, incomprehensible.			
The Formula of Concord Date: 1576	*Creeds of Christendom* Vol. 3, 149				
Westminster Confession Date: 1647	*Creeds of Christendom* Vol. 3, 606	There is but one only living and true God, who is infinite in being and perfection, a most pure spirit, invisible, without body, parts, or passions, immutable, immense, eternal, incomprehensible, almighty, most wise . . . working all things according to the counsel of his own immutable and most righteous will. . . .			

Between the eighth and sixteenth centuries, church theologians systematized and codified what was taught by the fathers. Shedd, *History of Christian Doctrine*, 177)

Document	Reference	Omniscience	Eternality	Immutability
Ante-Nicene Creed by Gregory Thaumaturgus Date: 270	P. Schaff *Creeds of Christendom* Vol. 2, 24–25	The wisdom which comprehends the constitution of all things. . . .	. . . is substantive eternal power. . . . the true Son of the true Father . . . Everlasting of Everlasting . . . a perfect Trinity not divided in glory eternity and sovereignty. . . .	The true Son of the true Father . . . Incorruptible of Incorruptible . . . the Trinity is ever the same unvarying and unchangeable.
Apostles' Creed (Italian) Date: 350	*Creeds of Christendom* Vol. 2, 50		We believe in God the Father Almighty, ruler and Creator of all ages and creatures.	
Athanasian Creed Date: 373	*Creeds of Christendom* Vol. 2, 66		. . . the Father eternal; the Son eternal; and the Holy Ghost eternal. And yet they are not three eternals, but one eternal.	Who although he be [is] God and Man; yet he is not two but one Christ. One; not by conversion of the Godhead into flesh; but by taking [assumption] of the Manhood into God.
Augsburg Confession Date: 1530	*Creeds of Christendom* Vol. 3, 7		. . . there is one divine essence, which is called and is God eternal. . . .	. . . there is one divine essence, which is called and is God . . . indivisible [without parts]. . . .
French Confession Date: 1559	*Creeds of Christendom* Vol. 3, 359	We believe and confess that there is one God, who is one sole and simple essence, spiritual, eternal, invisible, immutable, infinite, incomprehensible . . . who is all wise. . . .		
Formula of Concord Date: 1576	*Creeds of Christendom* Vol. 3, 149	The attributes of the divine nature are . . . to know all things. . . .	The attributes of the divine nature are . . . to be . . . eternal. . . .	
Westminster Confession Date: 1647	*Creeds of Christendom* Vol. 3, 606	There is but one only living and true God, who is infinite in being and perfection, a most pure spirit, invisible, without body, parts, or passions, immutable, immense, eternal, incomprehensible, almighty, most wise . . . working all things according to the counsel of his own immutable and most righteous will. . . .		

Is Neotheism in Consonance with Theological Tradition?

In *The God Who Risks*, John Sanders attempts to demonstrate the consonance between neotheism (which he calls "relational theism") and "theological tradition." By "theological tradition," Sanders means doctrines held by the church throughout history. According to Sanders, "one of the criteria for evaluating a theological proposal is consonance with the tradition" (Sanders 1998, 140). For the neotheist, divine relationality entails that God enters into "reciprocal give-and-take relations with us" (Sanders 1998, 140).[1] Sanders elaborates that "the model of providence defended here [neotheism] finds agreement with the *intentions* and *functions*, though not always the *material* content, of the theological tradition" (Sanders 1998, 141, italics added).

Sanders believes that we interpret the Scriptures as we do because of our presuppositions, which are influenced by a biblical and Hellenic synthesis, for church fathers as they were influenced by Hellenic thought" (Sanders 1998, 141). This is not to say that the early church fathers thought the Greeks had the total truth or that they sold out to Hellenism. However, they did use Hellenistic thought to defend and to explain the

---

1. For a classical theist, a "give-and-take" relationship entails God giving and our taking, for the neotheist a "give-and-take" relationship entails both God and humans giving and taking from each other. For example, we inform God as He learns from what we do.

Christian concept of God to their contemporaries (Sanders 1998, 141). Sanders says that the resulting synthesis between biblical and Hellenistic thought is a pre-understanding that rules out other (i.e. neotheistic) interpretations, which do not fit the classical notion of what God must be like (Sanders 1998, 141–42).

RESPONSE TO OUR PRE-UNDERSTANDING IS DUE TO HELLENIC INFLUENCE ON THE FATHERS

Sanders is correct that one has pre-understandings, and that pre-understandings affect interpretation. Sanders intimates that we need to question the truth of the traditional view due to its reliance on a synthesis between biblical and Hellenistic thought.

However, the question is not whether one has pre-understandings, but whether the pre-understandings are true. If the pre-understandings are true, there is no reason to question them. The neotheist has not demonstrated falsehood and so is begging the question. If it is true that our biblical interpretation is conditioned by our pre-understanding, then it is also the case that the neotheist biblical interpretation is conditioned by their pre-understanding.

Given that one's pre-understanding is *logically* prior to one's *interpretation* of the biblical text, one cannot argue from one's *interpretation* of the biblical text backwards to justify one's *pre-understanding*. One's *interpretation* already has been "colored" by the pre-understanding. The pre-understanding must be justified. On other grounds that are beyond our purview here, it suffices to say that the argument that all pre-understanding is relative is self-defeating because it presupposes a pre-understanding that is not relative.

RESPONSE TO HISTORICAL AGREEMENT WITH INTENTIONS

The interpretive intentions (purposes or goals) of the theistic tradition are fine with Sanders. However, this presents a problem because intentions (purposes for writing) do not exist in the text, per se (Veatch 1954, 12–16). Meaning exists in text; intentions are always one step removed from the text because they exist in the mind (Gilson 1988, 112–13). Intentions exist in text if the author states them clearly, but even then there likely are unstated intentions, for example the author's intention for expressing his intentions.[2] John 20:30–31 states, "Jesus did many other miraculous signs in the presence of his disciples, which are not recorded in this book. But these are written that you may believe that Jesus is the Christ, the Son of God, and that by believing you may have life in his name."

As to the intentions of the theological traditions, Sanders thinks that the church fathers' intentions were noble, for they intended to show that the Christian God is compatible with the best thinking of their day. They also sought to protect God from the notion of unworthy Greco-Roman deities (Sanders 1998, 141). Therefore, Sanders agrees with *why* the church fathers wrote. But this does not mean that He agrees with *what* they wrote.

RESPONSE TO HISTORICAL AGREEMENT WITH FUNCTION

Sanders professes agreement with the function of the theological tradition, and he summarizes how the neotheistic "risk" model functions. He believes that his model explains the doctrines of salvation, suffering and evil, prayer, and divine guidance (Sanders 1998, 278). However, if consonance of function is the criterion by which one's model is in consonance with theological tradition, then one must affirm that many cults,

---

2. The notion of intention has a broad semantic range, for intention can refer to the *efficient cause*—the will of the agent. Take, for example, the phrase "I didn't intend to say that." Intention can refer to *final causality* ("purpose or why someone wrote"). For example, John 20:31, "These things have been written that you may know that you have eternal life." Intentions may also deal with the *formal cause or meaning* in the text. For example, "This is the intent (meaning) of the author expressed in the text." Given the context, Sanders is referring to final causality. Sanders agrees with the reasons why the fathers wrote, but not with the meaning in what the fathers wrote.

other world religions, neoorthodox theologians, and liberal theologians are also in consonance with the early theological traditions. Yet most evangelicals will deny that neotheists are in consonance with the early theological traditions, since that would demand consonance with what was said.

RESPONSE TO HISTORICAL DISAGREEMENT WITH MATERIAL CONTENT

Sanders says that he does not always agree with the material content of traditional theology. The word *formal* denotes the "term" that is used, and the word *material* denotes "the meaning or content" of the term. Therefore, Sanders is stating that he does not always agree with what the tradition teaches, but he agrees with the "terms" being used. For example, formally, neotheists agree that God is omniscient. However, materially (actually) they disagree with the orthodox theological tradition, for they hold that God does not know the future. Formally, Neotheists think that God is sovereign. However, materially (actually) they disagree with the orthodox theological tradition because they affirm that God does not control all things. Formally, neotheists think that God is immutable. However, materially (actually) they deny that God is immutable, since they say that He "is the best learner" (Pinnock et al. 1994, 124).

Like cults and some other religions, neotheists use the same terms as orthodox Christianity, but they pour different meaning into the terms. If formal agreement is what is required for agreement with traditional theology, then almost any cult, worldview (such as finite-godism and panentheism), liberal theology, or neoorthodox view qualifies as consonant with the theological tradition.

In addition, Sanders dedicates an entire chapter in *The God Who Risks* to recasting the "material content" of what the church fathers said into a neotheistic mold. For example, Sanders says that Tertullian recognizes that God can change His mind (Sanders 1998, 143). That is just not consonant with the true content of Tertullian's writings. Tertullian actually affirmed that

God does *not* change His judgments; Tertullian argued that Marcionites who claimed that God can err were perverse for making such an assertion. He wrote that when one speaks of divine repentance, one should avoid relating it to human experience (*Five Books Against Marcion* 2.23–24).

Sanders also states that Tertullian taught that God has many emotions in common with us and that later on he uses this to state that God is affected by what we do (Sanders 1998, 143). On the contrary, Tertullian rebukes the Marcionites for attributing human emotions to God and says that God's emotions are according to His nature—immutable and infinite (*Five Books Against Marcion* 2.16).

Sanders asserts that Tertullian recognizes that God is passible because he mentions "the crucified God" who "suffered" on our behalf (Sanders 1998, 143). However, in this passage, Tertullian is refuting the Gnostic notion that Christ did not have a material body. Also, he acknowledges the two natures of Christ and what the person of Christ suffered through his humanity. If Christ had been a phantom after his resurrection, he would be a deceiver. Nothing in this passage indicates that God the Father suffered or that the Godhead suffered (*On the Flesh of Christ* 5). Tertullian's views are specifically contrary to the neotheistic notion of divine conditionality, and Tertullian clearly aligns with classical theists. It is the neotheists who recast the church fathers' teachings into their own neotheistic mold.[3]

Agreement in literary *functionality* ("what a text does"), *intentionality* ("why it is taught"), and *formality* ("what terms are used to accomplish the intentions") is not sufficient for consonance with traditional theology. These criteria are too broad. They take in cults, neoorthodox theologians, liberal

---

3. Sanders does this with the rest of the texts that he cites in *The God Who Risks*. We encourage readers to research the sources that are alluded to by Sanders, to read the actual text and the church fathers in their contexts. They will see that the church fathers did not believe in divine conditionality as espoused by neotheists.

theologians, and those in other religions and worldviews. Such faith positions may have the same goals as orthodox evangelical Christianity, but they cannot accurately be subsumed under the umbrella of biblical truth.

But if *material content* ("what was said, or the truths taught") is the criterion by which we measure whether a theological model is consonant with the orthodox theological Christian tradition, then liberal and neoorthodox theology, cults, other world religions, philosophies, and neotheism are not consonant with the theological Christian tradition.

A Response to Clark Pinnock's *Most Moved Mover*

INTRODUCTION

As this book was about to go to press, a major player in neotheism came out with a major book on the topic. Time did not permit integrating the content of Clark Pinnock's *Most Moved Mover* into our discussion throughout this volume, but its importance demands a response.[1]

While little is new in *Most Moved Mover*, what is new is significant, and what isn't new confirms our analysis in the foregoing chapters. Comments here will consider (1) basic tests for a theological belief, (2) similarities between neotheism and process theology, and (3) some crucial admissions Pinnock makes on behalf of neotheism.

THE BASIC TESTS FOR A THEOLOGICAL BELIEF

Pinnock acknowledges four factors that form the basis for his theology: (1) the Bible (ch. 1); (2) tradition (ch. 2); (3) reason (ch. 3); and (4) experience (ch. 4). He explains of this approach, "I adhere to the rule of Scripture within a trilateral hermeneutic" (19).

---

1. Clark Pinnock, *Most Moved Mover: A Theology of God's Openness* (Grand Rapids: Baker, 2001).

The Test of Scripture

Pinnock writes, "First, as an evangelical, my primary commitment is to Scripture not to tradition, reason, or experience" (19). At the same time, he says, "I accept diversity among the biblical witnesses and recognize the dialogical character of the Bible. . . . The Bible does not speak with a single voice" for "the Bible is a complex work by many authors whose views may vary and . . . the text is open to many plausible interpretations" (21). In fact, biblical authors do not merely "vary" in their viewpoints; they made many mistakes in offering prophecies that did not come true (50–51).

Interestingly, Pinnock says, "I also accept that the burden of proof lies on the open view insofar as it puts forward new ideas" (18). On top of this, he confesses: "I cannot claim that the Bible teaches the open view of God or any other subject simply and straightforwardly such that there is no counter testimony which probes and questions and objects" (21).

In short, on Pinnock's first and primary test for truth he accepts the burden of proof. However, he has not only a fallible interpretation (which we all have) but a fallible Bible on which to base it. Further, his interpretation is not only fallible, but it is not even probable, let alone highly probable or virtually certain on this "or any other subject." In short, he admits to being an agnostic interpreter of a fallible book and expects us to accept his admittedly innovative interpretation when the burden of proof is on him. Given all this, he fails his primary test on his own confession.

This is to say nothing of the fact that Pinnock fails to seriously engage any of the biblical texts in favor of crucial attributes, such as sovereignty, omniscience, immutability, and eternality, which biblical theists offer (see chaps. 2–8 above). So, granting his own test of Scripture, Pinnock fails to make his case.

The Test of Tradition

Pinnock says that "tradition is important . . . because theology ought not to be biblical in an isolated way. . . .

Theology needs to maintain continuity with the historic faith of the church" (21).

According to this test, neotheism is a miserable failure, as we have shown (see sections on theological tradition, chs. 2–8). The church fathers give overwhelming affirmation of each crucial attribute of God that is denied by neotheism. Many of Pinnock's statements virtually acknowledge neotheism's failure on this test. As to one crucial attribute, Pinnock admits that "the idea of exhaustive divine omnipotence has, nevertheless, been a persistent belief from early times, and few theologians have considered the possibility that God might have created a universe, the future of which could not be totally foreknown" (101). Indeed, one of Pinnock's noted exceptions, the Socinians (107), he acknowledges to be heretical.

Pinnock uses the "fallacy of diverting the issue" to attempt to hide the lack of historical support for his distinctive views about the nature of God. In this case, the diversion is to the libertarian view of free will (92f.). But this view is not unique to neotheism, since moderate Calvinists, Arminians, Molinists, and even Thomists have held the same view, while supporting the divine attributes of classical orthodoxy that Pinnock denies (e.g., immutability, simplicity, eternality, and complete omniscience).

Further, the very title of Pinnock's chapter 2, "Overcoming a Pagan Inheritance" both diverts the issue and begs the question. By pointing to alleged pagan influences on the orthodox view of God, Pinnock hopes to take the heat off neotheism for its denial of the whole history of orthodox theology on these crucial attributes. The fact is that each tenet of classical theism is supported by virtually all of history's orthodox theologians.

Pinnock attempts to blunt the unanimity of the Fathers by claiming that "concepts like timelessness and impassability are not written in stone." This reduces these doctrines to mere "opinions of the past." They are "not dogmas of the church" (109). As we have shown in this volume, one could reject by the same logic the infallibility and inerrancy of the Bible.

Further, the support from the fathers of the church is expressed by the documents produced in ecumenical councils. The statements of the councils themselves are contrary to neotheism (see Appendix 1). Hence, to ask "What church council has declared it [neotheism] to be impossible" (110) is misleading and misses the very point Pinnock proposed as a test for the truth of his view, namely, that "theology needs to maintain continuity with the historic faith of the church" (21). Neotheism clearly does not. Thus, it is hanged on its own gallows.

The Test of Reason

Regarding the test of reason, Pinnock argues that "serious theologians value coherence and intelligibility in their work. . . . They want their concepts to be internally consistent and coherent with other beliefs that they hold" (22). There is no disagreement here. It remains only to put neotheism to its own test.

Here is a selection of apparent inconsistencies within Pinnock's brand of neotheism.

First, God is "above time" (96), but He is not "outside of time" (98). How can He be both?

Second, Pinnock claims that God's time differs from ours (99). But how does God being "beyond time" and having a "different time" than ours differ from God being eternal? To claim that God's time is uncreated does not help, since an eternal number of moments is not possible, as the Kalam argument for God has shown. Further, how does an uncreated, eternal time that is "beyond time" in the created sense differ from saying God is not in time?

Third, God has limited "omniscience" (138). But how does this differ from saying God is not omniscient, since omniscience means unlimited knowledge, and it is contradictory to say that something is a limited unlimited. If something is self-contradictory, it is false.

Fourth, God combines opposite attributes in His being. In Pinnock's own words, "God is necessary and contingent, eternal and temporal, infinite and finite" (143). But how can opposites both be true? Positing a bipolar nature of God does not solve the problem for two reasons. First, it is an admission that neotheism is really a form of bipolar theism or process theology, which neotheists deny. Second, even in the bipolar view, one nature is non-temporal and immutable—the very facet of traditional theism that neotheists deny. Further, the other "pole," being contingent, temporal, and finite, is not really part of God but is the created universe. In this case they have backed into the very classical theistic view they are attempting to avoid.

Fifth, Pinnock decries the classical view of God's unchange-able nature again and again. Yet he holds that God is "un-changeable in essence," "God's essential nature remains the same," and "Nothing at all in His essential nature changes" (86). Why then is the traditional theist vilified for believing in an immutable God?

Sixth, Pinnock claims that God is "unchangeable in changeable ways" (86). "God is changeless in nature but ever changing in His experience." That is, "God changes in relation to creatures" (86). But how can God change without changing in His nature? How can God be separated from His experience, which admittedly changes? And if it is posited that He has an unchanging part of His nature and a changing part, then neotheists have turned to the dreaded view of process theology that they wish to avoid.

Seventh, God has an unchanging nature or essence in con-trast to His relationships with creatures (as in the sixth point), yet "the essence of a thing now depends on its relationships with other things" (121). But if essence is determined by chang-ing relationships, how can it remain unchanged. In fact, if es-sence is determined by changing relations, there is no *essence* at all. But to deny that there is an essence denies the orthodox teaching affirmed in the ecumenical creeds that God *has* an "essence."

Eighth, God is ontologically independent from the world. He is a necessary Being and the world is contingent (85–86).

But if God is necessary, then He has no potentiality to be other than He is. But without potentiality, one cannot change. Yet Pinnock believes that God can and does change. How can He change if He has no potential for it?

Ninth, on the one hand, Pinnock condemns classical theism for being influenced by the Greeks (ch. 5). On the other, he admits that his own view is influenced by modern process theology (141). He even acknowledges that a synthesis with philosophy can be good (113, 117). Apparently it is wrong for opponents of his view to be influenced by philosophy but acceptable if the influence is on proponents of his view.

Tenth, Pinnock claims to believe in inerrancy, and each year he signs the Evangelical Theological Society's statement to that effect. Yet he asserts that the Bible errs in making false predictions (50–51). Nor can he reconcile his views by redefining truth as *intention*, not *correspondence*. For on an intentional view of truth, almost any mistake can be true. This undermines the truth claim of almost all of Scripture. Further, elsewhere he himself embraces a correspondence view of truth (185).

Eleventh, he exhorts us to avoid making caricatures of the views of others (181). Yet he repeatedly calls the opposing view "fatalistic" and "deterministic" (167). The classical God is even dubbed "a solitary narcissistic being" by a neotheist theologian who is quoted (6).

Unavoidably, neotheism fails its own test for coherence and internal consistency (22). It has constructed the noose with which it has hanged itself.

The Test of Experience

Pinnock calls his final test for the truth of a theological view "existential fit," "practical adequacy," and a "model to meet the demands of life" (23). Here Pinnock waxes eloquent, making a persuasive case for his conclusions. Unfortunately, many of the conclusions made are not unique to neotheism and, hence, are irrelevant as evidence for his view. For example, synergism (or cooperation with God's grace), libertarian free will, non-fatalism, real petitionary prayer, resistible grace, the need to accept the gift of salvation, and faith that is not a form of works are all held by moderate Calvinists, Arminians, Molinists, and Thomists.

As to the other alleged benefits of neotheism, experience is a double-edged argument. A plausible argument can and has been made by classical theism (see ch. 10) for the practical superiority of the classical view of God.

What is more, one can question the whole experience argument being used as a test of truth. It seems much wiser to use experience as a *manifestation* of the truth rather than as a *test* for truth. Otherwise we fall into a kind of pragmatism. If something is known to be true from Scripture, it will work. But simply because a view works does not make it true. Lies often work well, but that pragmatic efficacy does not make them true.

THE SIMILARITIES WITH PROCESS THEOLOGY

The long-stated allegation that neotheism is strongly influenced by process theology is confirmed by Pinnock's own frank admission. Under the heading "The Relation to Process Philosophy," he writes, "Maybe modern influences, which create a distorting tilt in the direction of divine immanence, are present in my work" (141).

Pinnock confesses that "there are things about process theism that I find attractive and convictions that we hold in common." For example,

> We make the love of God a priority; hold to libertarian human freedom; are both critical of conventional [classical] theism; seek a more dynamic model of God; contend that God has real, and not merely rational, relationships with the world; believe that God is affected by what happens in the world; say that God knows what can be known, which does not amount to exhaustive foreknowledge; appreciate the value of philosophy in helping to shape theological convictions; connect positively to Wesleyan/Arminian traditions. (142–43)

As for the thought of Alfred North Whitehead, the father of radical, liberal process theology, Pinnock says, "Here is a theology that tries to work with modern science and has a dynamic metaphysic that doesn't equate God with everything superior and the world with everything inferior." Further, "I find the dialectic in its doctrine of God helpful, for example the idea that God is necessary and contingent, eternal and temporal, infinite and finite." Pinnock adds, "I think [process theology] is right about God affecting everything and being affected by everything. I agree with it that God is temporally everlasting rather than timelessly eternal" (143).

Pinnock concludes: "Candidly, I believe that conventional theists are more influenced by Plato, who was a pagan, than I am by Whitehead, who was a Christian" (143). First, this begs the question that Plato's influences on Christianity were all "pagan" when in fact orthodox Christianity rejected Plato's "pagan" dualism, finite godism, and reincarnation, and his views that there is a reality higher than God (the Good) and that we need no special revelation. Christians stood for absolute values and truth, heaven and hell, the immortality of man, the knowability of God, and other doctrines taught by Scripture but rejected by Plato.

Further, Whitehead was not a "Christian" in any orthodox sense of the word. So far as we can tell, he did not believe in even one of the fundamental orthodox doctrines of the faith, including the divine inspiration of Scripture, the Trinity, the deity of Christ, Christ's virgin birth, atoning death, bodily resurrection, physical ascension, or any other supernatural event. Nor did he hold to absolute truth, absolute values, or heaven and hell. How can he be called "Christian" in any meaningful sense?

It is an irrelevant diversion from the real issues for Pinnock to note some areas of disagreement with process thought, such as *ex nihilo* creation, miracles, and an ontologically independent God. The question is not whether Pinnock believes things that process theologians do not, but whether he holds common ground with them on matters that are not orthodox. Already we have found the answer to that question, and more is yet to be seen.

SOME CRUCIAL ADMISSIONS OF NEOTHEISM

Unexpected in Pinnock's work are his admissions of unorthodox belief. Among them, the following stand out:

- Pinnock holds that atheism may be better than some forms of traditional theism. He says, "Surley it is better that there be no belief in God than that the God who is believed in be an idol who diminishes and humiliates people" (2).
- Pinnock uses a "dialogical" method for determining truth (143), which yields a "synthesis" of views (150).
- Pinnock appears to hold to a view of God that is similar to the unorthodox Mormon view of God (141).
- Pinnock believs that God is bipolar as process theology teaches (141–44).

Three admissions that are even more serious, however, need to be given in Pinnock's own words:

God Has a Body

Pinnock brings a neotheistic skeleton out of the closet with the statement about God: "If he is with us in the world, if we are to take biblical metaphors seriously, *is God in some way embodied?*" (33, emphasis added). He answers affirmatively, "I do not believe that the idea is as foreign to the Bible's view of God as we have assumed" (33). "Is there perhaps something in God that corresponds with embodiment? Having a body is certainly not a negative thing because it makes it possible for us to be agents. Perhaps God's agency would be easier to envisage *if he were in some way corporeal*" (33–34, emphasis added). He adds, *"I do not feel obligated to assume that God is a purely spiritual being when his self-revelation does not suggest it"* (34, emphasis added). Surely Pinnock has read John 4:24 ("God is spirit") and Luke 24:39, when Jesus said, "Touch me and see;

a spirit does not have flesh and bones, as you see I have." In light of Pinnock's view that God may be corporeal, one must take more seriously the suggestion that there are similarities between Pinnock's view and that of the Mormons (141).

The Bible Made Mistakes

Pinnock has been known for his acceptance of the inerrancy of the Bible. Indeed, he still has books in print defending an inerrant Scripture, although subsequent statements have cast doubt as to whether he still holds to such a confession. Nonetheless, he annually signs the doctrinal basis of the Evangelical Theological Society, a prerequisite to renewing membership in the Society:

> The Bible alone, and the Bible in its entirety, is the Word of God written and is therefore inerrant in the autographs. God is a Trinity, Father, Son, and Holy Spirit, each an uncreated person, one in essence, equal in power and glory.

Any doubts that he now denies inerrancy are put to rest with his most recent statements. He writes that "there are fifteen imprecise prophetic forecasts" (50). For example, he said he believes that the city of Tyre was not destroyed as Ezekiel said it would be (29:17-20) in that "the city continued to be inhabited right up until Jesus' own day." Pinnock declares flatly, "Nebuchadnezzer did not do to Tyre exactly what Ezekiel has predicted" (50). In a revealing footnote Pinnock adds, "We may not want to admit it but prophecies often go unfulfilled—Joseph's parents never bowed to him (Gen. 37:9-10); the Assyrians did not destroy Jerusalem in the eighth century (Mic. 3:9-12); despite Isaiah, Israel's return from exile did not usher in a golden age (Is. 41:14-20) . . . " (51).

Jesus Erred

Finally Pinnock affirms a serious christological heresy that even Jesus made a false prediction: "despite Jesus, in the

322 THE BATTLE FOR GOD

destruction of the temple, some stones were left on the other (Mt. 24:2)" (51). Pinnock's point is that Jesus was wrong in what He predicted.

CONCLUSION

Summarizing Pinnock's beliefs in an evangelical context is reminiscent of the comment that error does not so much need refutation as it does a clear exposition. After reading that God has a body, the Bible is mistaken, and Jesus erred, we feel compelled to say simply, "We rest our case."

Sources

Alexander. *Epistles on the Arian Heresy.*

Alford, Henry. *The Greek Testament.* 4 vols. Vol 4: *Hebrews-Revelation.* London: Rivingtons, 1871-74.

Ambrosiaster. *Commentary on Paul's Epistles,* in *Ancient Christian Commentary,* vol. 7.

American Heritage Dictionary of the English Language. 4th ed. Boston: Houghton Mifflin, 2000.

Anselm of Canterbury. *Saint Anselm: Basic Writings: Proslogium; Monologion; Gaunilon's on Behalf of the Fool; Cur Deus Homo?* 2d ed. Trans. S. N. Deane. LaSalle, Ill.: Open Court, 1962.

——. *Trinity, Incarnation, and Redemption: Theological Treatises,* ed. J. Hopkins and H. Richardson. New York: Harper and Row, 1970.

——. *Truth, Freedom, and Evil: Three Philosophical Dialogues.* Trans. and ed. J. Hopkins and H. Richardson. New York: Harper and Row, 1967.

Aristides. *Apology.* Roberts, Alexander, and James Donaldson, eds. *The Ante-Nicene Fathers.* 10 vols. 1885-1887. Repr., Grand Rapids: Eerdmans, 1950-51. Herein cited as *ANF.*

Arminius, Jacobus. *The Writings of James Arminius,* 3 vols. Trans. J. Nichols and W. R. Bagnall. 1853 ed. repr. Grand Rapids: Baker, 1956.

Arnobius. *The Seven Books of Arnobius* 2.64 (*ANF,* Vol. 6).

Athenagoras. *A Plea for the Christians* 8 (*ANF,* Vol. 2).

Augustine. *Confessions.*

——. *Enchiridion.*

——. *Exposition on the Book of Psalms.*

——. *Letters*

——. *Of True Religion.*

——. *On Grace and Free Will.*

——. *On Patience.*

——. *On the Gospel of John.*

——. *On the Spirit and the Letter.*

——. *On the Trinity.*

——. *The City of God.* Trans. Marcus Dods. New York: Modern Library, 1983).

——. *Two Souls, Against the Manichaeans.*

Beckwith, Francis J. "Limited Omniscience and the Test for a Prophet: A Brief Philosophical Analysis," in *Journal of the Evangelical Theological Society* 36.3 (September 1993): 357–62.

——. "The Mormon God, Omniscience, and Eternal Progression: A Philosophical Analysis," in *Trinity Journal* 12.2 (Fall 1991): 128–38.

Beckwith, Francis J., and Stephen E. Parrish. *The Mormon Concept of God: A Philosophical Analysis.* Lewiston, New York: E. Mellen, 1991.

Behe, Michael. *Darwin's Black Box: The Biochemical Challenge to Evolution.* New York: Free Press, 1980.

Bettenson, Henry. *Documents of the Christian Church.* New York: Oxford University Press, 1971.

Boyd, Gregory A. *God of the Possible: A Biblical Introduction to the Open View of God.* Grand Rapids: Baker, 2000.

——. "The Bible and the Open View of the Future." Baptist General Convention Online Website, 18 Dec. 2000. http://www.bgc.bethel.edu/4know/bible.htm.

Bray, Gerald. *The Doctrine of God.* Downers Grove, Ill.: InterVarsity, 1993.

Brown, F., S. Driver, and C. Briggs. *Enhanced Brown-Driver-Briggs Hebrew and English Lexicon.* CD-ROM ed. Oak Harbor, Wash.: Logos Research Systems, 2000.

Bruce, F. F. *The Epistle to the Hebrews.* New International Commentary on the New Testament, rev. ed. Grand Rapids: Eerdmans, 1990.

Buchanan, George Wesley. *To the Hebrews.* The Anchor Bible. Garden City, N.Y.: Doubleday, 1972.

Calvin, John. *Commentaries.* ET, Edinburgh: Calvin Translation Society, 1847–51; repr. ed. Grand Rapids: Baker, 1979.

Institutes of the Christian religion. 2 vols. Ed. John T. McNeill. Trans. Ford Lewis Battles. Philadelphia: Westminster, 1960.

Caneday, A. B. "Putting God at Risk: A Critique of John Sanders's View of Providence," in *Trinity Journal* 20 NS (1999): 131–63.

Carson, D. A. *The Gospel According to John.* Grand Rapids: Eerdmans, 1991.

Chafer, Lewis S. *Systematic Theology.* 8 vols. Dallas: Dallas Seminary Press, 1947.

Charnock, Stephen. *The Existence and Attributes of God.* ET Grand Rapids: Sovereign Grace, 1971.

Chavalas, Mark W. "The Historian, the Believer, and the Word: A Study in the Supposed Conflict of Faith and Reason," *JETS* 36.2 (June 1993): 145–62.

Clark, Mary T., ed. *An Aquinas Reader.* New York: Doubleday, 1972.

Clement of Alexandria. *Stromata,* or *Miscellanies* 7 (*ANF,* Vol. 2).

——. *The Instructor.*

Clement of Rome. *The Epistle to the Corinthians.*

Cole, R. Alan. *Exodus.* Tyndale Old Testament Commentaries. Downers Grove, Ill.: InterVarsity, 1973.

Constitutions of the Holy Apostles.

Craig, William Lane. *The Cosmological Argument from Plato to Leibnitz.* New York: Barnes & Noble, 1979.

———. *The Only Wise God: The Compatibility of Divine Foreknowledge and Human Freedom.* Grand Rapids: Baker, 1987.

———. *The Kalam Cosmological Argument.* New York: Barnes & Noble, 1979).

Crellius. *De Deo et Ejus Attributis.*

Cyprian. *The Epistles of Cyprian; To the People of Thibaris.*

———. *The Treatises of Cyprian.*

Cyril of Jerusalem. *Catechetical Lectures (Nicene and Post-Nicene Fathers, 2.7).*

Didache.

Dionysius. *On John.*

Dunn, James D. G. *The Epistle to the Colossians and to Philemon: A Commentary on the Greek Text.* Grand Rapids: Eerdmans, 1996.

Edwards, Jonathan. *Selections from the Unpublished Writings of Jonathan Edwards, of America; Edited from the Original Mss., with Facsimiles and an Introduction, by the Rev. Alexander B. Grosart.* 1865. Repr. ed., Ligonier, Pa.: Soli Deo Gloria, 1992.

———. *The Works of Jonathan Edwards.* Ed. T. Edwards. 2 vols., 1842 ed. Repr. ed., New York: Garland, 1987.

Ellingworth, Paul. *Commentary on Hebrews.* New International Greek Testament Commentary. Grand Rapids: Eerdmans, 1993.

Erickson, Millard. *The Evangelical Left: Encountering Postconservative Evangelical Theology.* Grand Rapids: Baker, 1997.

Fitzmyer, Joseph A. *Romans: The Anchor Bible.* New York: Doubleday, 1993.

Garrigou-LaGrange, R. *God: His Existence and Nature.* St. Louis: Herder, 1946.

Geisler, Norman L. *Baker Encyclopedia of Christian Apologetics.* Grand Rapids: Baker, 1999.

———. *Chosen but Free.* Minneapolis: Bethany, 1999.

———. *Creating God in the Image of Man.* Minneapolis: Bethany, 1997.

———. *Decide for Yourself: How History Views the Bible.* Grand Rapids: Baker, 1982.

———. *Knowing the Truth About Creation.* Ann Arbor, Mich.: Servant, 1989.

———. *Thomas Aquinas: An Evangelical Appraisal.* Grand Rapids: Baker, 1991.

Geisler, Norman L., and William Watkins. *Worlds Apart: A Handbook on Worldviews.* Grand Rapids: Baker, 1989.

Geisler, Norman L., and Winfried Corduan. *Philosophy of Religion.* Grand Rapids: Zondervan, 1974.

Gerstner, John. *The Rational Biblical Theology of Jonathan Edwards.* Powhatan, Va.: Berea, 1991.

Gilby, Thomas, ed. *St. Thomas Aquinas Theological Texts.* Durham, N.C.: Labyrinth, 1982.

Gilson, Etienne. *God and Philosophy.* London: Oxford, 1941.

———. *Linguistics and Philosophy: An Essay on the Philosophical Constants of Language.* Trans. J. Lyon. Notre Dame, Ind.: University of Notre Dame Press, 1988.

Gregory of Nyssa. *Answer to Eunomius.*

Gregory Thaumaturgus. *A Metaphrase of the Book of Ecclesiastes.*

———. *Twelve Topics on the Faith (ANF,* Vol. 6).

Grudem, Wayne A. *Systematic Theology: An Introduction to Biblical Doctrine.* Grand Rapids: Zondervan, 1994.

Gundry, Stanley N. "Evangelical Theology: Where Should We Be Going?" in *Journal of the Evangelical Theological Society* 22.1 (March 1979): 3–13.

Harris, R. Laird, et al., eds. *Theological Wordbook of the Old Testament.* Chicago: Moody, 1980.

Hartshorne, Charles. *A Natural Theology for Our Time.* LaSalle, Ill.: Open Court, 1967.

———. *Omnipotence and Other Theological Mistakes.* Albany, N.Y.: State University of New York, 1984.

Hasker, William. *God, Time, and Knowledge.* Ithaca, N.Y.: Cornell University Press, 1989.

Hilary of Poitiers. *On the Trinity.*

Hippolytus. *Against the Heresy of Noetus.*

———. *The Refutation of All Heresies.*

Irenaeus. *Against Heresies (ANF,* Vol. 1).

———. *Epistle of Ignatius to Polycarp 3 (ANF,* Vol. 1).

———. *To the Ephesians (ANF,* Vol. 1).

Justin Martyr. *Dialogue with Trypho.*

———. *First Apology (ANF,* Vol. 1).

———. *Second Apology (ANF,* Vol. 1).

Kittel, Gerhard, and Gerhard Friedrich, eds. *Theological Dictionary of the New Testament.* Trans. and abr. G. W. Bromiley. Grand Rapids: Eerdmans, 1985.

Köhler, Ludwig, and Walter Baumgartner. *The Hebrew and Aramaic Lexicon of the Old Testament.* Rev. W. Baumgartner and J. J. Stamm. Leiden: Brill, 1994.

Kushner, Harold S. *When Bad Things Happen to Good People.* New York: Schocken, 1989.

Lactantius. *The Divine Institutes (ANF,* Vol. 7).

———. *The Epitome of the Divine Institutes (ANF,* Vol. 7).

Leith, John, ed. *Creeds of the Churches: A Reader in Christian Doctrine from the Bible to the Present.* Garden City, N.Y.: Anchor, 1963.

Louth, Andrew, ed., with Marco Conti. *Genesis 1–11. Ancient Christian Commentary,* Vol. 1. T.

Luther, Martin. *The Babylonian Captivity of the Church.*

———. *The Bondage of the Will.*

———. *What Luther Says: An Anthology,* 3 vols. Comp. E. M. Plass. St. Louis, Concordia, 1959.

———. *Works.* 55 vols. Ed. J. Pelikan. St. Louis: Concordia, 1955–86.

Mathetes. *The Epistle to Diognetus.*

McGrath, Alister. *The Christian Theology Reader.* Oxford: Blackwell, 1995.

Methodius. *Three Fragments on the Passion of Christ (ANF,* Vol. 6).

Melito of Sardis. *Philosopher, Remains of the Second and Third Century.*

Miley, John. *Systematic Theology.* Cincinnati: Jennings and Graham, 1892–94.

Mondin, Battista. *The Principle of Analogy in Protestant and Catholic Theology.* The Hague: M. Nijhoff, 1963.

Morris, Leon. *The Gospel According to John.* Grand Rapids: Eerdmans, 1995.

Mozley, J. K. *The Impassibility of God: A Survey of Christian Thought.* Cambridge: Cambridge University Press, 1926.

Muller, Richard A. "Incarnation, Immutability, and the Case for Classical Theism." *Westminster Theological Journal* 45.1 (Spring 1983), 22–41.

Nash, Ronald H. *The Concept of God: An Introduction.* Grand Rapids: Zondervan, 1983.

Novatian. *Treatise Concerning the Trinity (ANF,* Vol. 5).

Oden, Thomas. *Systematic Theology,* vol. 1: *The Living God.* San Francisco: Harper & Row, 1987.

———. "The Real Reformers Are Traditionalists," *Christianity Today* 42.2 (9 February 1998): 45.

Thomas Oden, gen. ed. *The Ancient Christian Commentary on Scripture: Old Testament.* Downers Grove, Ill.: InterVarsity, 2001. Cited herein as *Ancient Christian Commentary.*

Ogden, Shubert. *The Reality of God and Other Essays.*

Origen. *Against Celsus.*

———. *Commentary on the Epistles to the Romans,* in *Ancient Christian Commentary,* vol. 7.

———. *De Principiis* 2.4.4 (*ANF,* Vol. 4).

———. *Homilies.*

Orr, James, ed. *International Standard Bible Encyclopedia.* 1929. Repr. Grand Rapids: Eerdmans, 1957–60. Cited herein as *ISBE.*

Packer, J. I. *Concise Theology: A Guide to Historic Christian Beliefs.* Wheaton, Ill.: Tyndale, 1993.

Pannenberg, Wolfhart. *Systematic Theology,* 3 vols. Trans. G. W. Bromiley. Grand Rapids: Eerdmans, 1991.

Parker, Francis H., and Henry Veatch. *Logic as a Human Instrument.* New York: Harper, 1959.

Payne, J. Barton. *The Encylopedia of Biblical Prophecy.* Grand Rapids: Baker, 1973.

Peter of Alexandria. *Fragments.*

Pettinato, Giovanni. *The Archives of Ebla: An Empire Inscribed in Clay,* ET. Garden City, N.J.: Doubleday, 1981.

Pieper, Franz August. *Christian Dogmatics.* ET, 4 vols. St. Louis: Concordia, 1950–57.

Pinnock, Clark H. *A Wideness in God's Mercy: The Finality of Jesus Christ in a World of Religions.* Grand Rapids: Zondervan, 1992.

———. *Most Moved Mover: A Theology of God's Openness.* Grand Rapids: Baker, 2001.

Pinnock, Clark H., et al. *The Openness of God: A Biblical Challenge to the Traditional Understanding of God.* Downers Grove, Ill.: InterVarsity, 1994.

Plantinga, Alvin. *Does God have a Nature? The Aquinas Lecture, 1980.* Milwaukee: Marquette University Press, 1980.

———. *The Nature of Necessity.* Oxford: Clarendon, 1974.

Polycarp. *Martyrdom of Polycarp.*

Pope, William Burt. *A Compendium of Christian Theology: Being Analytical Outlines of a Course of Theological Study.* Rev. ed. New York: Hunt and Eaton, n.d.

Prestige, G. L. *God in Patristic Thought.* London: SPCK, 1959.

Preuss, Arthur. *God: His Knowability, Essence, and Attributes: A Dogmatic Treatise.* St. Louis: Herder, 1911.

Quenstedt, Johannes. *Theologia Didactico-Polemica* (1685). Cited in Heinrich Schmid, *The Doctrinal Theology of the Evangelical Lutheran Church.* Third rev. ed. Minneapolis: Augsburg, 1961.

Sanders, John. "Does God Know?" *Christianity Today.* 21 May 2001.

———. *The God Who Risks: A Theology of Providence.* Downers Grove, Ill.: InterVarsity, 1998.

Schaff, Philip. *The Creeds of Christendom: With a History and Critical Notes.* 3 vols. 1877. Repr., Grand Rapids: Baker, 1983. Cited herein as *Creeds.*

Shedd, William G. T. *Dogmatic Theology.* 2d ed. 3 vols. Nashville: Thomas Nelson, 1980.

Strong, A. H. *Systematic Theology.* 3 vols. Philadelphia: Judson, 1907–9.

Tatian. *Address to the Greeks.*

Tertullian. *Against Hermogenes.*

———. *On Fasting.*

Tertullian. *Against Marcion (ANF, Vol. 3).*

———. *Against Praxeas (ANF, Vol. 3).*

———. *On Exhortation to Chastity (ANF, Vol. 3).*

———. *On the Flesh of Christ (ANF, Vol. 3).*

Theophilus. *Theophilus to Autolycus.*

Thomas Aquinas. *Catena Aurea.*

———. *On Evil.*

———. *On the One and Triune God.*

———. *On the Power of God.*

———. *On Truth.*

———. *Philosophical Texts; Selected and Translated with Notes and an Introduction by Thomas Gilby.* London: Oxford University Press, 1951.

———. *Summa Theologica.*

Tillich, Paul. *Ultimate Concern: Tillich in Dialogue.* New York: Harper and Row, 1965.

Tozer, A. W. *The Knowledge of the Holy: The Attributes of God: Their Meaning in Christian Life.* New York: Harper, 1961.

Turretin, Francis. *Institutes of Elenctic Theology.* Trans. G. M. Giger; ed. J. T. Dennison Jr. Phillipsburg, N.J.: Presbyterian and Reformed, 1992.

Veatch, Henry. *Intentional Logic*. New Haven, Conn.: Yale University Press, 1952.

———. *Realism and Nominalism Revisited*. Milwaukee: Marquette University Press, 1954.

———. *Two Logics: The Conflict Between Classical and Neo-analytical Philosophy*. Evanston, Ill.: Northwestern University Press, 1969.

Vos, Geerhardus. "Omniscience," in *ISBE*.

Weaver, Richard M. *Ideas Have Consequences*. Chicago: University of Chicago Press, 1948.

Wenham, Gordon J. *Genesis 16–50*. Word Biblical Commentary. Dallas: Word, 1994.

Wesley, John. *The Works of John Wesley*. 3d ed. Peabody, Mass.: Hendrickson, 1984; CD-ROM: Rio, Wis.: Ages Software, 1996.

Westcott, Brooke Foss. *The Epistle to the Hebrews: The Greek Text with Notes and Essays*. 1903. Repr. ed. London: Macmillan, 1920.

Whitehead, Alfred North. *Process and Reality: An Essay in Cosmology*. Ed. D. R. Griffin and D. W. Sherburne. 1929 corr. ed. Repr. ed. New York: Free Press, 1979.

Wiley, H. Orton. *Christian Theology*, 3 vols. Kansas City: Beacon Hill, 1940–43.

Index